More Guns, Less Crime

A volume in the series
STUDIES IN LAW AND ECONOMICS
EDITED BY *William M. Landes and J. Mark Ramseyer*

Previously published:
POLITICS AND PROPERTY RIGHTS: THE CLOSING OF THE
OPEN RANGE IN THE POSTBELLUM SOUTH, *by Shawn E. Kantor*

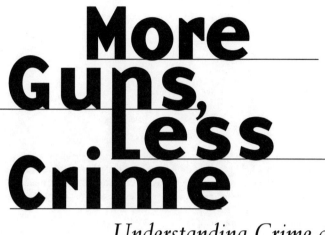

More Guns, Less Crime

*Understanding Crime and
Gun-Control Laws*

John R. Lott, Jr.

The University of Chicago Press
Chicago and London

John R. Lott, Jr., is the John M. Olin Visiting Law and Economics Fellow at the
University of Chicago. He has held positions at Stanford, UCLA, Wharton, Rice, and
Texas A&M and was the chief economist at the United States Sentencing Commission
during 1988 and 1989. He has published over seventy articles in academic journals.

The University of Chicago Press, Chicago 60637
The University of Chicago Press, Ltd., London
© 1998 by The University of Chicago
All rights reserved. Published 1998
Printed in the United States of America
07 06 05 04 03 02 01 00 99   8 9 10

ISBN: 0-226-49363-6 (cloth)

Library of Congress Cataloging-in-Publication Data

Lott, John R.
    More guns, less crime : understanding crime and gun-control laws /
John R. Lott, Jr.
        p.   cm. — (Studies in law and economics)
    Includes bibliographical references and index.
    ISBN 0-226-49363-6 (cloth : alk. paper)
        1. Firearms—Law and legislation—United States.   2. Firearms and
    crime—United States.   I. Title.   II. Series: Studies in law and
    economics (Chicago, Ill.)
    KF3941.L68   1998
    344.73'0533—dc21   97-51481
                                                            CIP

⊗ The paper used in this publication meets the minimum requirements of the
American National Standard for Information Sciences—Permanence of Paper for
Printed Library Materials, ANSI Z39.48–1992.

To Bill Landes and Sam Peltzman,
for all their support
and encouragement

Contents

Preface

Does allowing people to own or carry guns deter violent crime? Or does it simply cause more citizens to harm each other? Using the most comprehensive data set on crime yet assembled, this book examines the relationship between gun laws, arrest and conviction rates, the socioeconomic and demographic compositions of counties and states, and different rates of violent crime and property crime. The efficacy of the Brady Law, concealed-handgun laws, waiting periods, and background checks is evaluated for the first time using nationwide, county-level data.

The book begins with a description of the arguments for and against gun control and of how the claims should be tested. A large portion of the existing research is critically reviewed. Several chapters then empirically examine what facts influence the crime rate and answer the questions posed above. Finally, I respond to the political and academic attacks leveled against the original version of my work, which was published in the January 1997 issue of the *Journal of Legal Studies.*

I would like to thank my wife, Gertrud Fremling, for patiently reading and commenting on many early drafts of this book, and my four children for sitting through more dinnertime conversations on the topics covered here than anyone should be forced to endure. David Mustard also assisted me in collecting the data for the original article, which serves as the basis for some of the discussions in chapters 4 and 5. Ongoing research with Steve Bronars and William Landes has contributed to this book. Maxim Lott provided valuable research assistance with the polling data.

For their comments on different portions of the work included in this book, I would like to thank Gary Becker, Steve Bronars, Clayton Cramer, Ed Glaeser, Hide Ichimura, Jon Karpoff, C. B. Kates, Gary Kleck, David Kopel, William Landes, Wally Mullin, Derek Neal, Dan Polsby, Robert Reed, Tom Smith, seminar participants at the University of Chicago (the Economics and Legal Organization, the Rational Choice, and Divinity School workshops), Harvard University, Yale University, Stanford University, Northwestern University, Emory University, Fordham University, Valparaiso University, the American Law and Economics Association

Meetings, the American Society of Criminology, the Western Economic Association Meetings, and the Cato Institute. I also benefited from presentations at the annual conventions of the Illinois Police Association and the National Association of Treasury Agents. Further, I would like to express my appreciation to the John M. Olin Law and Economics Program at the University of Chicago Law School for its generous funding (a topic dealt with at length in chapter 7).

American culture is a gun culture—not merely in the sense that 75 to 86 million people own a total of about 200 to 240 million guns,[1] but in the broader sense that guns pervade our debates on crime and are constantly present in movies and the news. How many times have we read about shootings, or how many times have we heard about tragic accidental gun deaths—bad guys shooting innocent victims, bad guys shooting each other in drug wars, shots fired in self-defense, police shootings of criminals, let alone shooting in wars? We are inundated by images through the television and the press. Our kids are fascinated by computer war games and toy guns.

So we're obsessed with guns. But the big question is: What do we really know? How many times have most of us actually used a gun or seen a gun being used? How many of us have ever seen somebody in real life threatening somebody else with a gun, witnessed a shooting, or seen people defend themselves by displaying or firing guns?

The truth is that most of us have very little firsthand experience with using guns as weapons. Even the vast majority of police officers have never exchanged shots with a suspect.[2] Most of us receive our images of guns and their use through television, film, and newspapers.

Unfortunately, the images from the screen and the newspapers are often unrepresentative or biased because of the sensationalism and exaggeration typically employed to sell news and entertainment. A couple of instances of news reporting are especially instructive in illustrating this bias. In a highly publicized incident, a Dallas man recently became the first Texas resident charged with using a permitted concealed weapon in a fatal shooting.[3] Only long after the initial wave of publicity did the press report that the person had been savagely beaten and in fear for his life before firing the gun. In another case a Japanese student was shot on his way to a Halloween party in Louisiana in 1992. It made international headlines and showed how defensive gun use can go tragically wrong.[4] However, this incident was a rare event: in the entire United States during a year, only about 30 people are accidentally killed by private citizens who mistakenly believe the victim to be an intruder.[5] By comparison, police accidentally kill as many as 330 innocent individuals annually.[6] In neither the Louisiana case nor the Texas case did the courts find the shooting to be criminal.

While news stories sometimes chronicle the defensive uses of guns, such discussions are rare compared to those depicting violent crime committed with guns. Since in many defensive cases a handgun is simply brandished, and no one is harmed, many defensive uses are never even reported to the police. I believe that this underreporting of defensive gun use is large, and this belief has been confirmed by the many stories I received from people across the country after the publicity broke on my original study. On the roughly one hundred radio talk shows on which I discussed that study, many people called in to say that they believed having a gun to defend themselves with had saved their lives. For instance, on a Philadelphia radio station, a New Jersey woman told how two men simultaneously had tried to open both front doors of the car she was in. When she brandished her gun and yelled, the men backed away and fled. Given the stringent gun-control laws in New Jersey, the woman said she never thought seriously of reporting the attempted attack to the police.

Similarly, while I was on a trip to testify before the Nebraska Senate, John Haxby—a television newsman for the CBS affiliate in Omaha— privately revealed to me a frightening experience that he had faced in the summer of 1995 while visiting in Arizona. At about 10 A.M., while riding in a car with his brother at the wheel, they stopped for a red light. A man appeared wielding a "butcher's knife" and opened the passenger door, but just as he was lunging towards John, the attacker suddenly turned and ran away. As John turned to his brother, he saw that his brother was holding a handgun. His brother was one of many who had recently acquired permits under the concealed-handgun law passed in Arizona the previous year.

Philip Van Cleave, a former reserve deputy sheriff in Texas, wrote me, "Are criminals afraid of a law-abiding citizen with a gun? You bet. Most cases of a criminal being scared off by an armed citizen are probably not reported. But I have seen a criminal who was so frightened of an armed, seventy-year-old woman that in his panic to get away, he turned and ran right into a wall! (He was busy trying to kick down her door, when she opened a curtain and pointed a gun at him.)"

Such stories are not limited to the United States. On February 3, 1996, outside a bar in Texcoco, Mexico (a city thirty miles east of Mexico City), a woman used a gun to stop a man from raping her. When the man lunged at the woman, "ripping her clothes and trying to rape her," she pulled a .22-caliber pistol from her purse and shot her attacker once in the chest, killing him.[7] The case generated much attention in Mexico when a judge initially refused to dismiss murder charges against the woman because she was viewed as being responsible for the attempted rape, having "enticed" the attacker "by having a drink with him at the bar."[8]

If national surveys are correct, 98 percent of the time that people use guns defensively, they merely have to brandish a weapon to break off an attack. Such stories are not hard to find: pizza deliverymen defend themselves against robbers, carjackings are thwarted, robberies at automatic teller machines are prevented, and numerous armed robberies on the streets and in stores are foiled,[9] though these do not receive the national coverage of other gun crimes.[10] Yet the cases covered by the news media are hardly typical; most of the encounters reported involve a shooting that ends in a fatality.[11]

A typical dramatic news story involved an Atlanta woman who prevented a carjacking and the kidnapping of her child; she was forced to shoot her assailant:

> A College Park woman shot and killed an armed man she says was trying to carjack her van with her and her 1-year-old daughter inside, police said Monday. . . .
>
> Jackson told police that the gunman accosted her as she drove into the parking lot of an apartment complex on Camp Creek Parkway. She had planned to watch a broadcast of the Evander Holyfield–Mike Tyson fight with friends at the complex.
>
> She fired after the man pointed a revolver at her and ordered her to "move over," she told police. She offered to take her daughter and give up the van, but the man refused, police said.
>
> "She was pleading with the guy to let her take the baby and leave the van, but he blocked the door," said College Park Detective Reed Pollard. "She was protecting herself and the baby."
>
> Jackson, who told police she bought the .44-caliber handgun in September after her home was burglarized, said she fired several shots from the gun, which she kept concealed in a canvas bag beside her car seat. "She didn't try to remove it," Pollard said. "She just fired."[12]

Although the mother saved herself and her baby by her quick actions, it was a risky situation that might have ended differently. Even though there was no police officer to help protect her or her child, defending herself was not necessarily the only alternative. She could have behaved passively, and the criminal might have changed his mind and simply taken the van, letting the mother and child go. Even if he had taken the child, he might later have let the baby go unharmed. Indeed, some conventional wisdom claims that the best approach is not to resist an attack. According to a recent *Los Angeles Times* article, "'active compliance' is the surest way to survive a robbery. Victims who engage in active resistance . . . have the best odds of hanging on to their property. Unfortunately, they also have much better odds of winding up dead."[13]

Yet the evidence suggests that the College Park woman probably engaged in the correct action. While resistance is generally associated with higher probabilities of serious injury to the victim, not all types of resistance are equally risky. By examining the data provided from 1979 to 1987 by the Department of Justice's National Crime Victimization Survey,[14] Lawrence Southwick, confirming earlier estimates by Gary Kleck, found that the probability of serious injury from an attack is 2.5 times greater for women offering no resistance than for women resisting with a gun. In contrast, the probability of women being seriously injured was almost 4 times greater when resisting without a gun than when resisting with a gun. In other words, the best advice is to resist with a gun, but if no gun is available, it is better to offer no resistance than to fight.[15]

Men also fare better with guns, but the benefits are significantly smaller. Behaving passively is 1.4 times more likely to result in serious injury than resisting with a gun. Male victims, like females, also run the greatest risk when they resist without a gun, yet the difference is again much smaller: resistance without a gun is only 1.5 times as likely to result in serious injury than resistance with a gun. The much smaller difference for men reflects the fact that a gun produces a smaller change in a man's ability to defend himself than it does for a woman.

Although usually skewed toward the dramatic, news stories do shed light on how criminals think. Anecdotes about criminals who choose victims whom they perceive as weak are the most typical. While "weak" victims are frequently women and the elderly, this is not always the case. For example, in a taped conversation with police investigators reported in the *Cincinnati Enquirer* (October 9, 1996, p. B2), Darnell "Bubba" Lowery described how he and Walter "Fatman" Raglin robbed and murdered musician Michael Bany on December 29, 1995:

> Mr. Lowery said on the tape that he and Walter "Fatman" Raglin, who is also charged with aggravated robbery and aggravated murder and is on trial in another courtroom, had planned to rob a cab driver or a "dope boy."
>
> He said he gave his gun and bullets to Mr. Raglin. They decided against robbing a cab driver or drug dealer because both sometimes carried guns, he said.
>
> Instead, they saw a man walking across the parking lot with some kind

of musical instrument. He said as he looked out for police, Mr. Raglin approached the man and asked for money.

After getting the money, Mr. Raglin asked if the man's car was a stick or an automatic shift. Then Mr. Raglin shot the man.

Criminals are motivated by self-preservation, and handguns can therefore be a deterrent. The potential defensive nature of guns is further evidenced by the different rates of so-called "hot burglaries," where a resident is at home when a criminal strikes.[16] In Canada and Britain, both with tough gun-control laws, almost half of all burglaries are "hot burglaries." In contrast, the United States, with fewer restrictions, has a "hot burglary" rate of only 13 percent. Criminals are not just behaving differently by accident. Convicted American felons reveal in surveys that they are much more worried about armed victims than about running into the police.[17] The fear of potentially armed victims causes American burglars to spend more time than their foreign counterparts "casing" a house to ensure that nobody is home. Felons frequently comment in these interviews that they avoid late-night burglaries because "that's the way to get shot."[18]

To an economist such as myself, the notion of deterrence—which causes criminals to avoid cab drivers, "dope boys," or homes where the residents are in—is not too surprising. We see the same basic relationships in all other areas of life: when the price of apples rises relative to that of oranges, people buy fewer apples and more oranges. To the non-economist, it may appear cold to make this comparison, but just as grocery shoppers switch to cheaper types of produce, criminals switch to attacking more vulnerable prey. Economists call this, appropriately enough, "the substitution effect."

Deterrence matters not only to those who actively take defensive actions. People who defend themselves may indirectly benefit other citizens. In the Cincinnati murder case just described, cab drivers and drug dealers who carry guns produce a benefit for cab drivers and drug dealers without guns. In the example involving "hot burglaries," homeowners who defend themselves make burglars generally wary of breaking into homes. These spillover effects are frequently referred to as "third-party effects" or "external benefits." In both cases criminals cannot know in advance who is armed.

The case for allowing concealed handguns—as opposed to openly carried handguns—relies on this argument. When guns are concealed, criminals are unable to tell whether the victim is armed before striking, which raises the risk to criminals of committing many types of crimes.

On the other hand, with "open-carry" handgun laws, a potential victim's defensive ability is readily identified, which makes it easier for criminals to choose the more vulnerable prey. In interviews with felony prisoners in ten state correctional systems, 56 percent claimed that they would not attack a potential victim who was known to be armed. Indeed, the criminals in states with high civilian gun ownership were the most worried about encountering armed victims.[19]

Other examples suggest that more than just common crimes may be prevented by law-abiding citizens carrying concealed handguns. Referring to the July, 1984, massacre at a San Ysidro, California, McDonald's restaurant, Israeli criminologist Abraham Tennenbaum described

> what occurred at a [crowded venue in] Jerusalem some weeks before the California McDonald's massacre: three terrorists who attempted to machine-gun the throng managed to kill only one victim before being shot down by handgun-carrying Israelis. Presented to the press the next day, the surviving terrorist complained that his group had not realized that Israeli civilians were armed. The terrorists had planned to machine-gun a succession of crowd spots, thinking that they would be able to escape before the police or army could arrive to deal with them.[20]

More recently, on March 13, 1997, seven young seventh- and eighth-grade Israeli girls were shot to death by a Jordanian soldier while visiting Jordan's so-called Island of Peace. Reportedly, the Israelis had "complied with Jordanian requests to leave their weapons behind when they entered the border enclave. Otherwise, they might have been able to stop the shooting, several parents said."[21]

Obviously, arming citizens has not stopped terrorism in Israel; however, terrorists have responded to the relatively greater cost of shooting in public places by resorting to more bombings. This is exactly what the substitution effect discussed above would predict. Is Israel better off with bombings instead of mass public shootings? That is not completely clear, although one might point out that if the terrorists previously chose shooting attacks rather than bombings but now can only be effective by using bombs, their actions are limited in a way that should make terrorist attacks less effective (even if only slightly).[22]

Substitutability means that the most obvious explanations may not always be correct. For example, when the February 23, 1997, shooting at the Empire State Building left one person dead and six injured, it was not New York's gun laws but Florida's—where the gun was sold—that came under attack. New York City Mayor Rudolph W. Giuliani immediately called for national gun-licensing laws.[23] While it is possible that even stricter gun-sale regulations in Florida might have prevented this and other shootings, we might ask, Why did the gunman travel to New York and not simply remain in Florida to do the shooting? It is important to study whether states that adopt concealed-handgun laws similar to those in Israel experience the same virtual elimination of mass public shootings. Such states may also run the risk that would-be attackers will substitute bombings for shootings, though there is the same potential downside to successfully banning guns. The question still boils down to an empirical one: Which policy will save the largest number of lives?

THE NUMBERS DEBATE AND CRIME

Unfortunately, the debate over crime involves many commonly accepted "facts" that simply are not true. For example, take the claim that individuals are frequently killed by people they know.[24] As shown in table 1.1, according to the FBI's *Uniform Crime Reports*, 58 percent of the country's murders were committed either by family members (18 percent) or by

Table 1.1 Murderers and victims: relationship and characteristics

	Percent of cases involving the relationship	Percent of victims	Percent of offenders
Relationship		—	—
Family	18%		
Acquaintance			
(nonfriend and friend)	40		
Stranger	13		
Unknown	30		
Total	101		
Race			
Black		38%	33%
White		54	42
Hispanic		2	2
Other		5	4
Unknown		1	19
Total		100	100
Sex			
Female		29	9
Male		71	72
Unknown		0	19
Total		100	100

Source: U.S. Dept. of Justice, FBI staff, *Uniform Crime Reports*, (Washington, DC: U.S. Govt. Printing Office, 1992
Note: Nonfriend acquaintances include drug pushers and buyers, gang members, prostitutes and their clients, bar customers, gamblers, cab drivers killed by their customers, neighbors, other nonfriend acquaintances, and friends. The total equals more than 100 percent because of rounding. The average age of victims was 33; that of offenders was 30.

those who "knew" the victims (40 percent). Although the victims' relationship to their attackers could not be determined in 30 percent of the cases, 13 percent of all murders were committed by complete strangers.[25]

Surely the impression created by these numbers has been that most victims are murdered by close acquaintances. Yet this is far from the truth. In interpreting the numbers, one must understand how these classifications are made. In this case, "murderers who know their victims" is a very broad category. A huge but not clearly determined portion of this category includes rival gang members who know each other.[26] In larger urban areas, where most murders occur, the majority of murders are due to gang-related turf wars over drugs.

The Chicago Police Department, which keeps unusually detailed numbers on these crimes, finds that just 5 percent of all murders in the city from 1990 to 1995 were committed by nonfamily friends, neighbors, or roommates.[27] This is clearly important in understanding crime. The list of nonfriend acquaintance murderers is filled with cases in which the relationships would not be regarded by most people as particularly close: for example, relationships between drug pushers and buyers, gang members, prostitutes and their clients, bar customers, gamblers, and cabdrivers killed by their customers.

While I do not wish to downplay domestic violence, most people do not envision gang members or drug buyers and pushers killing each other when they hear that 58 percent of murder victims were either relatives or acquaintances of their murderers.[28] If family members are included, 17 percent of all murders in Chicago for 1990–95 involved family members, friends, neighbors, or roommates.[29] While the total number of murders in Chicago grew from 395 in 1965 to 814 in 1995, the number involving family members, friends, neighbors, or roommates remained virtually unchanged. What has grown is the number of murders by nonfriend acquaintances, strangers, identified gangs, and persons unknown.[30]

Few murderers could be classified as previously law-abiding citizens. In the largest seventy-five counties in the United States in 1988, over 89 percent of adult murderers had criminal records as adults.[31] Evidence for Boston, the one city where reliable data have been collected, shows that, from 1990 to 1994, 76 percent of juvenile murder victims and 77 percent of juveniles who murdered other juveniles had prior criminal arraignments.[32]

Claims of the large number of murders committed against acquaintances also create a misleading fear of those we know. To put it bluntly, criminals are not typical citizens. As is well known, young males from their mid-teens to mid-thirties commit a disproportionate share of crime,[33] but even this categorization can be substantially narrowed. We know that criminals tend to have low IQs as well as atypical personalities.

For example, delinquents generally tend to be more "assertive, unafraid, aggressive, unconventional, extroverted, and poorly socialized," while nondeliquents are "self-controlled, concerned about their relations with others, willing to be guided by social standards, and rich in internal feelings like insecurity, helplessness, love (or its lack), and anxiety."[34] Other evidence indicates that criminals tend to be more impulsive and put relatively little weight on future events.[35] Finally, we cannot ignore the unfortunate fact that crime (particularly violent crime, and especially murder) is disproportionately committed against blacks by blacks.[36]

The news media also play an important role in shaping what we perceive as the greatest threats to our safety. Because we live in such a national news market, we learn very quickly about tragedies in other parts of the country.[37] As a result, some events appear to be much more common than they actually are. For instance, children are much less likely to be accidentally killed by guns (particularly handguns) than most people think. Consider the following numbers: in 1995 there were a total of 1,400 accidental firearm deaths in the entire country. A relatively small portion of these involved children: 30 deaths involved children up to four years of age and 170 more deaths involved five- to fourteen-year-olds.[38] In comparison, 2,900 children died in motor-vehicle crashes, 950 children lost their lives from drowning, and over 1,000 children were killed by fire and burns. More children die in bicycle accidents each year than die from all types of firearm accidents.

Of course, any child's death is tragic, and it offers little consolation to point out that common fixtures in life from pools to heaters result in even more deaths. Yet the very rules that seek to save lives can result in more deaths. For example, banning swimming pools would help prevent drowning, and banning bicycles would eliminate bicycling accidents, but if fewer people exercise, life spans will be shortened. Heaters may start fires, but they also keep people from getting sick and from freezing to death. So whether we want to allow pools or space heaters depends not only on whether some people may be harmed by them, but also on whether more people are helped than hurt.

Similar trade-offs exist for gun-control issues, such as gun locks. As President Clinton has argued many times, "We protect aspirin bottles in this country better than we protect guns from accidents by children."[39] Yet gun locks require that guns be unloaded, and a locked, unloaded gun does not offer ready protection from intruders.[40] The debate is not simply over whether one wants to save lives or not; it involves the question of how many of these two hundred accidental gun deaths would have been avoided under different rules versus the extent to which such rules would reduce people's ability to defend themselves. Without looking at data, one can only guess the net effects.[41] Unfortunately, despite the best intentions, evidence indicates that child-resistant bottle caps actually have resulted in "3,500 additional poisonings of children under age 5 annually from [aspirin-related drugs] . . . [as] consumers have been lulled into a less-safety-conscious mode of behavior by the existence of safety caps."[42] If President Clinton were aware of such research, he surely wouldn't refer to aspirin bottles when telling us how to deal with guns.[43]

Another common argument made in favor of banning guns involves the number of people who die from guns each year: there were 17,790 homicides and 18,169 suicides in 1992 alone.[44] Yet just because a law is passed to ban guns, it does not automatically follow that the total number of deaths will decline. Given the large stock of guns in the country, and given the difficulties the government faces in preventing other illegal items, such as drugs, from entering the country, it is not clear how successful the government would be in eliminating most guns. This raises the important question of whether the law would primarily reduce the number of guns held by law-abiding citizens. How would such a law alter the relative balance of power between criminals and law-abiding citizens?

Suppose it were possible to remove all guns. Other questions would still arise. Would successfully removing guns discourage murders and other crimes because criminals would find knives and clubs poor alternatives? Would it be easier for criminals to prey on the weakest citizens, who would find it more difficult to defend themselves? Suicide raises other questions. It is simply not sufficient to point to the number of people who kill themselves with guns. The debate must be over what substitute methods are available and whether they appear sufficiently less attractive. Even evidence about the "success rate" of different methods of suicide is not enough, because questions arise over why people choose the method that they do. If people who were more intent than others on successfully killing themselves previously chose guns, forcing them to use other methods might raise the reported "success rate" for these other methods. Broader concerns for the general public also arise. For example, even if we banned many of the obvious ways of committing suicide, many methods exist that we could never really control. These substitute methods might endanger others in ways that shootings do not—for example, deliberately crashing one's car, throwing oneself in front of a train, or jumping off a building.

This book attempts to measure the same type of trade-off for guns. Our primary questions are the following: Will allowing citizens to carry concealed handguns mean that otherwise law-abiding people will harm each other? Will the threat of self-defense by citizens armed with guns primarily deter criminals? Without a doubt, both "bad" and "good" uses of guns occur. The question isn't really whether both occur; it is, rather, Which is more important? In general, do concealed handguns save or cost lives? Even a devoted believer in deterrence cannot answer this question without examining the data, because these two different effects clearly exist, and they work in opposite directions.

To some, however, the logic is fairly straightforward. Philip Cook argues that "if you introduce a gun into a violent encounter, it increases the chance that someone will die."[45] A large number of murders may arise from unintentional fits of rage that are quickly regretted, and simply keeping guns out of people's reach would prevent deaths.[46] Others point to the horrible public shootings that occur not just in the United States but around the world, from Tasmania, Australia, to Dunblane, Scotland.

The survey evidence of defensive gun use weighs importantly in this debate. At the lowest end of these estimates, again according to Philip Cook, the U.S. Department of Justice's National Crime Victimization Survey reports that each year there are "only" 80,000 to 82,000 defensive uses of guns during assaults, robberies, and household burglaries.[47] Other national polls weight regions by population and thus have the advantage, unlike the National Crime Victimization Survey, of not relying too heavily on data from urban areas.[48] These national polls should also produce more honest answers, since a law-enforcement agency is not asking the questions.[49] They imply much higher defensive use rates. Fifteen national polls, including those by organizations such as the *Los Angeles Times,* Gallup, and Peter Hart Research Associates, imply that there are 760,000 to 3.6 million defensive uses of guns per year.[50] Yet even if these estimates are wrong by a very large factor, they still suggest that defensive gun use is extremely common.

Some evidence on whether concealed-handgun laws will lead to increased crimes is readily available. Between October 1, 1987, when Florida's "concealed-carry" law took effect, and the end of 1996, over 380,000 licenses had been issued, and only 72 had been revoked because of crimes committed by license holders (most of which did not involve the permitted gun).[51] A statewide breakdown on the nature of those crimes is not available, but Dade County records indicate that four crimes involving a permitted handgun took place there between September 1987 and August 1992, and none of those cases resulted in injury.[52] Similarly, Multnomah County, Oregon, issued 11,140 permits over the period from January 1990 to October 1994; only five permit holders were involved in shootings, three of which were considered justified by grand juries. Of the other two cases, one involved a shooting in a domestic dispute, and the other involved an accident that occurred while a gun was being unloaded; neither resulted in a fatality.[53]

In Virginia, "Not a single Virginia permit-holder has been involved in violent crime."[54] In the first year following the enactment of concealed-carry legislation in Texas, more than 114,000 licenses were issued, and only 17 have so far been revoked by the Department of Public Safety (reasons not specified).[55] After Nevada's first year, "Law enforcement officials throughout the state could not document one case of a fatality that resulted from irresponsible gun use by someone who obtained a permit under the new law."[56] Speaking for the Kentucky Chiefs of Police Association, Lt. Col. Bill Dorsey, Covington assistant police chief, concluded that after the law had been in effect for nine months, "We haven't seen any cases where a [concealed-carry] permit holder has committed an offense with a firearm,"[57] In North Carolina, "Permit-holding gun owners have not had a single permit revoked as a result of use of a gun in a crime."[58] Similarly, for South Carolina, "Only one person who has received a pistol permit since 1989 has been indicted on a felony charge, a comparison of permit and circuit court records shows. That charge, . . . for allegedly transferring stolen property last year, was dropped by prosecutors after evidence failed to support the charge."[59]

During state legislative hearings on concealed-handgun laws, the most commonly raised concerns involved fears that armed citizens would attack each other in the heat of the moment following car accidents or accidentally shoot a police officer. The evidence shows that such fears are unfounded: although thirty-one states have so-called nondiscretionary concealed-handgun laws, some of them decades old, there exists only one recorded incident of a permitted, concealed handgun being used in a shooting following a traffic accident, and that involved self-defense.[60] No permit holder has ever shot a police officer, and there have been cases where permit holders have used their guns to save officers' lives.

Let us return to the fundamental issue of self-protection. For many people, the ultimate concern boils down to protection from violence. Unfortunately, our legal system cannot provide people with all the protection that they desire, and yet individuals are often prevented from defending themselves. A particularly tragic event occurred recently in Baltimore:

> Less than a year ago, James Edward Scott shot and wounded an intruder in the back yard of his West Baltimore home, and according to neighbors, authorities took away his gun.
>
> Tuesday night, someone apparently broke into his three-story row house again. But this time the 83-year-old Scott didn't have his .22-caliber rifle, and police said he was strangled when he confronted the burglar.
>
> "If he would have had the gun, he would be OK," said one neighbor

who declined to give his name, fearing retribution from the attacker, who had not been arrested as of yesterday. . . .

Neighbors said burglars repeatedly broke into Scott's home. Ruses [a neighbor] said Scott often talked about "the people who would harass him because he worked out back by himself."[61]

Others find themselves in a position in which either they no longer report attacks to the police when they have used a gun to defend themselves, or they no longer carry guns for self-defense. Josie Cash learned this lesson the hard way, though charges against her were ultimately dropped. "The Rockford [Illinois] woman used her gun to scare off muggers who tried to take her pizza delivery money. But when she reported the incident to police, they filed felony charges against her for carrying a concealed weapon."[62]

A well-known story involved Alan Berg, a liberal Denver talk-show host who took great delight in provoking and insulting those with whom he disagreed. Berg attempted to obtain a permit after receiving death threats from white supremacists, but the police first attempted to talk him out of applying and then ultimately rejected his request. Shortly after he was denied, Berg was murdered by members of the Aryan Nations.[63]

As a Chicago cabdriver recently told me, "What good is a police officer going to do me if you pulled a knife or a gun on me right now?"[64] Nor are rural, low-crime areas immune from these concerns. Illinois State Representative Terry Deering (Democrat) noted that "we live in areas where if we have a state trooper on duty at any given time in a whole county, we feel very fortunate. Some counties in downstate rural Illinois don't even have 24-hour police protection."[65] The police cannot feasibly protect everybody all the time, and perhaps because of this, police officers are typically sympathetic to law-abiding citizens who own guns.[66]

Mail-in surveys are seldom accurate, because only those who feel intensely about an issue are likely to respond, but they provide the best information that we have on police officers' views. A 1996 mail survey of fifteen thousand chiefs of police and sheriffs conducted by the National Association of Chiefs of Police found that 93 percent believed that law-abiding citizens should continue to be able to purchase guns for self-defense.[67] The Southern States Police Benevolent Association surveyed its eleven thousand members during June of 1993 (36 percent responded) and reported similar findings: 96 percent of those who responded agreed with the statement, "People should have the right to own a gun for self-protection," and 71 percent did not believe that stricter handgun laws would reduce the number of violent crimes.[68] A national reader survey

conducted in 1991 by *Law Enforcement Technology* magazine found that 76 percent of street officers and 59 percent of managerial officers agreed that
all trained, responsible adults should be able to obtain handgun-carry
permits.[69] By similarly overwhelming percentages, these officers and police chiefs rejected claims that the Brady law would lower the crime rate.

The passage of concealed-handgun laws has also caused former opponents in law enforcement to change their positions. Recently in Texas,
"vocal opponent" Harris County District Attorney John Holmes admitted, "I'm eating a lot of crow on this issue. It's not something I necessarily
like to do, but I'm doing it on this."[70] Soon after the implementation of
the Florida law, the president and the executive director of the Florida
Chiefs of Police and the head of the Florida Sheriff's Association all admitted that they had changed their views on the subject. They also admitted
that despite their best efforts to document problems arising from the law,
they have been unable to do so.[71] The experience in Kentucky has been
similar; as Campbell County Sheriff John Dunn says, "I have changed my
opinion of this [program]. Frankly, I anticipated a certain type of people
applying to carry firearms, people I would be uncomfortable with being
able to carry a concealed weapon. That has not been the case. These are
all just everyday citizens who feel they need some protection."[72]

If anything, the support among rank-and-file police officers for the
right of individuals to carry guns for self-protection is even higher than it
is among the general population. A recent national poll by the Lawrence
Research group (September 21–28, 1996) found that by a margin of 69 to
28 percent, registered voters favor "a law allowing law-abiding citizens
to be issued a permit to carry a firearm for personal protection outside
their home."[73] Other recent national polling by the National Opinion Research Center (March 1997) appears even more supportive of at least allowing some law-abiding citizens to carry concealed handguns. They
found that 53.5 percent supported "concealed carry only for those with
special needs," while 45 percent agreed that permits should be issued to
"any adult who has passed a criminal background check and a gun safety
course."[74] Perhaps just as telling, only 16 percent favored a ban on
handguns.[75]

The National Opinion Research Center poll also provides some in-
sights into who supports tighter restrictions on gun ownership; it claims
that "the less educated and those who haven't been threatened with a
gun are most supportive of gun control."[76] If this is true, it appears that
those most supportive of restrictions also tend to be those least directly
threatened by crime.[77]

State legislators also acknowledge the inability of the police to be always available, even in the most public places, by voting to allow them-

selves unusually broad rights to carry concealed handguns. During the 1996 legislative session, for example, Georgia "state legislators quietly gave themselves and a few top officials the right to carry concealed guns to places most residents can't: schools, churches, political rallies, and even the Capitol."[78] Even local prosecutors in California strenuously objected to restrictions on their rights to carry concealed handguns.[79]

Although people with concealed handgun permits must generally view the police as offering insufficient protection, it is difficult to discern any pattern of political orientation among celebrities who have concealed-handgun permits: Bill Cosby, Cybill Shepherd, U.S. Senator Dianne Feinstein (D–California), Howard Stern, Donald Trump, William F. Buckley, Arthur O. Sulzberger (chairman of the *New York Times*), union bosses, Laurence Rockefeller, Tom Selleck, Robert De Niro, and Erika Schwarz (the first runner-up in the 1997 Miss America Pageant). The reasons these people gave on their applications for permits were quite similar. Laurence Rockefeller's reason was that he carries "large sums of money"; Arthur Sulzberger wrote that he carries "large sums of money, securities, etc."; and William Buckley listed "protection of personal property when traveling in and about the city" as his reason.[80] Some made their decision to carry a gun after being victims of crime. Erika Schwarz said that after a carjacking she had been afraid to drive at night.[81]

And when the *Denver Post* asked Sen. Ben Nighthorse Campbell (R–Colo.) "how it looks for a senator to be packing heat," he responded, "You'd be surprised how many senators have guns." Campbell said that "he needed the gun back in the days when he exhibited his Native American jewelry and traveled long distances between craft shows."[82]

EMOTION, RATIONALITY, AND DETERRENCE

In 1995 two children, ten and eleven years old, dropped a five-year-old boy from the fourteenth floor of a vacant Chicago Housing Authority apartment.[83] The reason? The five-year-old refused to steal candy for them. Or consider the case of Vincent Drost, a promising musician in the process of composing a symphony, who was stabbed to death immediately after making a call from a pay telephone to his girlfriend. The reason? According to the newspapers, "His five teenage attackers told police they wanted to have some fun and simply wanted 'to do' somebody."[84] It is not difficult to find crimes such as "the fatal beating of a school teacher" described as "extremely wicked, shockingly evil." The defense attorney in this crime described the act as one of "insane jealousy."[85]

The notion of "irrational" crime is enshrined by forty-seven states that recognize insanity defenses.[86] Criminal law recognizes that emotions can overwhelm our normal judgments in other ways.[87] For example, under the Model Penal Code, intentional homicide results in the penalty for manslaughter when it "is committed under the influence of extreme mental or emotional disturbance for which there is reasonable explanation or excuse."[88] These mitigating factors are often discussed in terms of the "heat of passion" or "cooling time," the latter phrase referring to "the interval in which 'blood' can be expected 'to cool'" or the time required for "reason to reassert itself."[89] Another related distinction is drawn between first- and second-degree murder: "The deliberate killer is guilty of first-degree murder; the impulsive killer is not."[90] In practice, the true distinction between these two grades appears to be not premeditation but whether the act was done without emotion or "in cold blood," "as is the case [when] someone who kills for money . . . displays calculation and greed."[91]

Some academics go beyond these cases or laws to make more general claims about the motives behind crime. Thomas Carroll, an associate professor of sociology at the University of Missouri at Kansas City, states that "murder is an irrational act, [and] we don't have explanations for irrational behavior."[92] From this he draws the conclusion that "there's really no statistical explanation" for what causes murder rates to fluctuate. Do criminals respond to disincentives? Or are emotions and attitudes the determining factors in crime? If violent acts occur merely because of random emotions, stronger penalties would only reduce crime to the extent that the people least able to control such violent feelings can be imprisoned.

There are obvious difficulties with taking this argument against deterrence to its extreme. For example, as long as "even a handful" of criminals respond to deterrence, increasing penalties will reduce crime. Higher probabilities of arrest or conviction as well as longer prison terms might then possibly "pay" for themselves. As the cases in the previous section have illustrated, criminal decisions—from when to break into a residence, whom to attack, or whether to attack people by using guns or bombs—appear difficult to explain without reference to deterrence. Some researchers try to draw a distinction between crimes that they view as "more rational," like robbery and burglary, and others, such as murder. If such a distinction is valid, one might argue that deterrence would then at least be effective for the more "rational" crimes.

Yet even if we assume that most criminals are largely irrational, deterrence issues raise some tough questions about human nature, questions that are at the heart of very different views of crime and how to combat it. Still it is important to draw a distinction between "irrational" behavior and the notion that deterrence doesn't matter. One doesn't necessarily imply the other. For instance, some people may hold strange, unfathomable objectives, but this does not mean that they cannot be discouraged from doing things that bring increasingly undesirable consequences. While we may not solve the deeper mysteries of how the human mind works, I hope that the following uncontroversial example can help show how deterrence works.

Suppose that a hypothetical Mr. Smith is passed over for promotion. He keeps a stiff upper lip at work, but after he gets home, he kicks his dog. Now this might appear entirely irrational: the dog did not misbehave. Obviously, Mr. Smith got angry at his boss, but he took it out on his poor dog instead. Could we conclude that he is an emotional, irrational individual not responding to incentives? Hardly. The reason that he did not respond forcefully to his boss is probably that he feared the consequences. Expressing his anger at the boss might have resulted in his being fired or passed up for future promotions. An alternative way to vent his frustration would have been to kick his co-workers or throw things around the office. But again, Mr. Smith chose not to engage in such behavior because of the likely consequences for his job. In economic terms, the costs are too high. He manages to bottle up his anger until he gets home and kicks his dog. The dog is a "low-cost" victim.

Here lies the perplexity: the whole act may be viewed as highly irrational—after all, Mr. Smith doesn't truly accomplish anything. But still he tries to minimize the bad consequences of venting his anger. Perhaps we could label Mr. Smith's behavior as "semirational," a mixture of seemingly senseless emotion and rational behavior at the same time.

What about changing the set of punishments in the example above? What if Mr. Smith had a "killer dog," that bit anyone who abused it (equivalent to arming potential victims)? Or what if Mr. Smith were likely to be arrested and convicted for animal abuse? Several scenarios are plausible. First, he might have found another victim, perhaps a family member, to hit or kick. Or he might have modified his outwardly aggressive acts by merely yelling at family and neighbors or demolishing something. Or he might have repressed his anger—either by bottling up his frustration or finding some nonviolent substitute, such as watching a video, to help him forget the day's events.

Evidence of responding to disincentives is not limited to "rational" humans. Economists have produced a large number of studies that investigate whether animals take the costs of doing things into account.[93] Animal subjects have included both rats and pigeons, and the typical experiment measures the amount of some desired treat or standard laboratory food or fluid that is consumed in relation to the number of times the animal must push a lever to get the item. Other experiments alter the amount of the item received for a given number of lever pushes. These experiments have been tried in many different contexts. For example, does an animal's willingness to work for special treats like root beer or cherry cola depend upon the existence of unlimited supplies of water or standard laboratory food? The results from these experiments consistently show that as the "cost" of obtaining the food increases, the animal obtains less food. In economic terms, "Demand curves are downward sloping."

As for human beings, a large economics literature exists that overwhelmingly demonstrates that people commit fewer crimes if criminal penalties are more severe or more certain. Whether we consider the number of airliners hijacked in the 1970s,[94] evasion of the military draft,[95] or international data on violent and property crimes,[96] stiffer penalties or higher probabilities of conviction result in fewer violations of the law. Sociologists are more cautious, but the National Research Council of the U.S. National Academy of Sciences established the Panel on Research on Deterrent and Incapacitative Effects in 1978 to evaluate the many academic studies of deterrence. The panel concluded as follows: "Taken as a whole, the evidence consistently finds a negative association between crime rates and the risks of apprehension, conviction or imprisonment. . . . the evidence certainly favors a proposition supporting deterrence more than it favors one asserting that deterrence is absent."[97]

This debate on incentives and how people respond to them arises repeatedly in many different contexts. Take gun-buyback programs. Surely the intention of such programs is good, but why should we believe that they will greatly influence the number of guns on the street? True, the guns purchased are removed from circulation, and these programs may help to stigmatize gun ownership. Yet if they continue, one effect of such programs will be to increase the return to buying a gun. The price that a person is willing to pay for a gun today increases as the price for which it can be sold rises. In the extreme case, if the price offered in these gun-buyback programs ever became sufficiently high, people would simply buy guns in order to sell them through these programs. I am sure this would hardly distress gun manufacturers, but other than creating some socially useless work, the programs would have a dubious effect on crime. Empirical work on this question reveals no impact on crime from these programs.[98]

Introspection can go only so far. Ultimately, the issue of whether sanctions or other costs deter criminals can be decided only empirically. To what extent will concealed-handgun laws or gun-control laws raise these costs? To what extent will criminals be deterred by these costs? In chapter 2 we will consider how to test these questions.

AN OVERVIEW

The following chapters offer a critical review of the existing evidence on gun control and crime, with the primary focus on the central questions that concern us all: Does gun ownership save or cost lives, and how do the various gun laws affect this outcome?

To answer these questions I use a wide array of data. For instance, I have employed polls that allow us to track how gun ownership has changed over time in different states, as well as the massive FBI yearly crime rate data for all 3,054 U.S. counties from 1977 to 1992. I use additional, more recently available data for 1993 and 1994 later to check my results. Over the last decade, gun ownership has been growing for virtually all demographic groups, though the fastest growing group of gun owners is Republican women, thirty to forty-four years of age, who live in rural areas. National crime rates have been falling at the same time as gun ownership has been rising. Likewise, states experiencing the greatest reductions in crime are also the ones with the fastest growing percentages of gun ownership.

Overall, my conclusion is that criminals as a group tend to behave rationally—when crime becomes more difficult, less crime is committed. Higher arrest and conviction rates dramatically reduce crime. Criminals also move out of jurisdictions in which criminal deterrence increases. Yet criminals respond to more than just the actions taken by the police and the courts. Citizens can take private actions that also deter crime. Allowing citizens to carry concealed handguns reduces violent crimes, and the reductions coincide very closely with the number of concealed-handgun permits issued. Mass shootings in public places are reduced when law-abiding citizens are allowed to carry concealed handguns.

Not all crime categories showed reductions, however. Allowing concealed handguns might cause small increases in larceny and auto theft. When potential victims are able to arm themselves, some criminals turn away from crimes like robbery that require direct attacks and turn instead to such crimes as auto theft, where the probability of direct contact with victims is small.

There were other surprises as well. While the support for the strictest gun-control laws is usually strongest in large cities, the largest drops in violent crime from legalized concealed handguns occurred in the most urban counties with the greatest populations and the highest crime rates. Given the limited resources available to law enforcement and our desire to spend those resources wisely to reduce crime, the results of my studies have implications for where police should concentrate their efforts. For example, I found that increasing arrest rates in the most crime-prone areas led to the greatest reductions in crime. Comparisons can also be made across different methods of fighting crime. Of all the methods studied so far by economists, the carrying of concealed handguns appears to be the most cost-effective method for reducing crime. Accident and suicide rates were unaltered by the presence of concealed handguns.

Guns also appear to be the great equalizer among the sexes. Murder rates decline when either more women or more men carry concealed handguns, but the effect is especially pronounced for women. One additional woman carrying a concealed handgun reduces the murder rate for women by about 3–4 times more than one additional man carrying a concealed handgun reduces the murder rate for men. This occurs because allowing a woman to defend herself with a concealed handgun produces a much larger change in her ability to defend herself than the change created by providing a man with a handgun.

While some evidence indicates that increased penalties for using a gun in the commission of a crime reduce crime, the effect is small. Furthermore, I find no crime-reduction benefits from state-mandated waiting periods and background checks before people are allowed to purchase guns. At the federal level, the Brady law has proven to be no more effective. Surprisingly, there is also little benefit from training requirements or age restrictions for concealed-handgun permits.

Two

How to Test the Effects of Gun Control

THE EXISTING LITERATURE

Despite intense feelings on both sides of the gun debate, I believe everyone is at heart motivated by the same concerns: Will gun control increase or decrease the number of lives lost? Will these laws improve or degrade the quality of life when it comes to violent crime? The common fears we all share with regard to murders, rapes, robberies, and aggravated assaults motivate this discussion. Even those who debate the meaning of the Constitution's Second Amendment cannot help but be influenced by the answers to these questions.[1]

While anecdotal evidence is undoubtedly useful in understanding the issues at hand, it has definite limits in developing public policy. Good arguments exist on both sides, and neither side has a monopoly on stories of tragedies that might have been avoided if the law had only been different. While one side presents the details of a loved one senselessly murdered in a massacre like the December 1993 Colin Ferguson shooting on the Long Island Railroad, the other side points to claims that if only Texas had allowed concealed handguns, the twenty-two lives lost in Luby's restaurant in Killeen in October 1991 could have been saved. Less publicized but equally tragic stories have been just as moving.

Surveys have filled many important gaps in our knowledge; nevertheless, they suffer from many inherent problems. For example, how accurately can a person judge whether the presence of a gun actually saved her life or whether it really prevented a criminal from attacking? Might people's policy preferences influence how they answer the pollster's questions? Other serious concerns arise with survey data. Does a criminal who is thwarted from committing one particular crime merely substitute another victim or another type of crime? Or might this general deterrence raise the costs of these undesirable activities enough so that some criminals stop committing crimes? Survey data just has not been able to answer such questions.

To study these issues more effectively, academics have turned to statistics on crime. Depending on what one counts as academic research, there are at least two hundred studies on gun control. The existing work falls into two categories, using either "time-series" or "cross-sectional" data. Time-series data deal with one particular area (a city, county, or state) over many years; cross-sectional data look across many different geographic areas within the same year. The vast majority of gun-control studies that examine time-series data present a comparison of the average murder rates before and after the change in laws; those that examine cross-sectional data compare murder rates across places with and without certain laws. Unfortunately, these studies make no attempt to relate fluctuations in crime rates to changing law-enforcement factors like arrest or conviction rates, prison-sentence lengths, or other obvious variables.

Both time-series and cross-sectional analyses have their limitations. Let us first examine the cross-sectional studies. Suppose, as happens to be true, that areas with the highest crime rates are the ones that most frequently adopt the most stringent gun-control laws. Even if restrictions on guns were to lower the crime rates, it might appear otherwise. Suppose crime rates were lowered, but not by enough to reach the level of rates in low-crime areas that did not adopt the laws. In that case, looking across areas would make it appear that stricter gun control produced higher crime. Would this be proof that stricter gun control caused higher crime? Hardly. Ideally, one should examine how the high-crime areas that adopted the controls changed over time—not only relative to their past levels but also relative to areas without the controls. Economists refer to this as an "endogeneity" problem. The adoption of the policy is a reaction (that is, "endogenous") to other events, in this case crime.[2] To correctly estimate the impact of a law on crime, one must be able to distinguish and isolate the influence of crime on the adoption of the law.

For time-series data, other problems arise. For example, while the ideal study accounts for other factors that may help explain changing crime rates, a pure time-series study complicates such a task. Many potential causes of crime might fluctuate in any one jurisdiction over time, and it is very difficult to know which one of those changes might be responsible for the shifting crime rate. If two or more events occur at the same time in a particular jurisdiction, examining only that jurisdiction will not help us distinguish which event was responsible for the change in crime. Evidence is usually much stronger if a law changes in many different places at different times, and one can see whether similar crime patterns exist before and after such changes.

The solution to these problems is to combine both time-series and cross-sectional evidence and then allow separate variables, so that each year the national or regional changes in crime rates can be separated out and distinguished from any local deviations.[3] For example, crime may have fallen nationally between 1991 and 1992, but what this study is able to examine is whether there is an additional decline over and above that national drop in states that have adopted concealed-handgun laws. I also use a set of measures that control for the average differences in crime rates across places even after demographic, income, and other factors have been accounted for. No previous gun-control studies have taken this approach.

The largest cross-sectional gun-control study examined 170 cities in 1980.[4] While this study controlled for many differences across cities, no variables were used to deal with issues of deterrence (such as arrest or conviction rates or prison-sentence lengths). It also suffered from the bias discussed above that these cross-sectional studies face in showing a positive relationship between gun control and crime.

The time-series work on gun control that has been most heavily cited by the media was done by three criminologists at the University of Maryland who looked at five different counties (one at a time) from three different states (three counties from Florida, one county from Mississippi, and one from Oregon) from 1973 to 1992 (though a different time period was used for Miami).[5] While this study has received a great deal of media attention, it suffers from serious problems. Even though these concealed-handgun laws were state laws, the authors say that they were primarily interested in studying the effect in urban areas. Yet they do not explain how they chose the particular counties used in their study. For example, why examine Tampa but not Fort Lauderdale, or Jacksonville but not Orlando? Like most previous studies, their research does not account for any other variables that might also help explain the crime rates.

Some cross-sectional studies have taken a different approach and used the types of statistical techniques found in medical case studies. Possibly the best known paper was done by Arthur Kellermann and his many co-authors,[6] who purport to show that "keeping a gun in the home was strongly and independently associated with an increased risk of homicide."[7] The data for this test consists of a "case sample" (444 homicides that occurred in the victim's homes in three counties) and a "control" group (388 "matched" individuals who lived near the deceased and were the same sex and race as well as the same age range). After information was obtained from relatives of the homicide victim or the control subjects regarding such things as whether they owned a gun or had a drug or alcohol problem, these authors attempted to see if the probability of a homicide was correlated with the ownership of a gun.

There are many problems with Kellermann et al.'s paper that undercut the misleading impression that victims were killed by the gun in the home. For example, they fail to report that in only 8 of these 444 homicide cases could it be established that the "gun involved had been kept in the home."[8] More important, the question posed by the authors cannot be tested properly using their chosen methodology because of the endogeneity problem discussed earlier with respect to cross-sectional data.

To demonstrate this, suppose that the same statistical method—with a matching control group—was used to do an analogous study on the efficacy of hospital care. Assume that we collected data just as these authors did; that is, we got a list of all the people who died in a particular county over the period of a year, and we asked their relatives whether they had been admitted to a hospital during the previous year. We would also put together a control sample with people of similar ages, sex, race, and neighborhoods, and ask these men and women whether they had been in a hospital during the past year. My bet is that we would find a very strong positive relationship between those who spent time in hospitals and those who died, quite probably a stronger relationship than in Kellermann's study on homicides and gun ownership. If so, would we take that as evidence that hospitals kill people? I would hope not. We would understand that, although our methods controlled for age, sex, race, and neighborhood, the people who had visited a hospital during the past year and the people in the "control" sample who did not visit a hospital were really not the same types of people. The difference is pretty obvious: those hospitalized were undoubtedly sick, and thus it should come as no surprise that they would face a higher probability of dying.

The relationship between homicides and gun ownership is no different. The finding that those who are more likely to own guns suffer a higher homicide rate makes us ask, Why were they more likely to own guns? Could it be that they were at greater risk of being attacked? Is it possible that this difference arose because of a higher rate of illegal activities among those in the case study group than among those in the control group? Owning a gun could lower the probability of attack but still leave it higher than the probability faced by those who never felt the need to buy a gun to begin with. The fact that all or virtually all the homicide victims were killed by weapons brought into their homes by intruders makes this all the more plausible.

Unfortunately, the case study method was not designed for studying these types of social issues. Compare these endogeneity concerns with a laboratory experiment to test the effectiveness of a new drug. Some patients with the disease are provided with the drug, while others are given a placebo. The random assignment of who gets the drug and who receives the placebo is extremely important. A comparable approach to the link between homicide and guns would have researchers randomly place guns inside certain households and also randomly determine in which households guns would be forbidden. Who receives a gun would not be determined by other factors that might themselves be related to whether a person faces a high probability of being killed.

So how does one solve this causation problem? Think for a moment about the preceding hospital example. One approach would be to examine a change in something like the cost of going to hospitals. For example, if the cost of going to hospitals fell, one could see whether some people who would otherwise not have gone to the hospital would now seek help there. As we observed an increase in the number of people going to hospitals, we could then check to see whether this was associated with an increase or decrease in the number of deaths. By examining changes in hospital care prices, we could see what happens to people who now choose to go to the hospital and who were otherwise similar in terms of characteristics that would determine their probability of living.

Obviously, despite these concerns over previous work, only statistical evidence can reveal the net effect of gun laws on crimes and accidental deaths. The laws being studied here range from those that allow concealed-handgun permits to those demanding waiting periods or setting mandatory minimum sentences for using a gun in the commission of a crime. Instead of just examining how crime changes in a particular city or state, I analyze the first systematic national evidence for all 3,054 counties in the United States over the sixteen years from 1977 to 1992 and ask whether these rules saved or cost lives. I attempt to control for a change in the price people face in defending themselves by looking at the change in the laws regarding the carrying of concealed handguns. I will also use the data to examine why certain states have adopted concealed-handgun laws while others have not.

This book is the first to study the questions of deterrence using these data. While many recent studies employ proxies for deterrence—such as police expenditures or general levels of imprisonment—I am able to use arrest rates by type of crime and also, for a subset of the data, conviction rates and sentence lengths by type of crime.[9] I also attempt to analyze a question noted but not empirically addressed in this literature: the concern over causality related to increases in both handgun use and crime rates. Do higher crime rates lead to increased handgun ownership or the reverse? The issue is more complicated than simply whether carrying concealed firearms reduces murders, because questions arise about whether criminals might substitute one type of crime for another as well as the extent to which accidental handgun deaths might increase.

The Impact of Concealed Handguns on Crime

Many economic studies have found evidence broadly consistent with the deterrent effect of punishment.[10] The notion is that the expected penalty affects the prospective criminal's desire to commit a crime. Expectations about the penalty include the probabilities of arrest and conviction, and the length of the prison sentence. It is reasonable to disentangle the probability of arrest from the probability of conviction, since accused individuals appear to suffer large reputational penalties simply from being arrested.[11] Likewise, conviction also imposes many different penalties (for example, lost licenses, lost voting rights, further reductions in earnings, and so on) even if the criminal is never sentenced to prison.[12]

While these points are well understood, the net effect of concealed-handgun laws is ambiguous and awaits testing that controls for other factors influencing the returns to crime. The first difficulty involves the availability of detailed county-level data on a variety of crimes in 3,054 counties during the period from 1977 to 1992. Unfortunately, for the time period we are studying, the FBI's *Uniform Crime Reports* include arrest-rate data but not conviction rates or prison sentences. While I make use of the arrest-rate information, I include a separate variable for each county to account for the different average crime rates each county faces,[13] which admittedly constitutes a rather imperfect way to control for cross-county differences such as expected penalties.

Fortunately, however, alternative variables are available to help us measure changes in legal regimes that affect the crime rate. One such method is to use another crime category to explain the changes in the crime rate being studied. Ideally, one would pick a crime rate that moves with the crime rate being studied (presumably because of changes in the legal system or other social conditions that affect crime), but is unrelated to changes in laws regulating the right to carry firearms. Additional motivations for controlling other crime rates include James Q. Wilson's and George Kelling's "broken window" effect, where less serious crimes left undeterred will lead to more serious ones.[14] Finally, after telephoning law-enforcement officials in all fifty states, I was able to collect time-series, county-level conviction rates and mean prison-sentence lengths for three states (Arizona, Oregon, and Washington).

The FBI crime reports include seven categories of crime: murder and non-negligent manslaughter, rape, aggravated assault, robbery, auto theft, burglary, and larceny.[15] Two additional summary categories were included: violent crimes (including murder, rape, aggravated assault, and robbery) and property crimes (including auto theft, burglary, and larceny). Although they are widely reported measures in the press, these broader categories are somewhat problematic in that all crimes are given the same weight (for example, one murder equals one aggravated assault).

The most serious crimes also make up only a very small portion of this index and account for very little of the variation in the total number of violent crimes across counties (see table 2.1). For example, the average county has about eight murders, and counties differ from this number by an average of twelve murders. Obviously, the number of murders cannot be less than zero; the average difference is greater than the average simply because while 46 percent of the counties had no murders in 1992, some counties had a very large number of murders (forty-one counties had more than a hundred murders, and two counties had over one thousand murders). In comparison, the average county experienced 619 violent crimes, and counties differ from this amount by an average of 935. Not only does the murder rate contribute just a little more than 1 percent to the total number of violent crimes, but the average difference in murders across counties also explains just a little more than 1 percent of the differences in violent crimes across counties.

Even the narrower categories are somewhat broad for our purposes. For example, robbery includes not only street robberies, which seem the most likely to be affected by concealed-handgun laws, but also bank rob-

Table 2.1 The most common crimes and the variation in their prevalence across counties (1992)

	Average number of crimes	Percent of crime category	Dispersion	Percent of variation in general category due to each crime	Number of counties
Violent crime	619.1		934.50		2,853
Murder	7.8	1.3%	11.60	1.2%	2,954
Rape	35.4	5.7%	48.96	5.2%	2,853
Robbery	224.8	36.3%	380.70	40.7%	2,954
Aggravated assault	367.5	59.4%	534.80	57.2%	2,954
Property crime	4,078.2		5,672		2,954
Auto theft	533.9	13.1%	868	15.3%	2,954
Burglary	969.1	23.8%	1,331	23.4%	2,954
Larceny	2,575.2	63.1%	3.516	62.0%	2,954

Note: Dispersion provides a measure of variation for each crime category; it is a measure of the average difference between the overall average and each county's number of crimes. The total of the percents for specific crimes in the violent-crime category does not equal 100 percent because not all counties report consistent measures of rape. Other differences are due to rounding errors.

beries, for which, because of the presence of armed guards, the additional return to permitting citizens to be armed would appear to be small.[16] Likewise, larceny involves crimes of "stealth," which includes those committed by pickpockets, purse snatchers, shoplifters, and bike thieves, and crimes like theft from buildings, coin machines, and motor vehicles. However, while most of these fit the categories in which concealed-handgun laws are likely to do little to discourage criminals, pickpockets do come into direct contact with their victims.

This aggregation of crime categories makes it difficult to isolate crimes that might be deterred by increased handgun ownership and crimes that might be increasing as a result of a substitution effect. Generally, the crimes most likely to be deterred by concealed-handgun laws are those involving direct contact between the victim and the criminal, especially when they occur in places where victims otherwise would not be allowed to carry firearms. Aggravated assault, murder, robbery, and rape are both confrontational and likely to occur where guns were not previously allowed.

In contrast, crimes like auto theft of unattended cars seem unlikely to be deterred by gun ownership. While larceny is more debatable, in general—to the extent that these crimes actually involve "stealth"—the probability that victims will notice the crime being committed seems low, and thus the opportunities to use a gun are relatively rare. The effect on burglary is ambiguous from a theoretical standpoint. It is true that if nondiscretionary laws cause more people to own a guns, burglars will face greater risks when breaking into houses, and this should reduce the number of burglaries. However, if some of those who already own guns now obtain right-to-carry permits, the relative cost of crimes like armed street robbery and certain other types of robberies (where an armed patron may be present) should rise relative to that for burglary or residential robbery. This may cause some criminals to engage in burglaries instead of armed street robbery. Indeed, a recent Texas poll suggests that such substitution may be substantial: 97 percent of first-time applicants for concealed-handgun permits already owned a handgun.[17]

Previous concealed-handgun studies that rely on state-level data suffer from an important potential problem: they ignore the heterogeneity within states.[18] From my telephone conversations with many law-enforcement officials, it has become very clear that there was a large variation across counties within a state in terms of how freely gun permits were granted to residents prior to the adoption of nondiscretionary right-to-carry laws.[19] All those I talked to strongly indicated that the most populous counties had previously adopted by far the most restrictive practices in issuing permits. The implication for existing studies is that simply using state-level data rather than county data will bias the results against finding any impact from passing right-to-carry provisions. Those counties that were unaffected by the law must be separated from those counties where the change could be quite dramatic. Even cross-sectional city data will not solve this problem, because without time-series data it is impossible to determine the impact of a change in the law for a particular city.[20]

There are two ways of handling this problem. First, for the national sample, one can see whether the passage of nondiscretionary right-to-carry laws produces systematically different effects in the high- and low-population counties. Second, for three states—Arizona, Oregon, and Pennsylvania—I acquired time-series data on the number of right-to-carry permits for each county. The normal difficulty with using data on the number of permits involves the question of causality: Do more permits make crimes more costly, or do higher crime rates lead to more permits? The change in the number of permits before and after the change in the state laws allows us to rank the counties on the basis of how restrictive they had actually been in issuing permits prior to the change in the law. Of course there is still the question of why the state concealed-handgun law changed, but since we are dealing with county-level rather than state-level data, we benefit from the fact that those counties with the most restrictive policies regarding permits were also the most likely to have the new laws imposed upon them by the state.

Using county-level data also has another important advantage in that both crime and arrest rates vary widely within states. In fact, as indicated in table 2.2, the variation in both crime rates and arrest rates across states is almost always smaller than the average within-state variation across counties. With the exception of the rates for robbery, the variation in crime rates across states is from 61 to 83 percent of their average variation within states. (The difference in violent-crime rates arises because robberies make up such a large fraction of the total crimes in this category.) For arrest rates, the numbers are much more dramatic; the variation across states is as small as 15 percent of the average of the variation within states.

These results imply that it is no more accurate to view all the counties in the typical state as a homogenous unit than it is to view all the states in the United States as a homogenous unit. For example, when a state's arrest rate rises, it may make a big difference whether that increase is taking place in the most or least crime-prone counties. Widely differing estimates of the deterrent effect of increasing a state's average arrest rate may be made, depending on which types of counties are experiencing the changes in arrest rates and depending on how sensitive the crime rates are to arrest-rate changes in those particular counties. Aggregating these

Table 2.2 Comparing the variation in crime rates across states and across counties within states from 1977 to 1992

	Percent of variation across states relative to the average variation within states
Crime rates per 100,000 population	
Violent-crime rate	111%
Murder rate	75
Murder rate with guns (from 1982 to 1991)	61
Rape rate	69
Aggravated-assault rate	83
Robbery rate	166
Property-crime rate	66
Auto theft rate	74
Burglary rate	69
Larceny rate	61
Arrest rates (number of arrests divided by number of offenses)*	
Violent crimes	21
Murder	21
Rape	17
Robbery	21
Aggravated assault	32
Property crime	18
Burglary	23
Larceny	15
Auto theft	15
Truncating arrest rates to be no greater than one	
Violent crime	44
Murder	30
Rape	34
Robbery	25
Aggravated assault	41
Property crimes	43
Burglary	33
Larceny	46
Auto theft	31

Note: The percents are computed as the standard deviation of state means divided by the average within-state standard deviations across counties.

*Because of multiple arrests for a crime and because of the lags between the time when a crime occurs and the time an arrest takes place, the arrest rate for counties and states can be greater than one. This is much more likely to occur for counties than for states.

data may thus make it more difficult to discern the true relationship between deterrence and crime.

Another way of illustrating the differences between state and county data is simply to compare the counties with the highest and lowest crime rates to the states with the highest and lowest rates. Tables 2.3 and 2.4 list the ten safest and ten most dangerous states by murder and rape rates, along with those same crime rates for the safest and most dangerous counties in each state. (When rates were zero in more than one county, the number of counties is given.) Two conclusions are clear from these tables. First, even the states with the highest murder and rape rates have counties with no murders or rapes, and these counties in the most dangerous states are much safer than the safest states, according to the average state crime rates for the safest states. Second, while the counties with the highest murder rates tend to be well-known places like Orleans (New Orleans, Louisiana), Kings (Brooklyn, N.Y.), Los Angeles, and Baltimore, there are a few relatively small, rural counties that, for very short periods

Table 2.3 Murder rates: state and county variation in the states with the ten highest and ten lowest murder rates (1992)

States ranked by level of murder rate (10 highest; 10 lowest)	Murder rate per 100,000	County with highest murder rate	Highest county murder rate per 100,000	Number of counties with zero murder rate
Louisiana (1)	15.3	Orleans	57	5
New York (2)	13.2	Kings	28	13
Texas (3)	12.7	Delta	64	116
California (4)	12.66	Los Angeles	21	8
Maryland (5)	12.1	Baltimore	46	4
Illinois (6)	11.21	St. Clair	31	67
Arkansas (7)	10.8	Chicot	53	19
Georgia (8)	10.7	Taliaferro	224	62
North Carolina (9)	10.4	Graham	56	16
South Carolina (10)	10.35	Jasper	32	4
Nebraska (41)	3.2	Pierce	13	72
Utah (42)	2.99	Kane	20	15
Massachusetts (43)	2.97	Suffolk	12	2
Montana (44)	2.22	Meager	55	32
North Dakota (45)	1.9	Golden Valley	53	44
Maine (46)	1.7	Washington	5.5	7
New Hampshire (47)	1.5	Carroll	5.5	5
Iowa (48)	1.1	Wayne	14	71
Vermont (49)	0.7	Chittenden	2.2	9
South Dakota (50)	0.6	Bon Homme	14	49

Table 2.4 Rape rates: state and county variation in the states with the ten highest and ten lowest rape rates (1992)

States ranked by level of rape rate (10 highest; 10 lowest)	Rape rate per 100,000	County with highest rape rate	Highest county rape rate per 100,000	County with lowest rape rate	Lowest county rape rate per 100,000
Alaska (1)	98	North Slope	473	Matanuska-Susitina	14
Delaware (2)	86	Sussex	118	New Castle	74
Michigan (3)	79	Branch	198	Keweenaw	0
Washington (4)	71	Ferry	237	Garfield	0
South Carolina (5)	59	Dillon	97	2 counties	0
Nevada (6)	55	Washoe	82	5 counties	0
Florida (7)	53.7	Putnam	178	3 counties	0
Texas (8)	53.5	Rains	130	70 counties	0
Oregon (9)	53	Multnomah	95	3 counties	0
South Dakota (10)	50	Pennington	136	24 counties	0
Mississippi (41)	29	Harrison	108	11 counties	0
Pennsylvania (42)	27.4	Fulton	85	2 counties	0
Connecticut (43)	26.8	New Haven	38	Windham	1
Wisconsin (44)	26.4	Menominee	98	10 counties	0
North Dakota (45)	25	Morton	81	33 counties	0
Maine (46)	23	Franklin	41	Sagadahoc	0
West Virginia (47)	22	Cabell	99	8 counties	0
Montana (48)	21	Mineral	179	24 counties	0
Iowa (49)	13	Buchanan	62	40 counties	0
Vermont (50)	12	Chittenden	47	Orange	0

of time, garner the top spots in a state. The reverse is not true, however: counties with the lowest murder rates are always small, rural ones.

The two exceptions to this general situation are the two states with the highest rape rates: Alaska and Delaware. Alaska, possibly because of the imbalance of men and women in the population, has high rape rates over the entire state.[21] Even Matanuska-Susitina, which is the Alaskan borough with the lowest rape rate, has a higher rape rate than either Iowa or Vermont. Delaware, which has a very narrow range between the highest and lowest county rape rates, is another exception. However, at least part of the reason for a nonzero rape rate in New Castle county (although this doesn't explain the overall high rape rate in the state) is that Delaware has only three counties, each with a relatively large population, which virtually guarantees that some rapes will take place.

Perhaps the relatively small across-state variation as compared to within-state variations is not so surprising, given that states tend to average out differences as they encompass both rural and urban areas. Yet when coupled with the preceding discussion on the differing effects of concealed-handgun provisions on different counties in the same state, these numbers strongly imply that it is risky to assume that states are homogenous units with respect either to how crimes are punished or how the laws that affect gun usage are changed. Unfortunately, this emphasis on state-level data pervades the entire crime literature, which focuses on state- or city-level data and fails to recognize the differences between rural and urban counties.

However, using county-level data has some drawbacks. Because of the low crime rates in many low-population counties, it is quite common to find huge variations in the arrest and conviction rates from year to year. These variations arise both because the year in which the offense occurs frequently differs from the year in which the arrests and/or convictions occur, and because an offense may involve more than one offender. Unfortunately, the FBI data set allows us neither to link the years in which offenses and arrests occurred nor to link offenders with a particular crime. In counties where only a couple of murders occur annually, arrests or convictions can be many times higher than the number of offenses in a year. This data problem appears especially noticeable for counties with few people and for crimes that are relatively infrequent, like murder and rape.

One partial solution is to limit the sample to counties with large populations. Counties with a large number of crimes have a significantly smoother flow of arrests and convictions relative to offenses. An alternative solution is to take a moving average of the arrest or conviction rates over several years, though this reduces the length of the usable sample period, depending on how many years are used to compute this average. Furthermore, the moving-average solution does nothing to alleviate the effect of multiple suspects being arrested for a single crime.

Another concern is that otherwise law-abiding citizens may have carried concealed handguns even before it was legal to do so.[22] If nondiscretionary laws do not alter the total number of concealed handguns carried by otherwise law-abiding citizens, but merely legalize their previous actions, passing these laws seems unlikely to affect crime rates. The only real effect from making concealed handguns legal could arise from people being more willing to use them to defend themselves, though this might also imply that they would be more likely to make mistakes in using them.

It is also possible that concealed-firearm laws both make individuals safer and increase crime rates at the same time. As Sam Peltzman has pointed out in the context of automobile safety regulations, increasing safety may lead drivers to offset these gains by taking more risks as they drive.[23] Indeed, recent studies indicate that drivers in cars equipped with air bags drive more recklessly and get into accidents at sufficiently higher rates to offset the life-saving effect of air bags for the driver and actually increase the total risk of death for others.[24] The same thing is possible with regard to crime. For example, allowing citizens to carry concealed firearms may encourage them to risk entering more dangerous neighborhoods or to begin traveling during times they previously avoided:

> Martha Hayden, a Dallas saleswoman, said the right-to-carry law introduced in Texas this year has turned her life around.
>
> She was pistol-whipped by a thief outside her home in 1993, suffering 300 stitches to the head, and said she was "terrified" of even taking out the garbage after the attack.
>
> But now she packs a .357 Smith and Wesson. "It gives me a sense of security; it allows you to get on with your life," she said.[25]

Staying inside her house may have reduced Ms. Hayden's probability of being assaulted again, but since her decision to engage in these riskier activities is a voluntary one, she at least believes that this is an acceptable risk. Likewise, society as a whole might be better off even if crime rates were to rise as a result of concealed-handgun laws.

Finally, we must also address the issues of why certain states adopted concealed-handgun laws and whether higher offense rates result in lower arrest rates. To the extent that states adopted the laws because crime was rising, econometric estimates that fail to account for this relationship will underpredict the drop in crime and perhaps improperly blame some of the higher crime rates on the new police who were hired to help solve the problem. To explain this problem differently, crime rates may have risen even though concealed-handgun laws were passed, but the rates might have risen even higher if the laws had not been passed. Likewise, if the laws were adopted when crime rates were falling, the bias would be in the opposite direction. None of the previous gun-control studies deal with this type of potential bias.[26]

The basic problem is one of causation. Does the change in the laws alter the crime rate, or does the change in the crime rate alter the law? Do higher crime rates lower the arrest rate or the reverse? Does the arrest rate really drive the changes in crime rates, or are any errors in measuring crime rates driving the relationship between crime and arrest rates? Fortunately, we can deal with these potential biases by using well-known techniques that let us see what relationships, if any still exist after we try to explain the arrest rates and the adoption of these laws. For example, in examining arrest rates, we can see how they change due to such things as changes in crime rates and then see to what extent the unexplained portion of the arrest rates helps to explain the crime rate. We will find that accounting for these concerns actually strengthens the general findings that I will show initially. My general approach, however, is to examine first how concealed-handgun laws and crime rates, as well as arrest rates and crime rates, tend to move in comparison to one another before we try to deal with more complicated relationships.

Three

Gun Ownership, Gun Laws, and the Data on Crime

Who Owns Guns?

Before studying what determines the crime rate, I would like to take a look at what types of people own guns and how this has been changing over time. Information on gun-ownership rates is difficult to obtain, and the only way to overcome this problem is to rely on surveys. The largest, most extensive polls are the exit polls conducted during the general elections every two years. Recent presidential election polls for 1988 and 1996 contained a question on whether a person owned a gun, as well as information on the person's age, sex, race, income, place of residence, and political views. The available 1992 survey data did not include a question on gun ownership. Using the individual respondent data in the 1988 CBS News General Election Exit Poll and the 1996 Voter News Service National General Election Exit Poll, we can construct a very detailed description of the types of people who own guns. The Voter News Service poll collected data for a consortium of national news bureaus (CNN, CBS, ABC, NBC, Fox, and AP).

What stands out immediately when these polls are compared is the large increase in the number of people who identify themselves as gun owners (see figure 3.1). In 1988, 27.4 percent of voters owned guns.[1] By 1996, the number of voters owning guns had risen to 37 percent. In general, the percentages of voters and the general population who appear to own guns are extremely similar; among the general population, gun ownership rose from 26 to 39 percent,[2] which represented 76 million adults in 1996. Perhaps in retrospect, given all the news media discussions about high crime rates in the last couple of decades, this increase is not very surprising. Just as spending on private security has grown dramatically—reaching $82 billion in 1996, more than twice the amount spent in 1980 (even after taking into account inflation)—more people have been obtaining guns.[3] The large rise in gun sales that took place immediately before the Brady law went into effect in 1994 accounts for some of the increase.[4]

Three points must be made about these numbers. First, the form of

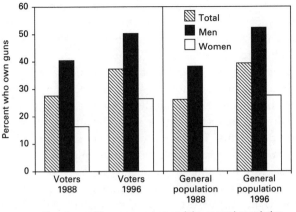

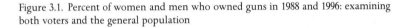

Gun ownership among voters and the general population

Figure 3.1. Percent of women and men who owned guns in 1988 and 1996: examining both voters and the general population

the question changed somewhat between these two years. In 1988 people were asked, "Are you any of the following? (Check as many as apply)," and the list included "Gun Owner." In 1996 respondents were asked to record yes or no to the question, "Are you a gun owner?" This difference may have accounted for part, though not all, of the change.[5] Second, Tom Smith, director of the General Social Survey, told me he guessed that voters might own guns "by up to 5 percent more" than nonvoters, though this was difficult to know for sure because in polls of the general population, over 60 percent of respondents claim to have voted, but we know that only around 50 percent did vote.[6] Given the size of the error in the General Social Survey regarding the percentage of those surveyed who were actual voters, it is nevertheless possible that nonvoters own guns by a few percentage points more than voters.[7]

Finally, there is strong reason to believe that women greatly under-report gun ownership. The most dramatic evidence of this arises from a comparison of the ownership rates for married men and married women. If the issue is whether women have immediate access to a gun in their house when they are threatened with a crime, it is the presence of a gun that is relevant. For example, the 1988 poll data show that 20 percent of married women acknowledged owning a gun, which doesn't come close to the 47 percent figure reported for married men. Obviously, some women interpret this poll question literally regarding personal owner-ship as opposed to family ownership. If married women were assumed to own guns at the same rate as married men, the gun-ownership rate in 1988 would increase from 27 to 36 percent.[8] Unfortunately, the 1996 data do not allow such a comparison, though presumably a similar effect is also occurring there. The estimates reported in the figures do not attempt to adjust for these three considerations.

The other finding that stands out is that while some types of people are more likely than others to own guns, significant numbers of people in all groups own guns. Despite all the Democrat campaign rhetoric during 1996, almost one in four voters who identify themselves as liberals and almost one in three Democrats own a gun (see figure 3.2). The most typical gun owner may be a rural, white male, middle-aged or older, who is a conservative Republican earning between $30,000 and $75,000. Women, however, experienced the greatest growth in gun ownership during this eight-year period, with an increase of over 70 percent: between the years 1988 and 1996, women went from owning guns at 41 percent of the rate of men to over 53 percent.

High-income people are also more likely to own guns. In 1996, people earning over $100,000 per year were 7 percentage points more likely to own guns than those making less than $15,000. The gap between those earning $30,000 to $75,000 and those making less than $15,000 was over 10 percentage points. These differences in gun ownership between high- and low-income people changed little between the two polls.

When comparing these poll results with the information shown in table 1.1 on murder victims' and offenders' race, the poll results imply

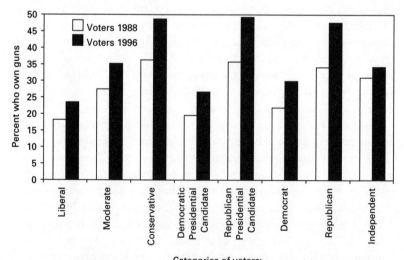

Categories of voters:
political views, candidate the respondent voted for, and respondent's party

Figure 3.2. Percent of different groups of voters who owned guns in 1988 and 1996

that, at least for blacks and whites, gun ownership does not explain the differential murder rates. For example, while white gun ownership exceeds that for blacks by about 40 percent in 1996 (see figure 3.3), and the vast majority of violent crimes are committed against members of the offender's own racial group, blacks are 4.6 times more likely to be murdered and 5.1 times more likely to be offenders than are whites. Blacks may underreport their gun ownership in these polls, but if the white gun-ownership rate is anywhere near correct, even a black gun-ownership rate of 100 percent could not explain by itself the difference in murder rates.

The polls also indicate that families that included union members tended to own guns at relatively high and more quickly growing rates (see figure 3.3). While the income categories by which people were classified in these polls varied across the two years, it is clear that gun ownership increased across all ranges of income. In fact, of the categories examined, only one experienced declines in gun ownership—people living in urban areas with a population of over 500,000 (see figure 3.4). Not too surprisingly, while rural areas have the highest gun-ownership rates and the lowest crime rates, cities with more than 500,000 people have the lowest gun-ownership rates and the highest crime rates (for example, in 1993 cities with over 500,000 people had murder rates that were over 60 percent higher than the rates in cities with populations between 50,000 and 500,000).

For a subset of the relatively large states, the polls include enough respondents to provide a fairly accurate description of gun ownership even at the state level, as shown in table 3.1. The 1988 survey was extensive enough to provide us with over 1,000 respondents for twenty-one

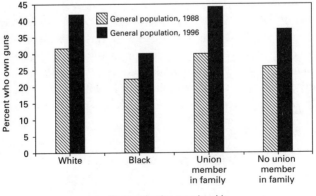

Figure 3.3. Percent of people by race and by union membership who own guns

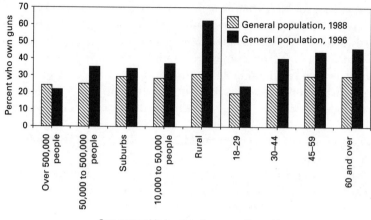

Gun ownership by size of community and by age

Figure 3.4. Percent of people living in different-size communities and in different age groups who owned guns in 1988 and 1996

states, and over 770 respondents for three other states. The 1996 survey was less extensive, with only fourteen of the states surveyed having at least 100 respondents. Since these fourteen states were relatively more urban, they tended to have lower gun-ownership rates than the nation as a whole.

The polls show that the increase in gun ownership was nationwide and not limited to any particular group. Of the fourteen states with enough respondents to make state-level comparisons, thirteen states had more people owning guns at the end of this period. Six states each had over a million more people owning guns. Only Massachusetts saw a decline in gun ownership.

States differ significantly in the percentage of people who own guns. On the lower end in 1988, in states like New York, New Jersey, and Connecticut, only 10 or 11 percent of the population owned guns. Despite its reputation, Texas no longer ranks first in gun ownership; California currently takes that title—approximately 10 million of its citizens own guns. In fact, the percentage of people who own guns in Texas is now below the national average.

UNDERSTANDING DIFFERENT GUN LAWS AND CRIME RATE DATA

While murder rates have exhibited no clear trend over the last twenty years, they are currently 60 percent higher than in 1965.[9] Driven by sub-

Table 3.1 Gun-ownership rates by state

State	CBS General Election Exit Poll (November 8, 1988) surveyed 34,245 people			Voter News Service General Election Exit Poll (November 5, 1996) surveyed 3,818 people			Change in states over time	
	Percent of voting population owning a gun[1] (1)	Percent of state's adults owning a gun[1] (2)	Estimated number of adults owning a gun, using column 2 (3)	Percent of voting population owning a gun[2] (4)	Percent of state's adults owning a gun[2] (5)	Estimated number of adults owning a gun, using column 5 (6)	Change in percent of adults owning a gun (7)	Change in the number of adults owning a gun (8)
United States	27.4%	26%	47.3 million	37%	38.9%	76.7 million	12.9%	29.4 million
California	23%	21%	6 million	33%	32%	10 million	11%	4 million
Connecticut	14%	10%	337,000	10%	12%	377,000	2%	40,000
Florida	28%	29%	3.6 million	35%	31%	4.4 million	2%	800,000
Illinois	19%	17%	1.9 million	34%	36%	4.3 million	19%	2.4 million
Indiana	29%	32%	1.74 million	32%	31%	1.8 million	−1%	60,000
Iowa	29%	31%	847,000	—	—	—	—	—
Maryland	23%	22%	1 million	—	—	—	—	—
Massachusetts	15%	16%	951,000	12%	11%	638,000	−5%	−313,000
Michigan	27%	28%	2.5 million	38%	37%	3.5 million	9%	1 million
Minnesota	33%	28%	1.2 million	—	—	—	—	—
Mississippi	40%	40%	1 million	—	—	—	—	—
Missouri	37%	31%	1.6 million	—	—	—	—	—
Nevada	30%	38%	404,000	—	—	—	—	—
New Jersey	12%	11%	810,000	14%	13%	1.04 million	2%	230,000
New Mexico	38%	41%	608,000	—	—	—	—	—

Table 3.1 Continued

| State | CBS General Election Exit Poll (November 8, 1988) surveyed 34,245 people | | | Voter News Service General Election Exit Poll (November 5, 1996) surveyed 3,818 people | | | Change in states over time | |
	Percent of voting population owning a gun[1] (1)	Percent of state's adults owning a gun[1] (2)	Estimated number of adults owning a gun, using column 2 (3)	Percent of voting population owning a gun[2] (4)	Percent of state's adults owning a gun[2] (5)	Estimated number of adults owning a gun, using column 5 (6)	Change in percent of adults owning a gun (7)	Change in the number of adults owning a gun (8)
New York	13%	11%	2 million	20%	18%	3.3 million	7%	1.3 million
North Carolina	35%	32%	2.1 million	45%	43%	4.8 million	11%	2.7 million
Ohio	25%	28%	2.97 million	32%	32%	3.57 million	4%	600,000
Oregon	40%	36%	996,000	—	—	—	—	—
Pennsylvania	24%	19%	2.2 million	30%	29%	3.5 million	10%	1.3 million
Texas	38%	37%	6.1 million	34%	34%	6.4 million	−3%	300,000
Vermont	34%	35%	193,000	—	—	—	—	—
Washington	33%	31%	1.5 million	—	—	—	—	—
Wisconsin	29%	29%	1.4 million	43%	45%	2.3 million	16%	900,000

Source: The polls used are the General Election Exit Polls from CBS (1988) and Voter News Service (1996). The estimated percent of the voting population owning a gun is obtained by using the weighting of responses supplied by the polling organizations. The estimated percent of the general population owning a gun uses a weight that I constructed from the census to account for the difference between the percentage of males and females; whites, blacks, Hispanics and others; and these groups by age categories that are in the voting population relative to the actual state-level populations recorded by the census.

[1] State poll numbers based upon at least 770 respondents per state.

[2] State poll numbers based upon at least one hundred respondents per state. Other states were surveyed, but the number of respondents in each state was too small to provide an accurate measure of gun ownership. These responses were still useful in determining the national ownership rate, even if they were not sufficient to help determine the rate in an individual state.

stantial increases in rapes, robberies, and aggravated assaults, violent crime was 46 percent higher in 1995 than in 1976 and 240 percent higher than in 1965. As shown in figure 3.5, violent-crime rates peaked in 1991, but they are still substantially above the rates in previous decades.

Such high violent-crime rates make people quite concerned about crime, and even the recent declines have not allayed their fears. Stories of people who have used guns to defend themselves have helped motivate thirty-one states to adopt nondiscretionary (also referred to as "shall-issue" or "do-issue") concealed-handgun laws, which require law-enforcement officials or a licensing agency to issue, without subjective discretion, concealed-weapons permits to all qualified applicants (see figure 3.6). This constitutes a dramatic increase from the eight states that had enacted nondiscretionary concealed-weapons laws prior to 1985. The requirements that must be met vary by state, and generally include the following: lack of a significant criminal record, an age restriction of either 18 or 21, various fees, training, and a lack of significant mental illness. The first three requirements, regarding criminal record, age, and payment of a fee, are the most common. Two states, Vermont and Idaho (with the exception of Boise), do not require permits, though the laws against convicted felons carrying guns still apply. In contrast, discretionary laws allow local law-enforcement officials or judges to make case-by-case decisions about whether to grant permits, based on the applicant's ability to prove a "compelling need."

When the data set used in this book was originally put together, county-level crime data was available for the period between 1977 and 1992. During that time, ten states—Florida (1987), Georgia (1989), Idaho (1990), Maine (1985),[10] Mississippi (1990), Montana (1991), Oregon (1990), Pennsylvania (1989), Virginia (1988),[11] and West Virginia (1989)—adopted nondiscretionary right-to-carry firearm laws. Pennsylvania is a special case because Philadelphia was exempted from the state law during the sample period, though people with permits from the surrounding Pennsylvania counties were allowed to carry concealed handguns into the city. Eight other states (Alabama, Connecticut, Indiana, New Hampshire, North Dakota, South Dakota, Vermont, and Washington) have had right-to-carry laws on the books for decades.[12]

Keeping in mind all the endogeneity problems discussed earlier, I have provided in table 3.2 a first and very superficial look at the data for the most recent available year (1992) by showing how crime rates varied with the type of concealed-handgun law. According to the data presented in the table, violent-crime rates were highest in states with the most restrictive rules, next highest in the states that allowed local authorities discretion in granting permits, and lowest in states with nondiscretionary rules.

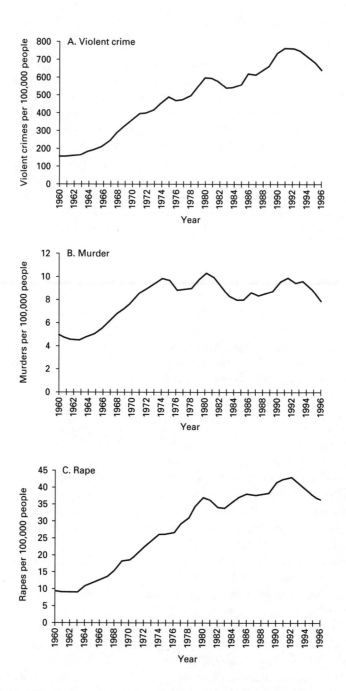

Figure 3.5. U.S. crime rates from 1960—1996 (from FBI's Uniform Crime Reports)

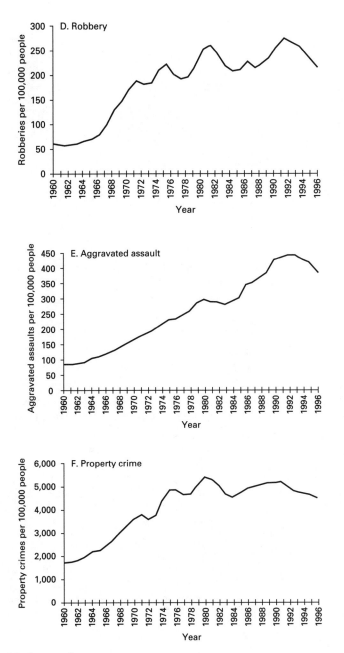

Figure 3.5. Continued

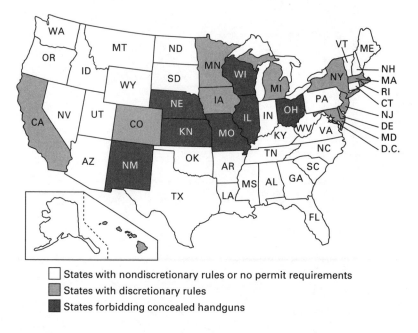

☐ States with nondiscretionary rules or no permit requirements
▨ States with discretionary rules
■ States forbidding concealed handguns

Figure 3.6. State concealed-handgun laws as of 1996

Table 3.2 Crime rates in states and the District of Columbia that do and do not allow the carrying of concealed handguns (1992)

Type of crime	States with nondiscretionary concealed-handgun laws	All other states	Percent higher crime rate in states without nondiscretionary laws	States with discretionary concealed-handgun laws	States forbidding concealed handguns
	Crime rate per 100,000 population				
Violent crime	378.8	684.5	81%	653.1	715.9
Murder	5.1	9.5	86%	7.3	11.6
Rape	35	43.6	25%	43.3	43.9
Aggravated assault	229.9	417.4	82%	380.9	451.7
Robbery	108.8	222.6	105%	220.9	224.1
Property crime	3,786.3	4,696.8	24%	4,666.3	4,725.5
Auto theft	334.2	533.4	60%	564.6	504
Burglary	840.3	1,074.7	28%	1,035.8	1,111.3
Larceny	2,611.8	3,088.7	18%	3,065.9	3,110.1

The difference is quite striking: violent crimes are 81 percent higher in states without nondiscretionary laws. For murder, states that ban the concealed carrying of guns have murder rates 127 percent higher than states with the most liberal concealed-carry laws. For property crimes, the difference is much smaller: 24 percent. States with nondiscretionary laws have less crime, but the primary difference appears in terms of violent crimes.

Since the primary data that we will focus on are at the county level, we are asking whether crime rates change in counties whose states adopt nondiscretionary concealed-handgun laws. We are also asking whether the crime rates change relative to other changes in counties located in states without such laws. Using a reference library (Lexis/Nexis) that contains an extensive collection of news stories and state laws, I conducted a search to determine the exact dates on which these laws took effect. In the states that adopted the laws during the year, the effects for their counties were scaled to equal that portion of the year during which the laws were in effect. Because of delays in implementing the laws even after they went into effect, I defined counties in states with nondiscretionary laws as being under the these laws beginning with the first full year for which the law was in effect. While all the tables shown in this book use the second measure, both measures produced similar results.

The number of arrests and offenses for each type of crime in every county from 1977 to 1992 was provided by the FBI's *Uniform Crime Reports;* in addition, however, I contacted the state department of corrections, attorney general, secretary of state, and state police offices in every state in an effort to compile data on conviction rates, sentence lengths, and concealed-weapons permits by county. The Bureau of Justice Statistics also released a list of contacts in every state that might provide state-level criminal justice data. Unfortunately, county data on the total number of outstanding concealed-carry pistol permits were available only for Arizona, California, Florida, Oregon, Pennsylvania, and Washington, and time-series county data before and after a change in the law were only available for Arizona (1994–96), Oregon (1990–92), and Pennsylvania (1986–92). Since the Oregon nondiscretionary law was passed in 1990, I sought data on the number of permits in 1989 by calling up every county sheriff in Oregon, and 25 of the 36 counties provided that information. (The remaining counties stated that records had not been kept.)[13] For Oregon, data on county-level conviction rates and sentence lengths were also available from 1977 to 1992.

One difficulty with the sentence-length data is that Oregon passed a sentencing-reform act that took effect in November 1989 and required criminals to serve 85 percent of their sentences; thus, judges may have correspondingly altered their sentencing practices. This change was phased in over time because the law only applied to crimes committed after it went into effect in 1989. In addition, the Oregon system did not keep complete records prior to 1987, and their completeness decreased as one looked further into the past. One solution to both of these problems is to allow the sentence-length variable to have different effects in each year.[14] A similar problem exists for Arizona, which adopted a truth-in-sentencing reform in the fall of 1994. We must note, finally, that Arizona differs from Oregon and Pennsylvania in that it already allowed handguns to be carried openly before passing its concealed-handgun law; thus, one might expect to find a somewhat smaller response to adopting a concealed-handgun law.

In addition to using separate variables to measure the average crime rate in each county,[15] I collected data from the Bureau of the Census to try to control for other demographic characteristics that might influence the crime rate. These data included information on the population density per square mile, total county population, and detailed information on the racial and age breakdown of the county (percent of population by each racial group and by sex between 10 and 19 years of age, between 20 and 29, between 30 and 39, between 40 and 49, between 50 and 64, and 65 and over).[16] While a large literature discusses the likelihood that younger males will engage in crime,[17] controlling for these other categories allows us to account for the groups considered most vulnerable (for example, females in the case of rape).[18] Recent evidence reported by Glaeser and Sacerdote confirms the higher crime rates experienced in cities and examines the effects on these rates of social and family influences as well as the changing pecuniary benefits from crime;[19] the present study, however, is the first to explicitly control for population density (see appendix 3 for a more complete discussion of the data).

An additional set of income data was also used. These included real per-capita personal income, real per-capita unemployment insurance payments, real per-capita income-maintenance payments, and real per-capita retirement payments per person over 65 years of age.[20] Unemployment insurance and income-maintenance payments from the Commerce Department's Regional Economic Information System (REIS) data set were included in an attempt to provide annual, county-level measures of unemployment and the distribution of income.

Finally, I recognize that other legal changes regarding how guns are used and when they can be obtained can alter the levels of crime. For example, penalties involving improper gun use might also have been changing simultaneously with changes in the requirements for obtaining permits to carry concealed handguns. In order to see whether such changes might confound my ability to infer the causes of any observed changes in crime rates, I read through various editions of *State Laws and Published Ordinances—Firearms* (published by the Bureau of Alcohol, Tobacco, and Firearms: 1976, 1986, 1989, and 1994). Except for the laws regarding machine guns and sawed-off shotguns, the laws involving the use of guns did not change significantly when the rules regarding concealed-handgun permits were changed.[21] A survey by Marvell and Moody that addresses the somewhat broader question of sentencing-enhancement laws for felonies committed with deadly weapons (firearms, explosives, and knives) from 1970 to 1992 also confirms this general finding: all but four of the legal changes were clustered from 1970 to 1981.[22] Yet Marvell and Moody's dates still allow us to examine the deterrent effect of criminal penalties specifically targeted at the use of deadly weapons during this earlier period.[23]

States also differ in terms of their required waiting periods for handgun purchases. Again using the Bureau of Alcohol, Tobacco, and Firearms' *State Laws and Published Ordinances—Firearms,* I identified states with waiting periods and conducted a Lexis search on the ordinances to determine exactly when those laws went into effect. Thirteen of the nineteen states with waiting periods instituted them prior to the beginning of the sample period.[24]

Four

Concealed-Handgun Laws and Crime Rates: The Empirical Evidence

While our initial comparison of crime rates in states with and without concealed-handgun laws was suggestive, obviously many other factors must be accounted for. The next three chapters use common statistical techniques known as regression analysis to control for these factors. (For those who are interested, a more complete discussion of regressions and statistical significance is provided in appendix 1.) The following discussion provides information on a wide range of law-enforcement activities, but the primary focus is on the link between the private ownership of guns and crime. What gun laws affect crime? Does increased gun ownership cause an increase or a decrease in murders? What is the impact of more lenient laws regarding gun ownership on accidental deaths and suicide?

The analysis begins by examining both county- and state-level crime data and then turns to evidence on the benefits of gun ownership for different groups, such as women and minorities. To test whether crime-rate changes are a result of concealed-handgun laws, it is not enough simply to see whether these laws lower crime rates; changes in crime rates must also be linked to the changes in the number of concealed-handgun permits. We must remember also that the laws are not all the same: different states adopt different training and age requirements for obtaining a permit. These differences allow us to investigate whether the form of the concealed-handgun law matters as well as to test the importance of other gun-control laws. Finally, evidence is provided on whether criminals move to other places when concealed-handgun laws are passed.

The book is organized to examine the simplest evidence first and then gradually considers more complicated issues. The first estimates measure whether the average crime rate falls in counties when they adopt concealed-handgun laws. By looking across counties or states at the same time that we examine them over time, we can test not only whether places with the most permits have the greatest reductions in crime, but also whether those with the greatest *increases* in permits have the greatest reductions in crime. Similarly, we can investigate how total gun ownership is related to the level of crime. Tracking gun ownership in individual states over time allows us to investigate how a crime in a state changes as its gun-ownership rates change.

USING COUNTY AND STATE DATA FOR THE UNITED STATES

The first group of estimates reported in table 4.1 attempts to explain the crime rates for nine different categories of crime. Each column in the table presents the changes in the crime rate for the crime described in the column heading. The numbers in each row represent the impact that a particular explanatory variable has on each crime rate. Three pieces of information are provided for most of the explanatory variables: (1) the percent change in the crime rate attributed to a particular change in the explanatory variable; (2) the percentage of the variation in the crime rate that can be explained by the variation in the explanatory variable;[1] and (3) one, two, or three asterisks denote whether a particular effect is statistically significant at least at the 1, 5, or 10 percent level, where the 1 percent level represents the most reliable result.[2]

While I am primarily interested in the impact of nondiscretionary laws, the estimates also account for many other variables: the arrest rate for each type of crime; population density and the number of people living in a county; measures of income, unemployment, and poverty; the percentage of the population that is a certain sex and race by ten-year age groupings (10 to 19 years of age, 20 to 29 years of age); and the set of variables described in the previous section to control for other county and year differences. The results clearly imply that nondiscretionary laws coincide with fewer murders, aggravated assaults, and rapes.[3] On the other hand, auto theft and larceny rates rise. Both changes are consistent with my discussion of the direct and substitution effects produced by concealed weapons.[4]

The results are also large, indicating how important the laws can be. When state concealed-handgun laws went into effect in a county, murders fell by about 8 percent, rapes fell by 5 percent, and aggravated assaults fell by 7 percent.[5] In 1992 the following numbers were reported: 18,469 murders; 79,272 rapes; 538,368 robberies; and 861,103 aggravated assaults in counties without nondiscretionary laws. The estimated coefficients suggest that if these counties had been subject to state concealed-

Table 4.1 The effect of nondiscretionary concealed-handgun laws on crime rates: National, County-Level, Cross-Sectional, Time-Series Evidence

Change in explanatory variable	Percent change in various crime rates for changes in explanatory variables								
	Violent crime	Murder	Rape	Aggravated assault	Robbery	Property crime	Burglary	Larceny	Auto theft
Nondiscretionary law adopted	−4.9%* (1%)	−7.7%* (2%)	−5.3%* (1%)	−7.01%* (1%)	−2.2%*** (.3%)	2.7%* (1%)	.05% (.02%)	3.3%* (1%)	7.1%* (1%)
Arrest rate for the crime category (e.g., violent crime, murder, etc.) increased by 100 percentage points	−0.48%* (9%)	−1.39%* (7%)	−0.81%* (4%)	−0.896%* (9%)	−0.57%* (4%)	−0.76%* (10%)	−2.4%* (11%)	−0.18%* (4%)	−0.18%* (3%)
Population per square mile increased by 1,000	6%* (5%)	−2% (1%)	−2% (1%)	0.58% (.4%)	31.6%* (17%)	0.48% (1%)	−7%* (9%)	3.7%* (4%)	48%* (36%)
Real per-capita personal income increased by $1,000	0.79%* (1%)	1.63%* (2%)	−0.59%*** (1%)	0.47% (1%)	0.47% (1%)	−1.02%* (3%)	−1.84%* (4%)	−1.23%* (2%)	1.5%* (2%)

Real per-capita unemployment Ins. increased by $100	−2.2%* (.07%)	−4.6%* (1%)	−4.7%* (1%)	−1.9%* (.05%)	0.7% (.01%)	3.8%* (2%)	6.0%* (3%)	1.9%* (.08%)	2.1%* (.06%)
Real per-capita income maintenance increased by $100	−0.7% (.3%)	2.5%** (1%)	−1.7% (.7%)	1.39% (.7%)	−3.2%* (1%)	1.9%* (2%)	3.9%* (4%)	0.2% (.1%)	3.3%* (2%)
Real per-capita retirement payments per person over 65 increased by $1,000	−0.197% (.5%)	−1.3% (3%)	−0.24% (.4%)	−0.68% (2%)	−0.55% (1%)	−0.87% (4%)	−1.06% (7%)	−0.63% (2%)	−0.93% (2%)
Population increased by 100,000	0.86% (1%)	−0.34% (.4%)	−2.94% (3%)	0.45%* (.06%)	−0.61%*** (.06%)	−2.18%* (6%)	−2.14%* (5%)	−3.10%* (6%)	−0.04%* (.05%)

Note: The percentage reported in parentheses is the percent of a standard deviation change in the endogenous variable that can be explained by one-standard-deviation change in the exogenous variable. Year and county dummies are not shown, and the results for demographic variables are shown in appendix. All regressions use weighted least squares, where the weighting is each county's population. Entire sample used for all counties over the 1977–1992 period.

*The result is statistically significant at the 1 percent level for a two-tailed t-test.

**The result is statistically significant at the 5 percent level for a two-tailed t-test.

***The result is statistically significant at the 10 percent level for a two-tailed t-test.

handgun laws and had thus been forced to issue handgun permits, murders in the United States would have declined by about 1,400.

Given the concern raised about increased accidental deaths from concealed weapons, it is interesting to note that the entire number of accidental handgun deaths in the United States in 1988 was only 200 (the last year for which these data are available for the entire United States).[6] Of this total, 22 accidental deaths were in states with concealed-handgun laws, while 178 occurred in states without these laws. The reduction in murders is as much as eight times greater than the total number of accidental deaths in concealed-handgun states. We will revisit the impact that concealed-handgun laws have on accidental deaths in chapter 5, but if these initial results are accurate, the net effect of allowing concealed handguns is clearly to save lives, even in the implausible case that concealed handguns were somehow responsible for all accidental handgun deaths.[7]

As with murders, the results indicate that the number of rapes in states without nondiscretionary laws would have declined by 4,200, aggravated assaults by 60,000, and robberies by 12,000.[8]

On the other hand, property-crime rates increased after nondiscretionary laws were implemented. If states without concealed-handgun laws had passed such laws, there would have been 247,000 more property crimes in 1992 (a 2.7 percent increase). The increase is small compared to the changes that we observed for murder, rape, and aggravated assault, though it is about the same size as the change for robbery. Criminals respond to the threat of being shot while committing such crimes as robbery by choosing to commit less risky crimes that involve minimal contact with the victim.[9]

It is possible to put a rough dollar value on the losses from crime in the United States and thus on the potential gains from nondiscretionary laws. A recent National Institute of Justice study estimates the costs to victims of different types of crime by measuring lost productivity; out-of-pocket expenses, such as those for medical bills and property losses; and losses from fear, pain, suffering, and lost quality of life.[10] While the use of jury awards to measure losses such as fear, pain, suffering, and lost quality of life may be questioned, the estimates provide us with one method of comparing the reduction in violent crimes with the increase in property crimes.

By combining the estimated reduction in crime from table 4.1 with the National Institute of Justice's estimates of what these crimes would have cost victims had they occurred, table 4.2 reports the gain from allowing concealed handguns to be $5.7 billion in 1992 dollars. The reduction in violent crimes represents a gain of $6.2 billion ($4.2 billion from

Table 4.2 The effect of nondiscretionary concealed-handgun laws on victims' costs: What if all states had adopted nondiscretionary laws?

Crime category	Change in number of crimes if states without nondiscretionary laws in 1992 had adopted them			Change in victims' costs if states without nondiscretionary laws in 1992 had adopted them		
	Estimates using county-level data	Estimates using county-level data and state time trends	Estimates using state-level data	Estimates using county-level data	Estimates using county-level data and state time trends	Estimates using state-level data
Murder	−1,410	−1,840	−1,590	−$4.2 billion	−5.57 billion	−$4.8 billion
Rape	−4,200	−3,700	−4,800	−$374 million	−$334 million	−$431 million
Aggravated assault	−60,400	−61,100	−93,900	−$1.4 billion	−$1.4 billion	−$2.2 billion
Robbery	−11,900	−10,990	−62,900	−$98 million	−$90 million	−$518 million
Burglary	1,100	−112,700	−180,800	$1.5 million	−$162 million	−$261 million
Larceny	191,700	−93,300	−180,300	$73 million	−$35 million	−$69 million
Auto theft	89,900	−41,500	−11,100	$343 million	−$2 million	−$42 million
Total change in victims' costs				−$5.7 billion	−$7.6 billion	−$8.3 billion

Note: Estimates of the costs of crime are in 1992 dollars, from the National Institute of Justice's study.

murder, $1.4 billion from aggravated assault, $374 million from rape, and $98 million from robbery), while the increase in property crimes represents a loss of $417 million ($343 million from auto theft, $73 million from larceny, and $1.5 million from burglary). However, while $5.7 billion is substantial, to put it into perspective, it equals only about 1.23 percent of the total losses to victims from these crime categories. These estimates are probably most sensitive to the value of life used (in the National Institute of Justice Study this was set at $1.84 million in 1992 dollars). Higher estimated values of life would obviously increase the net gains from the passage of concealed-handgun laws, while lower values would reduce the gains. To the extent that people are taking greater risks regarding crime because of any increased sense of safety produced by concealed-handgun laws,[11] the preceding numbers underestimate the total savings from allowing concealed handguns.

The arrest rate produces the most consistent effect on crime. Higher arrest rates are associated with lower crime rates for all categories of crime. Variation in the probability of arrest accounts for 3 to 11 percent of the variation in the various crime rates.[12] Again, the way to think about this is that the typical observed change in the arrest rate explains up to about 11 percent of the typical change in the crime rate. The crime most responsive to the arrest rate is burglary (11 percent), followed by property crimes (10 percent); aggravated assault and violent crimes more generally (9 percent); murder (7 percent); rape, robbery, and larceny (4 percent); and auto theft (3 percent).

For property crimes, the variation in the percentage of the population that is black, male, and between 10 and 19 years of age explains 22 percent of the ups and downs in the property-crime rate.[13] For violent crimes, the same number is 5 percent (see appendix 5). Other patterns also show up in the data. Not surprisingly, a higher percentage of young females is positively and significantly associated with the occurrence of a greater number of rapes.[14] Population density appears to be most important in explaining robbery, burglary, and auto theft rates, with the typical variation in population density explaining 36 percent of the typical change across observations in auto theft.

Perhaps most surprising is the relatively small, even if frequently significant, effect of a county's per-capita income on crime rates. Changes in real per-capita income account for no more than 4 percent of the changes in crime, and in seven of the specifications it explains at most 2 percent of the change. It is *not* safer to live in a high-income neighborhood if other characteristics (for example, demographics) are the same. Generally, high-income areas experience more violent crimes but fewer property crimes. The two notable exceptions to this rule are rape and auto theft: high-income areas experience fewer rapes and more auto theft. If the race, sex, and age variables are replaced with separate variables showing the percentage of the population that is black and white, 50 percent of the variation in the murder rate is explained by variations in the percentage of the population that is black. Yet because of the high rates at which blacks are arrested and incarcerated or are victims of crimes (for example, 38 percent of all murder victims in 1992 were black; see table 1.1), this is not unexpected.

One general caveat should be made in evaluating the coefficients involving the demographic variables. Given the very small portions of the total populations that are in some of these narrow categories (this is particularly true for minority populations), the effect on the crime rate from a one-percentage-point increase in the percentage of the population in that category greatly overstates the true importance of that age, sex, or race grouping. The assumption of a one-percentage-point change is arbitrary and is only provided to give the reader a rough idea of what these coefficients mean. For a better understanding of the impact of these variables, relatively more weight should be placed on the second number, which shows how much of the variation in the various crime rates can be explained by the normal changes in each explanatory variable.[15]

We can take another look at the sensitivity of the results from table 4.1 and examine the impact of different subsets of the following variables: the nondiscretionary law, the nondiscretionary law and the arrest rates, and the nondiscretionary law and the variables that account for the national changes in crime rates across years. Each specification yields results that show even more significant effects from the nondiscretionary law, though when results exclude variables that measure how crime rates differ across counties, they are likely to tell us more about which states adopt these laws than about the impact of these laws on crime.[16] The low-crime states are the most likely to pass these laws, and their crime rates become even lower after their passage. I will attempt to account for this fact later in chapter 6.

In further attempts to test the sensitivity of the results to the various control variables used, I reestimated the specifications in table 4.1 without using either the percentages of the populations that fall into the different sex, race, and age categories or the measures of income; this tended to produce similar though somewhat more significant results with respect to concealed-handgun laws. The estimated gains from passing concealed-handgun laws were also larger.

While these regressions account for nationwide changes in crime rates on average over time, one concern is that individual states are likely to have their own unique time trends. The question here is whether the states adopting nondiscretionary concealed-handgun laws experienced falling crime rates over the entire time period. This cannot be true for all states as a whole, because as figure 3.5 shows, violent crimes have definitely not been diminishing during the entire period. However, if this downward trend existed for the states that adopted nondiscretionary laws, the variables shown in table 4.1 could indicate that the average crime rate was lower after the laws were passed, even though the drop in the average level was due merely to a continuation of a downward trend that began before the law took effect. To address this issue, I reestimated the specifications shown in table 4.1 by including state dummy variables that were each interacted with a time-trend variable.[17] This makes it possible to account not only for the national changes in crime rates with the individual year variables but also for any differences in state-specific trends.

When these individual state time trends were included, all results indicated that the concealed-handgun laws lowered crime, though the coefficients were not statistically significant for aggravated assault and larceny. Under this specification, the passage of nondiscretionary concealed-handgun laws in states that did not have them in 1992 would have reduced murders in that year by 1,839; rapes by 3,727; aggravated assaults by 10,990; robberies by 61,064; burglaries by 112,665; larcenies by 93,274; and auto thefts by 41,512. The total value of this reduction in crime in 1992 dollars would have been $7.6 billion. With the exceptions of aggravated assault and burglary, violent-crime rates still experienced larger drops from the adoption of concealed-handgun laws than did property crimes.

Despite the concerns over the aggregation issues discussed earlier, economists have relied on state-level data in analyzing crime primarily because of the difficulty and extra time required to assemble county-level data. As shown in tables 2.2–2.4, the large within-state heterogeneity raises significant concerns about relying too heavily on state-level data.

To provide a comparison with other crime studies relying on state-level data, table 4.3 reestimates the specifications reported in table 4.1 using state-level rather than county-level data. While the results in these two tables are generally similar, two differences immediately manifest themselves: (1) the specifications now imply that nondiscretionary concealed-handgun laws lower all types of crime, and (2) concealed-handgun laws explain much more of the variation in crime rates, while arrest rates (with the exception of robbery) explain much less of the variation.[18] While concealed-handgun laws lower both violent- and property-crime rates, the rates for violent crimes are still much more sensitive to

Table 4.3 Aggregating the data: state-level, cross-sectional, time-series evidence

Change in explanatory variable	Percent change in various crime rates for changes in explanatory variables								
	Violent crime	Murder	Rape	Aggravated assault	Robbery	Property crime	Burglary	Larceny	Auto theft
Nondiscretionary law adopted	−10.1% (5.8%)	−8.62%** (5%)	−6.07%** (4.7%)	−10.9%* (6.5%)	−14.21%* (5.7%)	−4.19%** (4.8%)	−0.88% (.43%)	−8.25%* (7.6%)	−3.14% (3.8%)
Arrest rate for the crime category increased by 100 percentage points	−8.02%* (1.5%)	−7.3%* (5.3%)	−2.05%*** (69%)	−15.3%* (3.9%)	−10.5%* (14.4%)	−59.9% (8.1%)	−14.5%* (6.5%)	−71.5%* (7.6%)	−65.7%* (10.4%)

Note: Except for the use of state dummies in place of county dummies, the control variables are the same as those used in table 4.1 including year dummies, though they are not all reported. The percent reported in parentheses is the percent of a standard deviation change in the endogenous variable that can be explained by a one-standard-deviation change in the exogenous variable. All regressions use weighted least squares, where the weighting is according to each state's population. Entire sample used over the 1977 to 1992 period.

*The result is statistically significant at the 1 percent level for a two-tailed t-test.

**The result is statistically significant at the 5 percent level for a two-tailed t-test.

***The result is statistically significant at the 10 percent level for a two-tailed t-test.

the introduction of concealed handguns, falling two-and-one-half times more than those for property crimes.

Suppose we rely on the state-level results rather than the county-level estimates. We would then conclude that if all states had adopted nondiscretionary concealed-handgun laws in 1992, about 1,600 fewer murders and 4,800 fewer rapes would have been committed.[19] Overall, table 4.3 allows us to calculate that the estimated monetary gain from reductions in crime produced by nondiscretionary concealed-handgun laws was $8.3 billion in 1992 dollars (again, see table 4.2 for the precise breakdown). Yet, at least in the case of property crimes, the concealed-handgun law coefficients are sensitive to whether the regressions are run at the state or county level. This suggests that aggregating observations into units as large as states is a bad idea.[20]

DIFFERENTIAL EFFECTS ACROSS COUNTIES, BETWEEN MEN AND WOMEN, AND BY RACE AND INCOME

Let us now return to other issues concerning the county-level data. Criminal deterrence is unlikely to have the same impact across all counties. For instance, increasing the number of arrests can have different effects on crime in different areas, depending on the stigma attached to arrest. In areas where crime is rampant, the stigma of being arrested may be small, so that the impact of a change in arrest rates is correspondingly small.[21] To test this, the specifications shown in table 4.1 were reestimated by breaking down the sample into two groups: (1) counties with above-median crime rates and (2) counties with below-median crime rates. Each set of data was reexamined separately.

As table 4.4 shows, concealed-handgun laws do indeed affect high- and low-crime counties similarly. The coefficient signs are consistently the same for both low- and high-crime counties, though for two of the crime categories—rape and aggravated assault—concealed-handgun laws have statistically significant effects only in the relatively high-crime counties. For most violent crimes—such as murder, rape, and aggravated assault—concealed-weapons laws have much greater deterrent effects in high-crime counties. In contrast, for robbery, property crimes, auto theft, burglary, and larceny, the effect appears to be greatest in low-crime counties.

Table 4.4 also shows that the deterrent effect of arrests is significantly different, at least at the 5 percent level, between high- and low-crime counties for eight of the nine crime categories (the one exception being violent crimes). The results further reject the hypothesis that arrests would be associated with greater stigma in low-crime areas. Additional

Table 4.4 Aggregating the data: Do law-enforcement and nondiscretionary laws have the same effects in high- and low-crime areas?

Change in explanatory variable	Percent change in various crime rates for changes in explanatory variables								
	Violent crime	Murder	Rape	Aggravated assault	Robbery	Property crime	Burglary	Larceny	Auto theft
	Sample where county crime rates are above the median								
Nondiscretionary law adopted	−6.0%*	−9.9%*	−7.2%*	−4.5%*	−3.4%*	1.6%*	0.4%	3.0%*	5.2%*
Arrest rate for the crime category increased by 100 percentage points	−5.2%*	−12.3%*	−3.3%*	−6.3%*	−29.4%*	−53.5%*	−56.5%*	−59.6%*	−13.3%*
	Sample where county crime rates are below the median								
Nondiscretionary law adopted	−3.7%**	−4.4%**	−3.0%	−0.3%	−7.9%*	8.8%*	3%**	8.7%*	7.2%*
Arrest rate for the crime category increased by 100 percentage points	−5.2%*	−4.9%*	−6.6%*	−6.8%*	−3.7%*	−13.5%*	−27.1%*	−10%*	−1.4%*

Note: The control variables are the same as those used in table 4.1, including year and county dummies, though they are not reported. All regressions use weighted least squares, where the weighting is each county's population. Entire sample used over the 1977 to 1992 period.
*The result is statistically significant at the 1 percent level for a two-tailed t-test.
**The result is statistically significant at the 5 percent level for a two-tailed t-test.
***The result is statistically significant at the 10 percent level for a two-tailed t-test.

arrests in low- and high-crime counties generate extremely similar changes in the aggregate category of violent crime, but the arrest-rate coefficient for murder is almost three times greater in high-crime counties than in low-crime counties. If these results suggest any conclusion, it is that for most crimes, tougher measures have more of an impact in high-crime areas.

The effect of gun ownership by women deserves a special comment. Despite the relatively small number of women who obtain concealed-handgun permits, the concealed-handgun coefficient for explaining rapes in the first three sets of results is consistently similar in size to the effect that this variable has on other violent crime. January 1996 data for Washington and Oregon reveal that women constituted 18.6 and 22.9 percent, respectively, of those with concealed-handgun permits.[22] The set of women who were the most likely targets of rape probably chose to carry concealed handguns at much higher rates than women in general. The preceding results show that rapists are particularly deterred by handguns. As mentioned earlier, the National Crime Victimization Survey data show that providing a woman with a gun has a much greater effect on her ability to defend herself against a crime than providing a gun to a man. Thus even if few women carry handguns, the change in the "cost" of attacking women could still be as great as the change in the "cost" of attacking men, despite the much higher number of men who are becoming armed. To phrase this differently, if one more woman carries a handgun, the extra protection for women in general is greater than the extra protection for men if one more man carries a handgun.[23]

These results raise a possible concern as to whether women have the right incentive to carry concealed handguns. Despite the fact that women who carry concealed handguns make other women so much safer, it is possible that women might decide not to carry them because they see their own personal gain as much smaller than the total benefit to all women that carrying a concealed handgun produces. While the problem is particularly pronounced for women, people in general often take into account only the benefits that they individually receive from carrying a gun and not the crime-reduction benefits that they are generating for others.[24]

As mentioned in chapter 2, an important concern is that passing a nondiscretionary concealed-handgun law should not affect all counties equally. In particular, when states had discretionary laws, counties with the highest populations were also those that most severely restricted people's ability to carry concealed weapons. Adopting nondiscretionary laws therefore produced the greatest change in the number of permits in the more populous counties. Thus, a significant advantage of using this county data is that it allows us to take advantage of county-level variation in the impact of nondiscretionary concealed-handgun laws. To test this variation across counties, figures 4.1 and 4.2 repeat all the specifications in table 4.1 but examine instead whether the effect of the nondiscretionary law varies with county population or population density. (The simplest way to do this is to multiply the nondiscretionary-law variable by either the county population or population density.) While all the other coefficients remain virtually unchanged, this new interaction implies the same crime-reducing effects from the nondiscretionary law as reported earlier. In all but one case the coefficients are more significant and larger.

The coefficients are consistent with the hypothesis that the new laws induce the greatest changes in the largest counties, which have a much greater response in both directions to changes in the laws. Violent crimes fall more and property crimes rise more in the largest counties. The figures indicate how these effects vary for counties of different sizes. For example, when counties with almost 600,000 people (two standard deviations above the mean population) pass a concealed-handgun law, the murder rate falls by 12 percent. That is 7.4 times more than it was reduced for the average county (75,773 people).

Although the law-enforcement officials that I talked to continually mentioned population as being the key variable, I also reexamined whether the laws had different effects in more densely populated counties. Given the close relationship between county population and population density, it is not too surprising to find that the impact of concealed handguns in more densely populated areas is similar to their impact in more populous counties. The most densely populated areas are the ones most helped by concealed-handgun laws. Passing a concealed-handgun law lowers the murder rate in counties with about 3,000 people per square mile (the levels found in Fairfax, Virginia; Orleans, Louisiana, which contains New Orleans; and Ramsey, Minnesota, which contains St. Paul) by 8.5 percent, 12 times more than it lowers murders in the average county. The only real difference between the results for population and population density occur for the burglary rate, where concealed-handgun laws are associated with a small reduction in burglaries for the most densely populated areas.

Figures 4.3 and 4.4 provide a similar breakdown by income and by the percentage of the population that is black. Higher-income areas and counties with relatively more blacks both have particularly large drops in crime associated with concealed-handgun laws. Counties with a 37 percent black population experienced 11 percent declines in both murder and aggravated assaults. The differences with respect to income were not as large.[25]

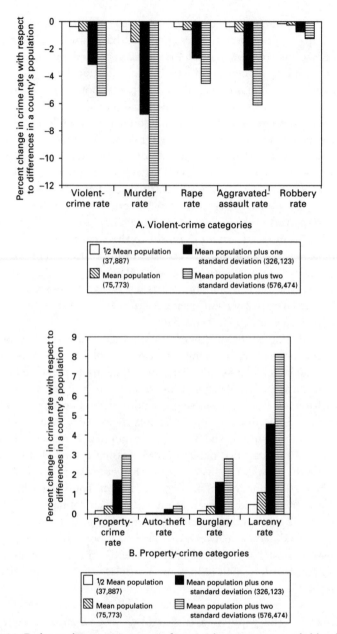

Figure 4.1. Do larger changes in crime rates from nondiscretionary concealed-handgun laws occur in more populous counties?

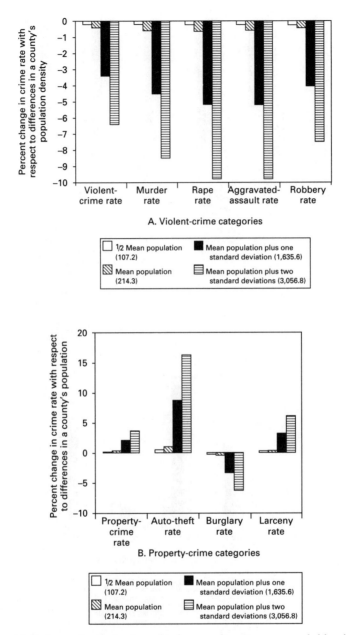

Figure 4.2. Do larger changes in crime rates from nondiscretionary concealed-handgun laws occur in more densely populated counties?

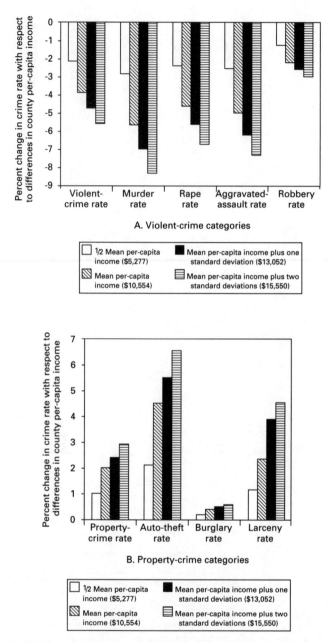

Figure 4.3. How does the change in crime from nondiscretionary concealed-handgun laws vary with county per-capita income?

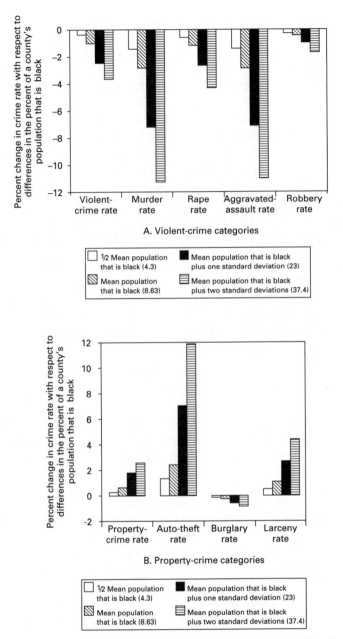

Figure 4.4. How does the change in crime from nondiscretionary concealed-handgun laws vary with the percent of a county's population that is black?

With the extremely high rates of murder and other crimes committed against blacks, it is understandable why so many blacks are concerned about gun control. University of Florida criminologist Gary Kleck says, "Blacks are more likely to have been victims of crime or to live in neighborhoods where there's a lot of crime involving guns. So, generally, blacks are more pro-control than whites are." Nationally, polls indicate that 83 percent of blacks support police permits for all gun purchases.[26] While many blacks want to make guns harder to get, the irony is that blacks benefit more than other groups from concealed-handgun laws. Allowing potential victims a means for self-defense is more important in crime-prone neighborhoods. Even more strikingly, the history of gun control in the United States has often been a series of attempts to disarm blacks.[27] In explaining the urgency of adopting the U.S. Constitution's Fourteenth Amendment, Duke University Law Professor William Van Alstyne writes,

> It was, after all, the defenselessness of the Negroes (denied legal rights to keep and bear arms by state law) from attack by night riders—even to protect their own lives, their own families, and their own homes—that made it imperative that they, as citizens, could no longer be kept defenseless by a regime of state law denying them the common right to keep and bear arms.[28]

Indeed, even in the 1960s much of the increased regulation of firearms stemmed from the fear generated by Black Panthers who openly carried guns.

Alexis Herman, the current Secretary of Labor, experienced firsthand the physical risks of growing up black in Alabama. Describing her difficult confirmation hearings, an Associated Press story included the following story:

> Anyone who thought the frustrations of waiting for confirmation would discourage her knew nothing about the lessons Herman learned from her father. They forgot that he sued to integrate the Democratic Party in Alabama, and later became the state's first black ward leader. They never heard about the night he put a pistol in his young daughter's hands and stepped out of the car to confront the Ku Klux Klan.
>
> "He taught me that you have to face adversity. He taught me to stand by my principles," Herman said in the interview. "He also taught me how to work within the system for change."
>
> Herman said her father never raised his voice, but he always kept a small silver pistol under the driver's seat of his DeSoto as he drove from community meeting to community meeting around Mobile. She always sat close by his side, unless the pistol was out. "The only way that I ever

knew trouble was around was that the gun would come out from under the driver's seat and he'd put it by his side," she said.

As they left the home of a minister one Christmas Eve, the pistol was on the car seat. She was 5. "It was a dark road, a dirt road to get back to the main highway," she recalled. "We were driven off the road by another car, and they were Klansmen."

She hid on the floor and her father pressed the pistol's white handle into her palm. "He told me, 'If anybody opens this door, I want you to pull this trigger.'" He locked the door behind him and walked ahead to keep them away from the car. She crouched in the dark, listening until the shouts and scuffling died down.

Eventually, the minister came to the car to drive Herman home. Her father, who had been beaten, rode in another car.[29]

Recently, after testifying before the Illinois state House of Representatives on whether to pass a concealed-handgun bill, I was approached by a black representative from Chicago who supported the bill.[30] He told me that, at least for Illinois, he was not surprised by my finding that areas with large minority populations gained the most from these laws. Noting the high rate at which young, black males are stopped by police and the fact that it is currently a felony to possess a concealed handgun, he said that an honest, law-abiding, young, black male would be "nuts" to carry a concealed handgun in Illinois. He mentioned a case that had occurred just a week earlier: Alonzo Spellman—a black professional football player for the Chicago Bears—had been arrested in Chicago after a routine traffic violation revealed that he had a handgun in his car.[31] Noting the inability of the police to protect people in heavily black areas when "bad guys" already had illegal guns, the representative said he believed that the current power imbalance between law-abiding people and criminals was greatest in black areas.

Perhaps it is not too surprising that blacks and those living in urban areas gain the most from being able to defend themselves with concealed handguns, since the absence of police appears most acute in black, central-city neighborhoods. Until 1983, the American Housing Survey annually asked sixty thousand households whether their neighborhoods had adequate police protection. Black, central-city residents were about twice as likely as whites generally to report that they did not have adequate protection, and six times more likely to say that they had considered moving because of an insufficient police presence in their neighborhoods.[32]

These results should at least give pause to the recent rush in California to pass city ordinances and state laws banning low-cost, "Saturday night specials." Indeed, the results have implications for many gun-control rules that raise gun prices. Law-abiding minorities in the most crime-prone areas produced the greatest crime reductions from being able to defend themselves. Unfortunately, however unintentionally, California's new laws risk disarming precisely these poor minorities.

USING OTHER CRIME RATES TO EXPLAIN THE CHANGES IN THE CRIME RATES BEING STUDIED

Other questions still exist regarding the specifications employed here. Admittedly, although arrest rates and average differences in individual counties are controlled for, more can be done to account for the changing environments that determine the level of crime. One method is to use changes in other crime rates to help us understand why the crime rates that we are studying are changing over time. Table 4.5 reruns the specifications used to generate figure 4.1A but includes either the burglary or robbery rates as proxies for other changes in the criminal justice system. Robbery and burglary are the violent- and property-crime categories that are the least related to changes in concealed-handgun laws, but they still tend to move up and down together with all the other types of crimes.[33]

Some evidence that burglary or robbery rates will measure other changes in the criminal justice system or other omitted factors that explain changing crime rates can be seen in their correlations with other crime categories. Indeed, the robbery and burglary rates are very highly correlated with the other crime rates.[34] The two sets of specifications reported in table 4.5 closely bound the earlier estimates, and the estimates continue to imply that the introduction of concealed-handgun laws coincided with similarly large drops in violent crimes and increases in property crimes. These results differ from the preceding results in that the nondiscretionary laws are not significant related to robberies. The estimates on the other control variables also remain essentially unchanged.[35]

CRIME: CHANGES IN LEVELS VERSUS CHANGES IN TRENDS

The preceding results in this chapter examined whether the average crime rate fell after the nondiscretionary laws went into effect. If changes in the law affect behavior with a lag, changes in the trend are probably more relevant; therefore, a more important question is, How has the crime trend changed with the change in laws? Examining whether there is a change in levels or a change in whether the crime rate is rising or falling could yield very different results. For example, if the crime rate

Table 4.5 Using crime rates that are relatively unrelated to changes in nondiscretionary laws as a method of controlling for other changes in the legal environment: controlling for robbery and burglary rates

Change in the explanatory variable	Percent change in various crime rates for changes in explanatory variables								
	Violent crime	Murder	Rape	Aggravated assault	Robbery	Property crime	Burglary	Larceny	Auto theft
	Controlling for robbery rates								
Nondiscretionary law adopted multiplied by county population (evaluated at mean county population)	-2.6%* 1%	-4.3%* 1.1%	-1.9%* 0.4%	-2.6%* 0.4%	—	1.4%* 0.5%	0.08% 0.04%	1.3%* 0.4%	3.7%* 0.5%
Arrest rate for the crime category increased by 100 percentage points	-0.038* 7%	-0.13* 7%	-0.07* 4%	-0.08* 8%	—	-0.06* 8%	-0.20* 9%	-0.015* 3%	-0.014* 2%

Table 4.5 Continued

Change in the explanatory variable	Percent change in various crime rates for changes in explanatory variables								
	Violent crime	Murder	Rape	Aggravated assault	Robbery	Property crime	Burglary	Larceny	Auto theft
					Controlling for burglary rates				
Nondiscretionary law adopted multiplied by *county population (evaluated at mean county population)	−2.4%* 1%	−4.3%* 1.1%	−2.0%* 0.4%	−2.6%* 0.4%	0.4% 0.04%	1.8%* 0.7%	—	1.4%* 0.4%	3.6%* 0.5%
Arrest rate for the crime category increased by 100 percentage points	−0.026* 5%	−0.13* 6%	−0.05* 3%	−0.05* 5%	−0.043* 3%	−0.05* 6%	—	−0.01* 2%	−0.01* 2%

Note: While not all the coefficient estimates are reported, all the control variables are the same as those used in table 4.1, including year and county dummies. All regressions use weighted least squares, where the weighting is each county's population. Net violent and property-crime rates are respectively net of robbery and burglary rates to avoid producing any artificial collinearity. Likewise, the arrest rates for those values omit the portion of the corresponding arrest rates due to arrests for robbery and burglary. While not reported, the coefficients for the robbery and burglary rates were extremely statistically significant and positive. Entire sample used over the 1977 to 1992 period.

*The result is statistically significant at the 1 percent level for a two-tailed t-test.

was rising right up until the law was adopted but falling thereafter, some values that appeared while crime rate was rising could equal some that appeared as it was falling. In other words, deceptively similar levels can represent dramatically different trends over time.

I used several methods to examine changes in the trends exhibited over time in crime rates. First, I reestimated the regressions in table 4.1, using year-to-year changes on all explanatory variables (see table 4.6). These regressions were run using both a variable that equals 1 when a nondiscretionary law is in effect as well as the change in that variable (called "differencing" the variable) to see if the initial passage of the law had an impact. The results consistently indicate that the law lowered the rates of violent crime, rape, and aggravated assault. Nondiscretionary laws discourage murder in both specifications, but the effect is only statistically significant when the nondiscretionary variable is also differenced. The property-crime results are in line with those of earlier tables, showing that nondiscretionary laws produce increases in property crime. Violent crimes decreased by an average of about 2 percent annually, whereas property crimes increased by an average of about 5 percent.

As one might expect, the nondiscretionary laws affected crime immediately, with an additional change spread out over time. Why would the entire effect not be immediate? An obvious explanation is that not everyone who would eventually obtain a permit to carry a concealed handgun did so right away. For instance, as shown by the data in table 4.7, the number of permits granted in Florida, Oregon, and Pennsylvania was still increasing substantially long after the nondiscretionary law was put into effect. Florida's law was passed in 1987, Oregon's in 1990, and Pennsylvania's in 1989.

Reestimating the regression results from table 4.1 to account for different time trends in the crime rates before and after the passage of the law provides consistent strong evidence that the deterrent impact of concealed handguns increases with time. For most violent crimes, the time trend prior to the passage of the law indicates that crime was rising. The results using the simple time trends for these violent-crime categories are reported in table 4.8. Figures 4.5 through 4.9 illustrate how the violent-crime rate varies before and after the implementation of nondiscretionary concealed-handgun laws when both the linear and squared time trends are employed. Comparing the slopes of the crime trends before and after the enactment of the laws shows that the trends become more negative to a degree that is statistically significant after the laws were passed.[36]

These results answer another possible objection: whether the findings are simply a result of so-called crime cycles. Crime rates rise or fall over

Table 4.6 Results of rerunning the regressions on differences

Exogenous variables	Δln(violent-crime rate)	Δln(Murder rate)	Δln(Rape rate)	Δln(Aggravated-assault rate)	Δln(robbery rate)	Δln(property-crime rate)	Δln(Burglary rate)	Δln(Larceny rate)	Δln(Auto-theft rate)
	All variables except for the nondiscretionary dummy differenced								
Nondiscretionary law adopted	−2.2%***	−2.6%	−5.2%*	−4.6%*	−3.3%****	5.2%*	3.5%*	5.2%*	12.8%*
First differences in the arrest rate for the crime category	−0.05%*	−0.15%*	−0.09%*	−0.09%*	−0.06%*	−0.08%*	−0.24%*	−0.02%*	−0.02%*
	All variables differenced								
First differences in the dummy for nondiscretionary law adopted	−2.7%*	−3.6%***	−3.9%*	−5.4%*	−0.7%	4.8%*	0.7%	6.2%*	24.2%*
First differences in the arrest rate for the crime category	−0.05%*	−0.15%*	−0.09%*	−0.09%*	−0.06%*	−0.08%*	−.24%*	−0.02%*	−0.02%*

Note: The variables for income; population; race, sex, and age of the population; and density are all in terms of first differences. While not all the coefficient estimates are reported, all the control variables used in Table 4.1 are used here, including year and county dummies. All regressions use weighted least squares, where the weighting is each county's population. Entire sample used over the 1977 to 1992 period.

*The result is statistically significant at the 1 percent level for a two-tailed t-test.

***The result is statistically significant at the 10 percent level for a two-tailed t-test.

****The result is statistically significant at the 11 percent level for a two-tailed t-test.

Table 4.7 Permits granted by state: Florida, Oregon, and Pennsylvania

Year	Florida	Oregon	Pennsylvania
1987	17,000[a]	N.A.	N.A.
1988	33,451	N.A.	267,335[c]
1989	51,335	N.A.	314,925
1990	65,636	N.A.	360,649
1991	67,043	N.A.	399,428
1992	75,578	22,197[b]	360,919
1993	95,187	32,049	426,011
1994	134,008	43,216	492,421
1995	163,757	65,394	571,208
1996	192,016	78,258	N.A.

[a]Estimate of the number of concealed-handgun permits issued immediately before Florida's law went into effect from David McDowall, Colin Loftin, and Brian Wiersema, "Easing Concealed Firearms Laws: Effects on Homicide in Three States," *Journal of Criminal Law and Criminology*, 86 (Fall 1995): 194.
[b]December 31, 1991.
[c]Number of permits issued under discretionary law.

time. If concealed-handgun laws were adopted at the peaks of these cycles (say, because concern over crime is great), the ensuing decline in crime might have occurred anyway without any help from the new laws. To deal with this, I controlled not only for national crime patterns but also for individual county patterns by employing burglary or robbery rates to explain the movement in the other crime rates. I even tried to control for individual state trends. Yet the simplest way of concisely illustrating that my results are not merely a product of the "normal" ups and downs in crime rates is to look again at the graphs in figures 4.5–4.9. With the exception of aggravated assault, the drops not only begin right when the laws pass but also take the crime rates well below what they had been before the passage of the laws. It is difficult to believe that, on the average, state legislatures could have timed the passage of these laws so accurately as to coincide with the peaks of crime waves; nor can the resulting declines be explained simply as reversions to normal levels.

WAS THE IMPACT OF NONDISCRETIONARY CONCEALED-HANDGUN LAWS THE SAME EVERYWHERE?

Just as we found that the impact of nondiscretionary laws changed over time, we expect to find differences across states. The reason is the same in both cases: deterrence increases with the number of permits. While the information obtained from state government officials only pertained to why permits were issued at different rates across counties within a

Table 4.8 Change in time trends for crime rates before and after the adoption of nondiscretionary laws

| | Percent change in various crime rates for change in explanatory variable | | | | | | | |
	Violent crime	Murder	Rape	Aggravated assault	Robbery	Property crime	Auto theft	Burglary	Larceny
Change in the crime rate from the difference in the annual change in crime rates in the years before and after the change in the law (annual rate after the law − annual rate before the law)	−0.9%*	−3%*	−1.4%*	−0.5%*	−2.7%*	−0.6%*	−0.3%**	−1.5%*	−0.1%

Note: The control variables are the same as those used in table 4.1, including year and county dummies, though they are not reported, because the coefficient estimates are very similar to those reported earlier. All regressions use weighted least squares, where the weighting is each county's population. Entire sample used over the 1977 to 1992 period.

*The result is statistically significant at the 1 percent level for a two-tailed t-test.

**The result is statistically significant at the 5 percent level for a two-tailed t-test.

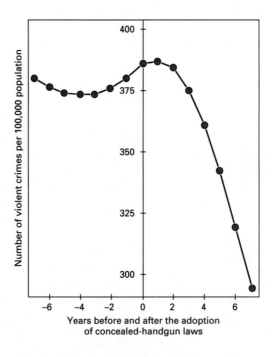

Figure 4.5. The effect of concealed-handgun laws on violent crimes

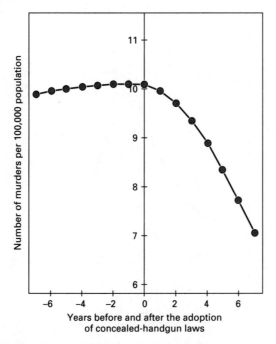

Figure 4.6. The effect of concealed-handgun laws on murders

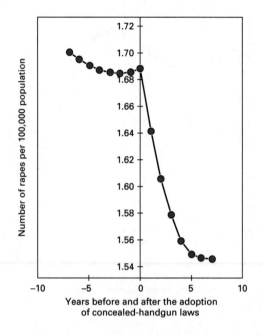

Figure 4.7. The effect of concealed-handgun laws on rapes

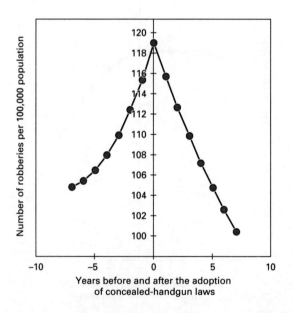

Figure 4.8. The effect of concealed-handgun laws on robbery rates

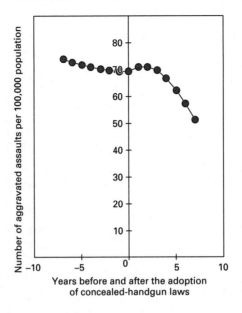

Figure 4.9. The effect of concealed-handgun laws on aggravated assaults

given state, the rate at which new permits are issued at the state level may also vary based upon population and population density. If this is true, then it should be possible to explain the differential effect that non-discretionary laws have on crime in each of the states that passed such laws in the same way that we examined differences across counties.

Table 4.9 reexamines my earlier regressions, where I took into account that concealed-handgun laws have different effects across counties, depending upon how lenient officials had been in issuing permits under a previously discretionary system. The one change from earlier tables is that a different coefficient is used for the counties in each of the ten states that changed their laws during the 1977 to 1992 period. At least for violent crimes, the results indicate a very consistent effect of nondiscretionary concealed-handgun laws across states. Nine of the ten states experienced declines in violent-crime rates as a result of these laws, and eight of the ten states experienced declines in murder rates; in the states where violent crimes, murders, or robberies rose, the increases were very small. In fact, the largest increases were smaller than the smallest declines in the states where those crime rates fell.

Generally, the states with the largest decreases in any one category tended to have relatively large decreases across all the violent-crime categories, although the "leader" in each category varied across all the

Table 4.9 State-specific impact of nondiscretionary concealed-handgun laws

	Violent crime	Murder	Rape	Aggravated assault	Robbery	Property crime	Auto theft	Burglary	Larceny
Florida	-4%	-10%	-8%	-4%	0.3%	1%	2%	0.3%	2%
Georgia	0.2	-2	0.5	-0.2	0	1	1	1	1
Idaho	-3	-1	0.1	-3	-7	-1	-3	-3	-1
Maine	-17	-5	1	-24	-8	1	-4	-2	2
Mississippi	-3	0.6	3	-8	0	-0.2	3	2	-1
Montana	-10	-5	-10	-12	-6	-4	-5	5	-4
Oregon	-3	-1	-1	-3	-4	-2	3	-4	-2
Pennsylvania	-1	-3	-1	1	-2	1	3	-1	3
Virginia	-2	1	-1	-2	-2	-1	-2	-2	-1
West Virginia	-1	-11	-5	-1	1	3	0	4	2
Summary of the coefficients' signs									
Negative	9	8	6	9	6	5	4	5	5
Positive	1	2	4	1	4	5	6	5	5

Note: The table uses arrest rates adjusted for counties wherein the adoption of nondiscretionary concealed-handgun laws was most likely to represent a real change from past practice by multiplying the nondiscretionary-law variables by the population in each county. The percents are evaluated at the mean county population.

violent-crime categories.[37] Likewise, the states with relatively small crime decreases (for example, Georgia, Oregon, Pennsylvania, and Virginia) tended to exhibit little change across all the categories.

Property crimes, on the other hand, exhibited no clear pattern. Property crimes fell in five states and increased in five states, and the size of any decrease or increase was quite small and unsystematic.

Ideally, any comparison across states would be based on changes in the number of permits issued rather than simply the enactment of the nondiscretionary law. States with the largest increases in permits should show the largest decreases in crime rates. Unfortunately, only a few states have recorded time-series data on the number of permits issued. I will use such data in chapter 5. For the moment, it is still useful to see whether the patterns in crime-rate changes found earlier across counties are also found across states. In particular, we would like to know whether the largest declines occurred in states with the largest or most dense populations, which we believed had the greatest increase in permits. The justification for the county-level differences was very strong because it was based on conversations with individual state officials, but those officials were not asked to make judgments across states (nor was it likely that they could do so). Further, there is much more heterogeneity across counties, and a greater number of observations. The relationship posited earlier for county populations also seems particularly tenuous when dealing with state-level data because a state with a large population could be made up of a large number of counties with small populations.

With this list of reservations in mind, let us look at the results we get by using state-level density data. Table 4.10 provides the results with respect to population density, and we find that, just as in the case of counties, larger declines in crime were recorded in the most densely populated states. The differences are quite large: the most densely populated states experienced decreases in violent crimes that were about three times greater than the decreases in states with the average density. The results were similar when state populations were taken into account.

OTHER GUN-CONTROL LAWS AND DIFFERENT TYPES OF CONCEALED-HANDGUN LAWS

Two common restrictions on handguns arise from (1) increased sentencing penalties for crimes involving the use of a gun and (2) waiting periods required before a citizen can obtain a permit for a gun. How did these two types of laws affect crime rates? Could it be that these laws—rather than concealed-handgun laws—explain the deterrent effects? To answer this question, I reestimated the regressions in tables 4.1 and 4.3 by

Table 4.10 Effects of concealed-handgun laws across states related to differences in state population density

State population density	Violent crimes	Murder	Rape	Aggravated assault	Robbery	Property crimes	Auto theft	Burglary	Larceny
1/2 Mean 179 per square mile	−2.7%	−3.2%	−5%	−1%	−7%	−1%	3%	−5%	1%
Mean 358 per square mile	−5.4	−6.3	−10	−2	−14	−1	6	−10	2
Plus 1 standard deviation 778 per square mile	−11.8	−13.7	−21	−4	−29	−3	12	−22	4
Plus 2 standard deviations 1,197 per square mile	−18.2	−21.1	−32	−6	−45	−5	19	−33	7

Note: The regressions used for this table multiplied the variable for whether the law was enacted by that state's population density. The control variables used to generate these estimates are the same as those used in table 4.1, including year and county dummies, though they are not reported, because the coefficient estimates are very similar to those reported earlier. All regressions use weighted least squares, where the weighting is each state's population.

(1) adding a variable to control for state laws that increase sentencing penalties when crimes involve guns and (2) adding variables to measure the impact of waiting periods.[38] It is not clear whether adding an extra day to a waiting period had much of an effect; therefore, I included a variable for when the waiting period went into effect along with variables for the length of the waiting period in days and the length in days squared to pick up any differential impact from longer lengths. In both sets of regressions, the variable for nondiscretionary concealed-handgun laws remains generally consistent with the earlier results.[39] While the coefficients for arrest rates are not reported here, they also remain very similar to those shown previously.

So what about these other gun laws? The pattern that emerges from table 4.11 is much more ambiguous. The results for county-level data suggest that harsher sentences for the use of deadly weapons reduce violent crimes, especially crimes of aggravated assault and robbery. While the same county-level data frequently imply an impact on murder, rape, aggravated assault, and robbery, the effects are quite inconsistent. For example, simply requiring the waiting period appears to raise murder and rape rates but lower the rates for aggravated assault and robbery. The lengths of waiting periods also result in inconsistent patterns: longer periods at first lower and then raise the murder and rape rates, with the reverse occurring for aggravated assault. Using state- level data fails to confirm any statistically significant effects for the violent-crime categories. First, it reveals no statistically significant or economically consistent relationship between either the presence of waiting periods or their length and violent-crime rates. The directions of the effects also differ from those found using county data. Taken together, the results make it very difficult to argue that waiting periods (particularly long ones) have an overall beneficial effect on crime rates. In addition, one other finding is clear: laws involving sentence length and waiting periods do not alter my earlier findings with respect to nondiscretionary laws; that is, the earlier results for nondiscretionary laws cannot merely be reflecting the impact of other gun laws.

THE IMPORTANCE OF THE TYPES OF CONCEALED-HANDGUN LAWS ADOPTED: TRAINING AND AGE REQUIREMENTS

Finally, we need to consider how concealed-handgun laws vary across states and whether the exact rules matter much. Several obvious differences exist: whether a training period is required, and if so, how long that period is; whether any minimum age limits are imposed; the number of

Table 4.11 Controlling for other gun laws

Exogenous variables	Violent crime	Murder	Rape	Aggravated assault	Robbery	Property crime	Burglary	Larceny	Auto theft
				County-level Regressions					
Nondiscretionary law adopted	-4.2%*	-8.7%*	-6%*	-5.5%*	-2%	3.6%*	1%	4.5%*	8.2%*
Enhanced sentencing law adopted	-4%	-0.3%	1.1%	-1.5%***	-2.9%***	-0.001%	-2%	1.2%***	-1.8%**
Waiting law adopted	2.3%	23%*	25%*	-9.4%**	-9%***	2%	2%	-0.3%	-8%**
Percent change in crime by increasing the waiting period by one day: linear effect	-0.08%	-9.4%*	-13.6%*	6.5%*	-11%*	-1.5%***	-4.5%*	1.2%	-1%
Percent change in crime by increasing the waiting period by one day: squared effect	-0.08%	0.55%*	0.8%*	-0.5%*	0.73%*	0.019%	0.23%*	-0.17%*	0.099%

State-level regressions

Nondiscretionary law adopted	−10.1%*	−8.1%**	−5.7%***	−10.2%*	−13.3%*	−3.4%	−7.6%*	−2.2%	−1%
Enhanced sentencing law adopted	3.5%	3%	3%	−2.8%	1%	3%***	0.5%	3.7%**	2%
Waiting law adopted	10%	6.8%	22%*	2.6%	15%	3.3%	6.5%	2.3%	−3.1%
Percent change in crime by increasing the waiting period by one day: linear effect	−3%	−3%	−10%*	−0.65%	−10%**	−0.95%	−2.2%	−0.53%	−2.4%
Percent change in crime by increasing the wating period by one day: squared effect	0.12%	−0.13%	0.59%*	−0.041%	0.59%**	−0.021%	0.05%	−0.06%	−0.25%

Note: The control variables are the same as those used in table 4.1, including year and county dummies, though they are not reported, because the coefficient estimates are very similar to those reported earlier. All regressions use weighted least squares, where the weighting is each county's population.
*The result is statistically significant at the 1 percent level for a two-tailed t-test.
**The result is statistically significant at the 5 percent level for a two-tailed t-test.
***The result is statistically significant at the 10 percent level for a two-tailed t-test.

years for which the permit is valid; where people are allowed to carry the gun (for example, whether schools, bars, and government buildings are excluded); residency requirements; and how much the permit costs. Six of these characteristics are reported in table 4.12 for the thirty-one states with nondiscretionary laws.

A major issue in legislative debates on concealed-handgun laws is whether citizens will receive sufficient training to cope with situations that can require difficult, split-second decisions. Steve Grabowski, president of the Nebraska state chapter of the Fraternal Order of Police, notes that "police training is much more extensive than that required for concealed-handgun permits. The few hours of firearms instruction won't prepare a citizen to use the gun efficiently in a stress situation, which is a challenge even for professionals."[40] Others respond that significantly more training is required to use a gun offensively, as a police officer may be called on to do, than defensively. Law-abiding citizens appear reticent to use their guns and, as noted earlier, in the majority of cases simply brandishing the gun is sufficient to deter an attack.

Reestimating the earlier regressions, I included measures for whether a training period was required, for the length of the training period, and for the age limit.[41] The presence or length of the training periods typically show no effect on crime, and although the effects are significant for robbery, the size of the effect is very small. On the other hand, age limits display quite different and statistically significant coefficients for different crimes. The 21-year-old age limit appears to lower murder rates, but it tends to reduce the decline in rape and overall violent-crime rates that is normally associated with nondiscretionary concealed-handgun laws. Because of these different effects, it is difficult to draw firm conclusions regarding the effect of age limits.

RECENT DATA ON CRIME RATES

After I originally put the data together for this study, and indeed after I had written virtually all of this book, additional county-level data became available for 1993 and 1994 from the FBI's *Uniform Crime Reports.* These data allow us to evaluate the impact of the Brady law, which went into effect in 1994. They also allow us to double-check whether the results shown earlier were mere aberrations.

Table 4.13 reexamines the results from tables 4.1, 4.8, and 4.11 with these new data, and the findings are generally very similar to those already reported. The results in section A that correspond to table 4.1 imply an even larger drop in murder rates related to the passage of concealed-handgun laws (10 percent versus 7.7 percent previously), though

Table 4.12 Current characteristics of different nondiscretionary concealed-handgun laws

State with nondiscretionary law	Last significant modification	Permit duration (years)	Training length (hours)	Age require-ment	Initial fee	Renewal fee	Issuing agency
Alabama	1936	1	None	21	$15–25	$6	Sheriff
Alaska	1994	5	12	21	$123	$57	Dept. of Public Safety
Arizona	1995	4	16	21	$50	?	Dept. of Public Safety
Arkansas	1995	4	5	21	$100	?	State Police
Connecticut	1986	5	5	21	$35	$35	State Police
Florida	1995	3	5	21	$85	$70	Dept. of State
Georgia	1996	5	None	21	$32		Judge of Probate Court
Idaho	1996	4	7	21	$56	$24	Sheriff
Indiana	1980	4	None	18	$25	$15	Chief of Police or Sheriff
Kentucky	1996	3	8 hrs Classroom + firing-range training	21	$60	$60	Sheriff
Louisiana	1996	4	9[a]	21	$100	?	Dept. of Public Safety

Table 4.12 Continued

State with nondiscretionary law	Last significant modification	Permit duration (years)	Training length (hours)	Age require- ment	Initial fee	Renewal fee	Issuing agency
Maine	1985	4	5	21	$35	$20	Chief of Police or Sheriff
Mississippi	1990	4	None	21	$100	$50	Dept. of Public Safety
Montana	1991	4	None	18	$50	$25	Sheriff
Nevada	1995	5		21	$60	$25	Sheriff
New Hampshire	1923	2	None	21	$4		Chief of Police
North Carolina	1995	4	5	21	$90		Sheriff
North Dakota	1985	3	None	21	$25	$80	Bureau of Criminal Investigation
Oklahoma	1995	4	8	23	$125	$125	State Bureau of Criminal Investigation
Oregon	1993	4	5	21	$65	$50	Sheriff
Pennsylvania	1995	5	None	21	$17.50	$17.50	Chief of Police or Sheriff
South Carolina	1996	4		21	$50	$50	State Law Enforcement Division

State							Issuing Authority
South Dakota	1986	4	None	18	$6		Chief of Police or Sheriff
Tennessee	1996	4		21	$100		Dept. of Public Safety
Texas	1995	4	10–15	21	$140[b]	Set by department	Dept. of Public Safety
Utah	1995	2		21	$64	$5	Dept. of Public Safety
Vermont (unregulated)	None	None	None	None	None	None	None
Virginia	1995	2	5	21	<$50	<$50	Clerk of Circuit Court
Washington	1995	5	None	21	$36+ $24 FBI fee	$33	Judge; Chief of Police, or Sheriff
West Virginia	1996	5	5	18	$50	$50	Sheriff
Wyoming	1994	5	–5	21	$50	$50	Attorney General

[a]This training period is waived for those who receive a permit directly from their local sheriff.
[b]The fee is reduced to $70 for those who are over 60 years of age.

Table 4.13 Earlier results reexamined using additional data for 1993 and 1994

Change in explanatory variable	Percent change in various crime rates for changes in explanatory variables				
	Violent crime	Murder	Rape	Aggravated assault	Robbery
Section A: Nondiscretionary law adopted	−4.4%*	−10.0%*	−3.0%*	−5.7%*	0.6%
Section B: The difference in the annual change in crime rates in the years before and after the change in the law (annual rate after the law minus annual rate before the law)	−0.5%*	−2.9%*	−1.7%*	−0.3%*	−2.2%*
Section C: Brady law adopted	3%	−2.3%	3.9%**	3.7%**	−3.9%

Note: This table uses county-level, violent-crime data from the Uniform Crime Report that were not available until the rest of the book was written. Here I was not able to control for all the variables used in table 4.1. All regressions use weighted least squares, where the weighting is each county's population. Section C also controls for the other variables that were included in Table 4.11 to account for changes in other gun laws. Section A corresponds to the regressions in table 4.1, section B to those in table 4.8, and section C to those in table 4.11, except that a dummy variable for the Brady law was added for those states that did not previously have at least a five-day waiting period.
*The result is statistically significant at the 1 percent level for a two-tailed t-test.
**The result is statistically significant at the 10 percent level for a two-tailed t-test.

the declines in the rates for overall violent crime as well as rape and aggravated assault are smaller. Robbery is also no longer statistically significant, and the point estimate is even positive. As noted earlier, given the inverted V shape of crime-rate trends over time, comparing the average crime rates before and after the passage of these laws is not enough, since crime rates that are rising before the law and falling afterward can produce similar average crime rates in the two periods. To deal with this, section B of table 4.13 corresponds to the results reported earlier in table 4.8. The estimates are again quite similar to those reported earlier. The effect on rape is larger than those previously reported, while the effects for aggravated assault and robbery are somewhat smaller. All the results indicate that concealed-handgun laws reduce crime, and all the findings are statistically significant.

Finally, section C of table 4.13 provides some very interesting estimates of the Brady law's impact by using a variable that equals 1 only for those states that did not previously have at least a five-day waiting period. The claims about the criminals who have been denied access to guns as a result of this law are not necessarily evidence that the Brady law lowers crime rates. Unfortunately, these claims tell us nothing about whether criminals are ultimately able to obtain guns illegally. In addition, to the extent that law-abiding citizens find it more difficult to obtain guns, they may be less able to defend themselves. For example, a woman who is being stalked may no longer be able to obtain a gun quickly to scare off an attacker. Numerous newspaper accounts tell of women who were attempting to buy guns because of threats by former lovers and were murdered or raped during the required waiting period.[42]

The evidence from 1994 indicates that the Brady law has been associated with significant increases in rapes and aggravated assaults, and the declines in murder and robbery have been statistically insignificant. All the other gun-control laws examined in table 4.11 were also controlled for here, but because their estimated impacts were essentially unchanged, they are not reported.

WHAT HAPPENS TO NEIGHBORING COUNTIES IN ADJACENT STATES WHEN NONDISCRETIONARY HANDGUN LAWS ARE ADOPTED?

> If you put more resources in one place, it will displace some of the crime.
>
> Al L'Ecuyer, West Boylston
> (Massachusetts) Police Chief[43]

Up to this point we have asked what happens to crime rates in places that have adopted nondiscretionary laws. If these laws do discourage criminals, however, they may react in several ways. We already have discussed two: criminals could stop committing crimes, or they could commit other, less dangerous crimes like those involving property, where the probability of contact with armed victims is low. Yet as the epigraph for this section notes, a third possibility is that criminals may commit crimes in other areas where potential victims are not armed. A fourth outcome is also possible: eliminating crime in one area can help eliminate crime in other areas as well. This last outcome may occur if criminals had been using the county that adopted the law as a staging area. Crime-prone, poverty-stricken areas of cities may find that some of their crime spills over to adjacent areas.

This section seeks to test what effect concealed-handgun laws and higher arrest rates have on crime rates in adjacent counties in neighboring states. Since concealed-handgun laws are almost always passed at the state level, comparing adjacent counties in neighboring states allows us to examine the differential effect of concealed-handgun laws. Evidence that changes in a state's laws coincide with changes in crime rates in neighboring states will support the claim that the laws affect criminals. If these laws do not affect criminals, neighboring states should experience no changes in their crime rates.

Although any findings that nondiscretionary concealed-handgun laws cause criminals to leave the jurisdictions that adopt these laws would provide additional evidence of deterrence, such findings would also imply that simply looking at the direct effect of concealed-handgun laws on crime overestimates the total gain to society from these laws. In the extreme, if the entire reduction in crime from concealed-handgun laws was simply transferred to other areas, society as a whole would be no better off with these laws, even if individual jurisdictions benefited. While the evidence would confirm the importance of deterrence, adopting such a law in a single state might have a greater deterrent impact than if the entire nation adopted the law. The deterrent effect of adopting nondiscretionary concealed-handgun laws in additional states could also decline as more states adopted the laws.

To investigate these issues, I reran the regressions reported in table 4.1, using only those counties that were within fifty miles of counties in neighboring states. In addition to the variable that examines whether your own state has a nondiscretionary concealed-handgun law, I added three new variables. One variable averages the dummy variables for whether adjacent counties in neighboring counties have such laws. A second variable examines what happens when your county and your neighboring county adopt these laws. Finally, the neighboring counties' arrest rates are added, though I do not bother reporting them, because the evidence indicates that only the arrest rates in your own county, not your neighboring counties, matter in determining your crime rate.

The results reported in table 4.14 confirm that deterrent effects do spill over into neighboring areas. For all the violent-crime categories, adopting a concealed-handgun law reduces the number of violent crimes in your county, but these results also show that criminals who commit murder, rape, and robbery apparently move to adjacent states without the laws. The one violent-crime category that does not fit this pattern is aggravated assault: adopting a nondiscretionary concealed-handgun law lowers the number of aggravated assaults in neighboring counties. With respect to the benefits of all counties adopting the laws, the last column

Table 4.14 Estimates of the impact of nondiscretionary concealed-handgun laws on neighboring counties

Type of crime	Percent change in own crime rate		
	Own county has nondiscretionary law	Average neighbor has nondiscretionary law	Average neighbor and own county have nondiscretionary law
Violent crime	−5.5%	0	−5.7%
Murder	−7.6%	3.5%	−4.1%
Rape	−6.2%	6%	0
Robbery	−4%	2.8%	−1.1%
Aggravated assault	−7.4%	−3.3%	−10.7%
Property crime	1%	1%	2%
Auto theft	−1.3%	2%	3.4%
Burglary	1%	4.7%	−1%
Larceny	9%	−2%	10.8%

shows that all categories of violent crime are reduced the most when all counties adopt such laws. The results imply that murder rates decline by over 8 percent and aggravated assaults by around 21 percent when a county and its neighbors adopt concealed-handgun laws.

As a final test, I generated the figures showing crime trends before and after a neighbor's adoption of the law by the method previously used, in addition to the time trends for before and after one's own adoption of the concealed-handgun laws. The use of an additional squared term allows us to see if the effect on crime is not linear. Figure 4.10 is a graphic display of the findings for violent crime, though the results for the individual violent-crime categories are equally dramatic. In all violent-crime categories, the adoption of concealed-handgun laws produces an immediate and large increase in violent-crime rates for neighboring counties, though unlike the direct effect of these laws on the crime rate in one's own county, the spillover effect in neighboring counties is relatively short-lived.

Overall, these results provide strong additional evidence for the deterrent effect of nondiscretionary concealed-handgun laws. They imply that the earlier estimate of the total social benefit from these laws may have overestimated the initial benefits, but underestimated the long-term benefits as more states adopt these laws. In the long run, the negative spillover effect subsides, and the adoption of these laws in all neighboring states has the greatest deterrent effect on crime.

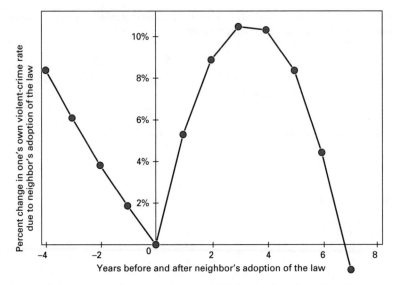

Figure 4.10. Impact on violent crime from a neighbor's adoption of nondiscretionary concealed-handgun law

CONCLUSIONS

The empirical work provides strong evidence that concealed-handgun laws reduce violent crime and that higher arrest rates deter all types of crime. The results confirm what law-enforcement officials have said— that nondiscretionary laws cause a greatest change in the number of permits issued for concealed handguns in the most populous, urbanized counties. This provides additional support for the claim that the greatest declines in crime rates are related to the greatest increases in concealed-handgun permits. The impact of concealed-handgun laws varies with a county's level of crime, its population and population density, its per-capita income, and the percentage of the population that is black. Despite the opposition to these laws in large, urban, densely populated areas, those are the areas that benefit the most from the laws. Minorities and women tend to be the ones with the most to gain from being allowed to protect themselves.

Some of the broader issues concerning criminal deterrence discussed in chapter 1 were evaluated, and the hypotheses used produced information about the locations where increased police efforts had the most significant deterrent effects on crime. Splitting the data set into high- and low-crime counties shows that arrest rates do not affect crime rates equally in all counties: the greatest return to increasing arrest rates is in the most crime-prone areas.

The results also confirm some of the potential aggregation problems with state-level data. The county-level data explain about six times more variation in violent-crime rates and eight times more variation in property-crime rates than do state-level data. Generally, the effect of concealed-handgun laws on crime appeared much greater when state-level regressions were estimated. However, one conclusion is clear: the very different results for state and county-level data should make us very cautious in aggregating crime data. The differences in county characteristics show that dramatically greater differences exist among counties within any state than among different states. Whether increased arrest rates are concentrated in the highest-crime counties in a state or spread out equally across all counties makes a big difference in their impact on crime. Likewise, it is a mistake to think that concealed-handgun laws change crime rates in all counties in a state equally. The data should definitely remain as disaggregated as possible.

The three sets of estimates that rely on county-level data, state-level data, or county-level data that accounts for how the law affected different counties have their own strengths and weaknesses. While using county-level data avoids the aggregation problems present with state-level data, the initial county-level regressions rely heavily on variation in state laws and thus are limited to comparing the variation in these fifty jurisdictions. If weight is thus given to any of the results, it would appear that the greatest weight should be given to the county-level regressions that interact the nondiscretionary-law variable with measures of how liberally different counties issued permits under the preexisting discretionary systems. These regressions not only avoid the aggregation problems but also take fullest advantage of the relationship between county-level variations in crime rates and the impact of nondiscretionary laws. They provide the strongest evidence that concealed-handgun laws reduce all types of crime. Despite these different approaches, one result is clear: the results are remarkably consistent with respect to the deterrent effect of nondiscretionary concealed-handgun laws on violent crime. Two of these three sets of estimates imply that concealed-handgun laws also result in lower property-crime rates, although these rates decline less than the rates for violent crimes.

This study represents a significant change in the general approach to crime studies. This is the first study to use cross-sectional time-series evidence at both the county and state levels. Instead of simply using either cross-sectional state- or city-level data, this study has made use of the much larger variations in arrest rates and crime rates between rural and urban areas, and it has been possible to control for whether the lower crime rates resulted from the gun laws themselves or from other differences in these areas (for example, low crime rates) that lead to the adoption of these laws.

Five

The Victims and the Benefits from Protection

C O N C E A L E D - H A N D G U N   L A W S ,   T H E
M E T H O D   O F   M U R D E R ,   A N D   T H E
C H O I C E   O F   M U R D E R   V I C T I M S

Do laws allowing individuals to carry concealed hand-guns cause criminals to change the methods they use to commit murders? For example, the number of murders perpetrated with guns may rise after such laws are passed, even though the total number of murders falls. While concealed-handgun laws raise the risk of committing murders with guns, murderers may also find it relatively more dangerous to kill using other methods once people start carrying concealed handguns, and they may therefore choose to use guns to put themselves on a more even basis with their potential prey. Using data on the methods of murder from the Mortality Detail Records provided by the U.S. Department of Health and Human Services, I reran the murder-rate regression from table 4.1 on counties with populations over 100,000 during the period from 1982 to 1991. I then separated murders committed with guns from all other murders. Table 5.1 shows that carrying concealed handguns appears to have been associated with approximately equal drops in both categories of murders. Carrying concealed handguns appears to make all types of murders relatively less attractive.

We may also wonder whether concealed-handgun laws have any effect on the types of people who are likely to be murdered. The *Supplementary Homicide Reports* of the FBI's *Uniform Crime Reports* contain annual, state-level data from 1977 to 1992 on the percent of victims by sex, race, and age, as well as information on the whether the victims and the offenders knew each other (whether they were members of the same family, knew each other but were not members of the same family, were strangers, or no relationship was known).[1] Table 5.2, which uses the same setup as in table 4.1, is intended to explain these characteristics of the victims. The regressions indicate no statistically significant relationship between the concealed-handgun law and a victim's sex, race, relationships with offenders, or age (the last is not shown). However, while they are not quite

Table 5.1 Do concealed-handgun laws influence whether murders are committed with or without guns? Murder methods for counties with more than 100,000 people from 1982 to 1991

Exogenous variables	ln(Total murders)	ln(Murder with guns)	ln(murders by nongun methods)
Nondiscretionary law adopted	−9.7%*	−9.0%**	−8.9%**
Arrest rate for murder increased by 100 percentage points	−0.15%*	−0.10%*	−0.14%*

Note: While not all the coefficient estimates are reported, all the control variables are the same as those used in table 4.1, including the year and county dummies. All regressions use weighted least squares, where the weighting is each county's population. The first column uses the UCR numbers for counties with more than 100,000 people. The second column uses the numbers on total gun deaths available from the Mortality Detail Records, and the third column takes the difference between the UCR numbers for total murders and Mortality Detail Records of gun deaths. Endogenous variables are in murders per 100,000 population.
*The result is statistically significant at the 1 percent level for a two-tailed t-test.
**The result is statistically significant at the 10 percent level for a two-tailed t-test.

statistically significant, two of the estimates appear important and imply that in states with concealed-handgun laws victims know their nonfamily offenders 2.6 percentage points more frequently than not, and that the number of victims for whom it was not possible to determine whether a relationship existed declined by 2.9 percentage points.

This raises the question of whether the possible presence of concealed handguns causes criminals to prefer committing crimes against people they know, since presumably they would be more likely to know if an acquaintance carried a concealed handgun. The principal relationship between age and concealed handguns is that the concealed weapon deters crime against adults more than against young people—because only adults can legally carry concealed handguns—but the effect is statistically insignificant.[2] Some of the benefits from allowing adults to carry concealed handguns may be conferred on younger people whom these adults protect. In addition, when criminals who attack adults leave states that pass concealed-handgun laws, there might also be fewer criminals left to attack the children.

The arrest rates for murder produces more interesting results. The percent of white victims and the percent of victims killed by family members both declined when arrest rates were increased, while the percent of black victims and the percent killed by non—family members

Table 5.2 Changes in characteristics of murder victims: annual, state-level data from the *Uniform Crime Reports, Supplementary Homicide Reports,* from 1977 to 1992

	Percent change in various endogenous variables for changes in explanatory variables									
	By victim's sex			By victim's race			By victim's relationship to offender			
Change in explanatory variable	Percent of Male Victims	Percent of Female Victims	Percent of victims, sex unknown	Percent of victims that are white	Percent of victims that are black	Percent of victims that are Hispanic	Percent of victims where the offender is known to victim but is not in family	Percent of victims where the offender is in the family	Percent of victims where the offender is a stranger	Percent of victims where the relationship is unknown
Nondiscretionary law adopted	0.39	−0.44	0.05	0.01	0.70	−0.87	2.58	−0.25	0.54	−2.88
Arrest rate for murder increased by 100 percentage points	0.068	−0.14	0.07	−2.02**	1.32**	0.33	1.74**	−1.45*	0.79	−1.08

To interpret this table, the first coefficient (0.39) implies that the percent of male victims increases by 0.39 percentage points if a state adopts a nondiscretionary concealed-handgun law. While not all the coefficient estimates are reported, all the control variables are the same as those used in table 2.3, including the year and state dummies. All regressions use weighted least squares, where the weighting is each state's population.

*The result is statistically significant at the 1 percent level for a two-tailed t-test.

**The result is statistically significant at the 5 percent level for a two-tailed t-test.

whom they knew both increased. The results imply that higher arrest rates have a much greater deterrent effect on murders involving whites and family members. One explanation is that whites with higher incomes face a greater increase in expected penalties for any given increase in the probability of arrest.

MASS PUBLIC SHOOTINGS

Chapter 1 noted the understandable fear that people have of mass public shootings like the one on the Long Island Railroad or at the top of the Empire State Building. To record the number of mass public shootings by state from 1977 to 1992, a search was done of news-article databases (Nexis) for the same period examined in the rest of this study. A mass public shooting is defined as one that occurred in a public place and involved two or more people either killed or injured by the shooting. The crimes excluded involved gang activity; drug dealing; a holdup or a robbery; drive-by shootings that explicitly or implicitly involved gang activity, organized crime, or professional hits; and serial killings, or killings that took place over the span of more than one day. The places where public shootings occurred included such sites as schools, churches, businesses, bars, streets, government buildings, public transit facilities, places of employment, parks, health care facilities, malls, and restaurants.

Unlike my earlier data, these data are available only at the state level. Table 5.3 shows the mean rate at which such killings occurred both before and after the adoption of the nondiscretionary concealed-handgun laws in the ten states that changed their laws during the 1977 to 1992 period and, more broadly, for all states that either did or did not have such laws during the period. In each case the before-and-after means are quite statistically significantly different at least at the 1 percent level,[3] with the rates being dramatically lower when nondiscretionary concealed-handgun laws were in effect. For those states from which data are available before and after the passage of such laws, the mean per-capita death rate from mass shootings in those states plummets by 69 percent.[4]

To make sure that these differences were not due to some other factor, I reestimated the specifications used earlier to explain murder rates for the state-level regressions with time trends before and after the adoption of the nondiscretionary concealed-handgun laws. The variable being explained is now the total number of deaths or injuries due to mass public shootings in a state.[5]

Figure 5.1 shows that although the total number of deaths and injuries from mass public shootings actually rises slightly immediately after a

Table 5.3 Mass shooting deaths and injuries

	Mean death and injury rate per year for years in which the states do not have nondiscretionary concealed-handgun laws (1)	Mean death and injury rate per year for years in which the states do have nondiscretionary concealed-handgun laws (2)
	A. Comparing the before-and-after mean mass shooting deaths and injuries for states that changed their concealed-handgun laws during the 1977–1992 period[1]	
Number of mass shooting deaths and injuries for the ten states that changed their laws during the 1977–1992 period	1.63	1.19
Mass shooting deaths and injuries per 100,000 population for the ten states that changed their laws during the 1977–1992 period	0.039	0.012
	B. Comparing the mean mass shooting deaths and injuries for all states with nondiscretionary concealed-handgun laws and those without such laws[2]	
Number of mass shooting deaths and injuries	2.09	0.89
Mass shooting deaths and injuries per 100,000 population	0.041	0.037

[1]Column 1 for section A has 128 observations; column 2 has 32 observations.
[2]Column 1 for section B has 656 observations; column 2 has 160 observations.

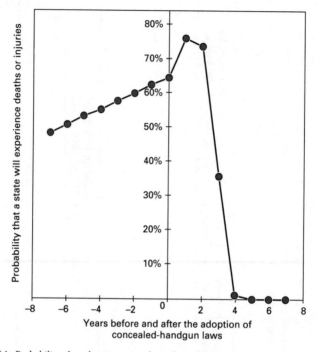

Figure 5.1. Probability that the ten states that adopted concealed-handgun laws during the 1977–1992 period experienced deaths or injuries from a shooting spree in a public place

nondiscretionary concealed-handgun law is implemented, it quickly falls after that, with the rate reaching zero five years after the law is enacted.[6] Why there is an initial increase is not immediately obvious, though during this early period relatively few people have concealed-handgun permits. Perhaps those planning such shootings do them sooner than they otherwise would have, before too many citizens acquire concealed-handgun permits. One additional qualification should also be made. While nondiscretionary concealed-handgun laws reduced deaths and injuries from mass public shootings to zero after five years in the ten states that changed their laws during the 1977 to 1992 period, a look at the mean death and injury rates from mass public shootings in the eight states that passed such laws before 1977 shows that these rates were quite low but definitely not zero. This tempers the conclusion here and implies that while deaths and injuries from mass public shootings fall dramatically after nondiscretionary concealed-handgun laws are passed, it is unlikely that the true rate will drop to zero for the average state that adopts these laws.

COUNTY DATA FOR ARIZONA, PENNSYLVANIA, AND
OREGON, AND STATE DATA FOR FLORIDA

One problem with the preceding results was the use of county population as a proxy for how restrictive counties were in allowing concealed-
handgun permits before the passage of nondiscretionary laws. Since I am
still going to control county-specific levels of crime with county dummies, a better measure would have been to use the actual change in the
number of gun permits before and after the adoption of a concealed-
handgun law. The per-capita number of permits provides a more direct
measure of the expected costs that criminals face in attacking people.
Knowing the number of permits also allows us to calculate the benefit
from issuing an additional permit.

Fortunately, the information on the number of permits issued by
county is available for three states: Arizona, Oregon, and Pennsylvania.
Florida also provides yearly permit data at the state level. Arizona and
Oregon also provided additional information on the conviction rate and
the mean prison-sentence length. However, for Oregon, because the
sentence-length variable is not directly comparable over time, it is interacted with all the individual year variables, so that we can still retain any
cross-sectional information in the data. One difficulty with the Arizona
sentence-length and conviction data is that they are available only from
1990 to 1995, and since the nondiscretionary concealed-handgun law did
not take effect until July 1994, we cannot control for all the other variables that we control for in the other regressions.

Unlike Oregon and Pennsylvania, Arizona did not allow private citizens
to carry concealed handguns prior to July 1994 (and permits were not actually issued until the end of the year), so the value of concealed-handgun
permits equals zero for this earlier period. Unfortunately, however, because Arizona changed its law so recently, I cannot control for all the variables that I controlled for in the other regressions. Florida's data are even
more limited, but they allow the study of the simple relationship between
crime and permits at the state level for a relatively long period of time.

The results in table 5.4 for Pennsylvania and table 5.5 for Oregon provide a couple of consistent patterns.[7] The most economically and statistically important relationship involves the arrest rate: higher arrest rates
consistently imply lower crime rates, and in twelve of the sixteen regressions the effect is statistically significant. Five cases for Pennsylvania (violent crime, murder, aggravated assault, robbery, and burglary) show that
arrest rates explain more than 15 percent of the change in crime rates.[8]
Automobile theft is the only crime for which the arrest rate is insignificant in both tables.

Table 5.4 Crime and county data on concealed-handgun permits: Pennsylvania counties with populations greater than 200,000

Percent change in the crime rate	Violent crime	Murder	Rape	Aggravated assault	Robbery	Property crime	Auto theft	Burglary	Larceny
				Crimes per 100,000 population					
Due to a 1 percent change in the number of right-to-carry pistol permits/population over 21 between 1988 and each year since the law was implemented	−5.3%**	−26.7%*	−5.7%**	−4.8%**	1.2%	−0.12%	1.5%	−1.4%	0.7%
Due to a 1 percent change in the arrest rate for the crime category	−0.79%*	−0.37%*	−0.08%	−0.76%*	−0.84%*	−0.41%**	−0.065%	−1.1%*	0.13%

Note: While not all the coefficient estimates are reported, all the control variables are the same as those used in table 4.1, including year and county dummies. All regressions use weighted least squares, where the weighting is each county's population. The nondiscretionary-law-times-county-population variable that was used in the earlier regressions instead of the variable for change in right-to-carry permits was tried here and produced very similar results. I also tried controlling for either the robbery or burglary rates, but I obtained very similar results.
*The result is statistically significant at the 1 percent level for a two-tailed t-test.
**The result is statistically significant at the 10 percent level for a two-tailed t-test.

Table 5.5 Crime and county data on concealed-handgun permits: Oregon data

Percent change in the crime rate	Crimes per 100,000 population						
	Murder	Rape	Aggravated assault	Robbery	Auto theft	Burglary	Larceny
Due to a 1 percent change in the number of right-to-carry pistol permits/population over 21 between 1988 and each year since the law was implemented	−37%****	−6.7%	−4.8%	−4.7%	12%	2.7%	−9%**
Due to a 1 percent change in the arrest rate for the crime category	−0.34%*	−1%*	−0.4%*	−0.4%*	−.04%	−0.7%*	−0.9%*
Due to a 1 percent change in the conviction rate for the crime category	−0.2%*	−0.09%*	−1.5%***	−0.19%*	−0.37%*	−0.27%*	−0.86%*

Note: While not all the coefficient estimates are reported, all the control variables are the same as those used in table 4.1, including year and county dummies. I also controlled for sentence length, but the different reporting practices used by Oregon over this period make its use somewhat problematic. To deal with this problem, the sentence-length variable was interacted with year-dummy variables. Thus, while the variable is not consistent over time, it is still valuable in distinguishing penalties across counties at a particular point in time. The categories for violent and property crimes are eliminated because the mean sentence-length data supplied by Oregon did not allow us to use these two categories. All regressions use weighted least squares, where the weighting is each county's population.

*The result is statistically significant at the 1 percent level for a two-tailed t-test.

**The result is statistically significant at the 5 percent level for a two-tailed t-test.

***The result is statistically significant at the 10 percent level for a two-tailed t-test.

****The result is statistically significant at the 11 percent level for a two-tailed t-test.

For Pennsylvania, murder and rape are the only crimes for which per-capita concealed-handgun permits explain a greater percentage of the variation in crime rates than does the arrest rate. However, increased concealed-handgun licensing explains more than 10 percent of the variation in murder, rape, aggravated assault, and burglary rates. Violent crimes, with the exception of robbery, show that greater numbers of concealed-handgun permits lower violent crime rates, while property crimes exhibit very little relationship. The portion of the variation for property crimes that is explained by concealed-handgun licensing is only about one-tenth as large as the variation for violent crimes that is explained by such licensing, which is not too surprising, given the much more direct impact that concealed handguns have on violent crime.[9] The regressions for Oregon weakly imply a similar relationship between concealed-handgun use and crime, but the effect is only strongly statistically significant for larceny; it is weakly significant for murder.

The Oregon data also show that higher conviction rates consistently result in significantly lower crime rates. The change in conviction rates explains 4 to 20 percent of the change in the corresponding crime rates;[10] however, for five of the seven crime categories, increases in conviction rates appear to produce a smaller deterrent effect than increases in arrest rates.[11] The greatest differences between the deterrent effects of arrest and conviction rates produce an interesting pattern. For rape, increasing the arrest rate by 1 percent produces more than ten times the deterrent effect of increasing the conviction rate for those who have been arrested by 1 percent. For auto theft, arrest seems more important than conviction: a 1 percent increase in the arrest rate reduces crime by about ten times more than the same increase in convictions. These results are consistent with the assumption that arrests produce large penalties in terms of shame or negative reputation.[12] In fact, the existing evidence shows that the reputational penalties from arrest and conviction can dwarf the legally imposed penalties.[13] This is some of the first evidence that the reputational penalties from arrests alone provide significant deterrence for some crimes.

One possible explanation for these results is that Oregon simultaneously passed both the nondiscretionary concealed-handgun law and a waiting period. The statistics in table 4.11 suggest that the long waiting period imposed by the Oregon law (fifteen days) increased murder by 5 percent, rape by 2 percent, and robbery by 6 percent. At least in the case of murder, which is weakly statistically significant in any case, the estimates from tables 4.11 and 5.5 together indicate that if Oregon had not adopted its waiting period, the drop in murder resulting from the concealed-handgun law would have been statistically significant at the 5 percent level.

The results for sentence length are not shown, but the t-statistics are frequently near zero, and the coefficients indicate no clear pattern. One possible explanation for this result is that all the changes in sentencing rules produced a great deal of noise in this variable, not only over time but also across counties. For example, after 1989, whether a crime was prosecuted under the pre- or post-1989 rules depended on when the crime took place. If the average time between when the offense occurred and when the prosecution took place differed across counties, the recorded sentence length could vary even if the actual time served was the same.

Florida's state-level data showing the changes in crime rates and changes in the number of concealed-handgun permits are quite suggestive (see figure 5.2). Cuba's Mariel Boat Lift created a sudden upsurge in Florida's murder rate from 1980 through 1982. By 1983 the murder rate had return to its pre-Mariel level, and it remained relatively constant or exhibited a slight upward trend until the state adopted its nondiscretionary concealed-handgun law in 1987. Murder-rate data are not available for 1988 because of changes in the reporting process, but the available evidence indicates that the murder rate began to drop when the law was adopted, and the size of the drop corresponded with the number of concealed-handgun permits outstanding. Ironically, the first post-1987 upward movement in murder rates occurred in 1992, when Florida began to require a waiting period and background check before issuing permits.

Finally, a very limited data set for Arizona produces no significant relationship between the change in concealed-handgun permits and the various measures of crime rates. In fact, the coefficient signs themselves indicate no consistent pattern; the fourteen coefficients are equally divided between negative and positive signs, though six of the specifications imply that the variation in the number of concealed-handgun permits explains at least 8 percent of the variation in the corresponding crime rates.[14] This is likely to occur for several reasons. The sample is extremely small (only 64–89 observations, depending on which specification), and we have only a year and a half over which to observe the effect of the law. In addition, if Arizona holds true to the pattern observed in other states, the impact of these laws is smallest right after the law passes.

The results involving either the mean sentence length for those sentenced in a particular year or the actual time served for those ending their sentences also imply no consistent relationship between sentence length and crime rates. While the coefficients are negative in eleven of

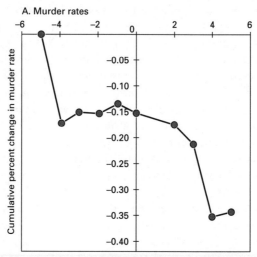

A. Murder rates

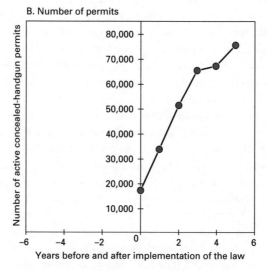

B. Number of permits

Figure 5.2A. Cumulative percent change in Florida's murder rate

Figure 5.2B. Concealed-handgun permits after implementation of the law in Florida

the fourteen specifications, they provide weak evidence of the deterrent effect of longer prison terms: only two coefficients are negative and statistically significant.

The Brady law also went into effect during this period.[15] Using the Arizona data to investigate the impact of the Brady law indicates that its only discernible effect was in the category of aggravated assault, where the statistics imply that it increased the number of aggravated assaults by 24 percent and the number of rapes by 3 percent. Yet it is important to remember that the data for Arizona covered only a very short period of time when this law was in effect, and other factors influencing crime could not be taken into account. While I do not believe that the Brady law was responsible for this large increase in assaults, I at least take this as evidence that the law did not reduce aggravated assaults and as confirmation of the belief that relying on this small sample for Arizona is problematic.

Overall, Pennsylvania's results provide more evidence that concealed-handgun ownership reduces violent crime, murder, rape, aggravated assault, and burglary. For Oregon, the evidence implies that murder and larceny decrease. While the Oregon data imply that the effect of handgun permits on murder is only marginally statistically significant, the point estimate is extremely large economically, implying that a doubling of permits reduces murder rates by 37 percent. The other coefficients for Pennsylvania and Oregon imply no significant relationship between the change in concealed-handgun ownership and crime rates. The evidence from the small sample for Arizona implies no relationship between crime and concealed-handgun ownership. All the results also support the claim that higher arrest and conviction rates deter crime, although—perhaps partly because of the relatively poor quality of the data—no systematic effect appears to arise from longer prison sentences.

PUTTING DOLLAR VALUES ON THE CRIME-REDUCTION BENEFITS AND PRIVATE COSTS OF ADDITIONAL CONCEALED-HANDGUN PERMITS

By combining evidence that additional concealed handguns reduce crime with the monetary estimates of victim losses from crime produced by the National Institute of Justice, it is possible to attach a monetary value to the benefits of additional concealed-handgun permits. While the results for Arizona imply no real savings from reduced crime, the estimates for Pennsylvania indicate that potential costs to victims are reduced by $5,079 for each additional concealed-handgun permit, and for Oregon, the savings are $3,439 per permit. As noted in the discussion of table 4.2, the results are largely driven by the effect of concealed handguns in lowering murder rates (with savings of $4,986 for Pennsylvania and $3,202 for Oregon).[16]

These estimated gains appear to far exceed the private costs of owning a concealed handgun. The purchase price of handguns ranges from $100 or less for the least-expensive .25-caliber pistols to over $700 for the newest, ultracompact, 9-millimeter models.[17] The permit-filing fees can range from $19 every five years in Pennsylvania to a first-time, $65 fee with subsequent five-year renewals at $50 in Oregon, which also requires several hours of supervised safety training. Assuming a 5 percent real interest rate and the ability to amortize payments over ten years, purchasing a $300 handgun and paying the licensing fees every five years in Pennsylvania implies a yearly cost of only $43, excluding the time costs incurred. The estimated expenses are higher for Oregon, because of the higher fees and the costs in time and money of obtaining certified safety instruction. Even if these annual costs double, however, they are still quite small compared to the social benefits. While ammunition purchases and additional annual training would increase annualized costs, the long life span of guns and their resale value work to reduce the above estimates.

The results imply that handgun permits are being issued at much lower than optimal rates, perhaps because of the important externalities not directly captured by the handgun owners themselves. While the crime-reducing benefits of concealed handguns are shared by all those who are spared being attacked, the costs of providing this protection are borne exclusively by permit holders.

ACCIDENTAL DEATHS AND SUICIDES

Even if nondiscretionary handgun permits reduce murder rates, we are still left with the question of what happens to the rates for accidental death. As more people carry handguns, accidents may be more likely. Earlier, we saw that the number of murders prevented exceeded the entire number of accidental deaths. In the case of suicide, the nondiscretionary laws increase the probability that a gun will be available when an individual feels particularly depressed; thus, they could conceivably lead to an increase in the number of suicides. While only a small portion of accidental deaths are attributable to guns (see appendix 4), the question remains whether concealed-handgun laws affect the total number of deaths through their effect on accidental deaths.

To get a more precise answer to this question, I used county-level data from 1982 to 1991 in table 5.6 to test whether allowing concealed handguns increased accidental deaths. Data are available from the Mortality

Table 5.6 Did nondiscretionary concealed-handgun laws increase the number of accidental deaths? (1982–91 county-level data)

	Deaths per 100,000 population			
	Ordinary least squares, natural logarithm of endogenous variable		Tobit	
Change in explanatory variable	Accidental deaths from handguns	Accidental deaths from nonhandgun sources	Accidental deaths from handguns	Accidental deaths from nonhandgun sources
Nondiscretionary law adopted	0.48%	9.9%**	0.574 more deaths	1.331 more deaths
Percent change in crime (for Tobit number of deaths per 100,000) for an increase in population of one person per square mile	−0.07%*	0.09%*	−0.004%	−0.016%
Percent change in crime (for Tobit number of deaths per 100,000) for an increase in $1,000 of real per-capita personal income	2.67%	−5.7%*	4.4%	−9%*

Note: While not all the coefficient estimates are reported, all the control variables are the same as those used in table 4.1, including year and county dummies. Absolute t-statistics are in parentheses. All regressions weight the data by each county's population.
*The result is statistically significant at the 1 percent level for a two-tailed t-test.
**The result is statistically significant at the 10 percent level for a two-tailed t-test.

Detail Records (provided by the U.S. Department of Health and Human Services) for all counties from 1982 to 1988 and for counties with populations over 100,000 from 1989 to 1991. The specifications are identical to those shown in all the previous tables, with the exceptions that they no longer include variables related to arrest or conviction rates and that the variables to be explained are either measures of the number of accidental deaths from handguns or measures of accidental deaths from all other nonhandgun sources.

While there is some evidence that the racial composition of the population and the level of welfare payments affect accident rates, the impact of nondiscretionary concealed-handgun laws is consistently both quite small economically and insignificant statistically. The first estimate in column 1 implies that accidental deaths from handguns rose by about 0.5 percent when concealed-handgun laws were passed. With only 200 accidental handgun deaths nationwide during 1988 (22 accidental handgun deaths occurred in states with nondiscretionary laws), the implication is that enacting concealed-handgun laws in states that currently do not have them would increase the number of deaths by less than one (.851 deaths).

With 186 million people living in states without concealed-handgun laws in 1992,[18] the third specification implies that implementing such laws across those remaining states would have resulted in about nine more accidental handgun deaths.[19] Combining this finding with earlier estimates from table 4.1, we find that if the rest of the country had adopted concealed-handgun laws in 1992, the net reduction in total deaths would have been approximately 1,405 to 1,583.

One caveat should be added to these numbers, however: both columns 2 and 4 indicate that accidental deaths from nonhandgun sources increased by more than accidental deaths from handguns after the nondiscretionary concealed-handgun laws were implemented. To the extent that the former category increased because of uncontrolled factors that also increase accidental deaths from handguns, the results presented here are biased toward finding that concealed-handgun laws have increased accidental deaths from handguns.

Finally, I examined similar specifications using data on suicide rates. The possibility exists that if a person becomes depressed while away from home, the presence of a concealed handgun might encourage that person to act impulsively, whereas an enforced delay might ultimately prevent a suicide. If anything, the results implied a statistically insignificant and small increase in suicides (less than one-tenth of 1 percent). Hence it is reasonable to conclude that no relationship exists between concealed-handgun laws and suicide rates.

TOTAL GUN OWNERSHIP AND CRIME

Traditionally, people have tried to use cross-county comparisons of gun ownership and crime rates to determine whether gun ownership enhances or detracts from safety.[20] Worldwide, there is no relationship between gun ownership and crime rates. Many countries, such as Switzerland, Finland, New Zealand, and Israel, have high gun-ownership rates and low crime rates, while many other countries have both low gun-ownership rates and either high or low crime rates. For example, in 1995 Switzerland's murder rate was 40 percent lower than Germany's despite having a three-times higher gun-ownership rate. Yet, making a reliable comparison across countries is an arduous task simply because it is difficult to obtain gun-ownership data both over time and across countries, and to control for all the other differences across the legal systems and cultures across countries. International comparisons are also risky because polls underreport ownership in countries where gun ownership is illegal, and they are conducted by different polling organizations that ask questions in widely differing ways. How crime is measured also varies across countries.

Fortunately, more consistent data are available to investigate the relationship between total gun ownership in the United States and crime. In chapter 3 I presented poll data from general-election surveys that offer consistent polling across states, showing how gun ownership varied across states for 1988 and 1996. There is broad variation in gun ownership across states, and the crime rates also vary across states and over time. Even with rather few observations, however, these data suggest that we may be able to answer an obvious question: Is the crime rate higher in states with more guns?

To test the relationship between gun ownership and crime, I attempted to examine the relationship between the percentage of the adult population owning guns and the crime rate after accounting for the arrest rate, real personal income, population per square mile, regional dummy variables (for the Northeast, Midwest, and South), the percentage of blacks among each state's population, and a variable to pick up the average change in crime rates between 1988 and 1995. This last variable was also intended to help pick up any differences in the results that arise from the slightly different poll methods in the two years. Ideally, one would want to construct the same type of cross-sectional, time-series data set over many years and states that was used in the earlier discussions; unfortunately, however, such extensive poll data on gun ownership are not available. Because we lack the most recent data for the above-named variables, all the variables except for the percentage of the state's adult population that owns guns is for 1995.

Table 5.7 The relationship between state crime rates and the general election poll data on the percent of the state's adult population owning guns

Crime rates	Percent change in the crime rate from a 1 percentage point increase in a state's gun-ownership rate	Estimated change in victim costs from a 1 percent increase in the number of guns nationwide
Violent crime	−4.1*	
Murder	−3.3*	$2.7 billion
Rape	0	
Aggravated assault	−4.3*	$44 million
Robbery	−4.3*	$200 million
Property crime	−1.5**	
Burglary	−1.6*	$54 million
Larceny	−1.3	$38 million
Auto theft	−3.2*	$17 million
Total savings		$3.1 billion

Note: While the other coefficient values are not reported here, these regression results control for the arrest rate, real personal income, population per square mile, regional dummy variables (for the Northeast, Midwest, South, and the intercept picking up the West), the percent of the state's population that is black, and a year-dummy variable for 1996 to pick up the average change in crime rate between the years. All regressions use weighted least squares, where the regressions are weighted by the state populations.
*The result is statistically significant at the 1 percent level for a two-tailed t-test.
**The result is statistically significant at the 5 percent level for a two-tailed t-test.

As table 5.7 shows, a strong negative relationship exists between gun ownership and all of the crime rates except for rape, and the results are statistically significant for seven of the nine categories. Indeed, the effect of gun ownership on crime is quite large: a 1 percent increase in gun ownership reduces violent crime by 4.1 percent. The estimates from the National Institute of Justice of the costs to victims of crime imply that increasing gun ownership nationwide by 1 percent would reduce victim costs by $3.1 billion, though we must bear in mind that these conclusions are based on a relatively small sample. Similar estimates for accidental gun deaths or suicides reveal no significant relationships.

CONCLUSION

Nondiscretionary concealed-handgun laws have equal deterrent effects on murders committed both with and without guns. Despite differences in the rates at which women and men carry guns, no difference exists in the total benefit they derive in terms of reduced murder rates. The evidence strongly rejects claims that criminals will be more likely to use firearms when their potential victims are armed. Furthermore, the increased presence of concealed handguns under nondiscretionary laws does not raise the number of accidental deaths or suicides from handguns.

As in other countries, people who engage in mass public shootings are deterred by the possibility that law-abiding citizens may be carrying guns. Such people may be deranged, but they still appear to care whether they will themselves be shot as they attempt to kill others. The results presented here are dramatic: states that adopted nondiscretionary laws during the 1977–1992 period virtually eliminated mass public shootings after four or five years. These results raise serious concerns over state and federal laws banning *all* guns from schools and the surrounding area. At least permitting school employees access to guns would seem to make schools less vulnerable to mass shootings.

One prominent concern about leniency in permitting people to carry concealed handguns is that the number of accidental deaths might rise, but I can find no statistically significant evidence that this occurs. Even the largest estimate of nine more accidental deaths per year is extremely small in comparison to the number of lives saved from fewer murders.

The evidence for Pennsylvania and Oregon also provides the first estimates of the annual social benefits that accrue from private expenditures on crime reduction. Each additional concealed-handgun permit reduces total losses to victims by between three and five thousand dollars. The results imply that handgun permits are being obtained at much lower than optimal rates in two of the three states for which I had the relevant data, perhaps because the individual owners bear all the costs of owning their handguns but receive only a small fraction of the total benefits. The evidence implies that concealed handguns are the most cost-effective method of reducing crime that has been analyzed by economists; they provide a higher return than increased law enforcement or incarceration, other private security devices, or social programs like early educational intervention.[21]

The general-election exit-poll data may also be used to calculate the change in total costs to crime victims when more people own guns. These preliminary estimates are quite dramatic, indicating that, nationwide, each 1 percent increase in the number of people owning guns reduces victim costs by over 3 billion dollars.

The data continue to supply strong evidence supporting the economic notion of deterrence. Higher arrest and conviction rates consistently and dramatically reduce the crime rate. Consistent with other recent work,[22] the results imply that increasing the arrest rate, independent of the probability of eventual conviction, imposes a significant penalty on criminals. Perhaps the most surprising result is that the deterrent effect of a 1 percent increase in arrest rates is much larger than the same increase in the probability of conviction. It was also surprising that while longer prison terms usually implied lower crime rates, the results were normally not statistically significant.

Six

What Determines Arrest Rates and the Passage of Concealed-Handgun Laws?

The regressions used in previous chapters took both the arrest rate and the passage of nondiscretionary concealed-handgun laws as given. This chapter deals with the unavoidably complicated issue of determining whether the variables I am using to explain the crime rate are in themselves determined by other variables. Essentially, the findings here confirm the deterrence effect of concealed-handgun laws and arrest rates.

Following the work of Isaac Ehrlich, I now let the arrest rate depend on crime rates as well as on population measures and the resources invested in police.[1] The following crime and police measures were used: the lagged crime rates; measures of police employment and payroll per capita, per violent crime, and per property crime at the state level (these three measures of employment are also broken down by whether police officers have the power to make arrests). The population measures were as follows: income; unemployment insurance payments; the percentages of county population by age, sex, and race (already used in table 4.1); and county and year dummy variables.[2] In an attempt to account for political influences, I further included the percentage of a state's population belonging to the National Rifle Association, along with the percentage voting for the Republican presidential candidate.[3]

Because presidential candidates and political issues vary from election to election, the variables for the percentage voting Republican are not perfectly comparable across years. To account for these differences across elections, I used the variable for the percentage voting Republican in a presidential election for the years closest to that election. Thus, the percent of the vote obtained in 1980 was multiplied by the individual year variables for the years from 1979 to 1982, the percent of the vote obtained in 1984 was multiplied by the individual year variables for the years from 1983 to 1986, and so on through the 1992 election. A second set of regressions explaining the arrest rate also includes the change in the log of the crime rates as a proxy for the difficulties that police forces may face in adjusting to changing circumstances.[4] The time period studied in all these regressions, however, is more limited than in the previous tables because the state-level data on police employment and payroll available from the U.S. Department of Justices' Expenditure and Employment data set for the criminal justice system covered only the years from 1982 to 1992.

Aside from the concern over what determines the arrest rate, we want to answer another question: Why did some states adopt nondiscretionary concealed-handgun laws while others did not? As noted earlier, if states adopted such laws because crime rates were either rising or expected to rise, our preceding regression estimates (using ordinary least-squares) will underestimate the drop in crime. Similarly, if such laws were adopted because crime rates were falling, the bias is in the opposite direction— the regression will overestimate the drop in crime. Thus, in order to explain whether a county was likely to be in a state that had adopted concealed-handgun laws, I used the rates for both violent crime and property crime, along with the change in those crime rates.[5] To control for general political differences that might affect the chances for the passage of these laws, I also included the percentage of a state's population that belonged to the National Rifle Association; the Republican presidential candidate's percentage of the statewide vote; the percentage of blacks and whites in a state's population; the total population in the state; regional dummy variables for whether the state is in the South, Northeast, or Midwest; and year dummy variables.

The regressions reported here are different from those reported earlier because they allow us to let the crime rate depend on the variables for the concealed-handgun law and the arrest rate, as well as other variables, but the variables for the concealed-handgun law and the arrest rate are in turn dependent on other variables.[6] While these estimates use the same set of control variables employed in the preceding tables, the results differ from all my previous estimates in one important respect: nondiscretionary concealed-handgun laws are associated with large, significant declines in all nine crime categories. I tried estimating a specification that mimicked the regressions in Ehrlich's study. Five of the nine crime categories implied that a change of one standard deviation in the predicted value of the nondiscretionary-law variable explains at least 10 percent of a change of one standard deviation in the corresponding crime rates. Nondiscretionary concealed-handgun laws explain 11 percent of the variation in violent crime, 7.5 percent of the variation in murder, 6 percent for rape, 10 percent for aggravated assault, and 5 percent for robbery. In fact, concealed-handgun laws explain a greater percentage of the change in murder rates than do arrest rates.

A second approach examined what happened to the results when the arrest rate was determined not only by past crime rates but also by the change in the crime rate in the previous year. The concern here is that rapid changes in crime rates make it more difficult for police agencies to maintain the arrest rates they had in the past. With the exception of robbery, the new set of estimates using the change in crime rates to explain arrest rates indicated that the effect of concealed-handgun laws was usually more statistically significant but economically smaller. For example, in the new set of estimates, concealed-handgun laws explained 3.9 percent of the variation in murder rates compared to 7.5 percent for the preceding estimates. While these results imply that even crimes involving relatively little contact between victims and criminals experienced declines, nondiscretionary concealed-handgun laws reduced violent crimes by more than they reduced property crimes.

Both sets of estimates provide strong evidence that higher arrest rates reduce crime rates. Among violent crimes, rape consistently appears to be the most sensitive to higher arrest rates. Among property crimes, larceny is the most sensitive to higher arrest rates.

The estimates explaining which states adopt concealed-handgun laws show that the states adopting these laws are relatively Republican with large National Rifle Association memberships and low but rising rates of violent crime and property crime. The set of regressions used to explain the arrest rate shows that arrest rates are lower in high-income, sparsely populated, Republican areas where crime rates are increasing. This evidence calls into question claims that police forces are not catching criminals in high-crime, densely populated areas.

I reestimated the state-level data using similar specifications. The coefficients on the variables for both arrest rates and concealed-handgun laws remained consistently negative and statistically significant. The state-level data again implied a much stronger effect from the passage of concealed-handgun laws and a much weaker effect from higher arrest rates. In order to use the longer data series available for the nonpolice employment and payroll variables, I even reestimated the regressions without those variables. This produced similar results.[7]

Finally, using the predicted values for the arrest rates allows us to investigate the significance of another weakness of the data. The arrest-rate data suffers not only from some missing observations but also from some instances where it is undefined when the crime rate in a county equals zero. This last issue is problematic only for murders and rapes in low-population counties. In these cases, both the numerator and denominator in the arrest rate equal zero, and it is not clear whether I should count this as an arrest rate equal to 100 or 0 percent, neither of which is correct, as it is truly undefined. The previously reported evidence arising from regressions that were run only on the larger counties (population over 10,000) sheds some light on this question, since these counties have fewer observations with undefined arrest rates. In addition, if the earlier reported evidence that adopting nondiscretionary concealed-handgun laws changed the number of permits the least in the lower-population counties, one would expect relatively little change in counties with missing observations.

The analysis presented in this section allowed us to try another, more appropriate approach to deal with this issue.[8] I created predicted arrest rates for these observations using the regressions that explain the arrest rate, and then I reestimated the regressions with the new, larger samples. While the coefficient for murder declined, implying a 5 percent drop when nondiscretionary laws are adopted, the coefficient for rape increased, implying a drop of more than 10 percent. Only very small changes appeared in the other estimates. All coefficients were statistically significant. The effect of arrest rates also remained negative and statistically significant. As one final test to deal with the problems that arise from using the arrest rates, I reestimated the regressions using only the predicted values for the nondiscretionary-law variable. In this case the coefficients were always negative and statistically significant, and they indicate that these laws produce an even larger negative effect on crime than the effect shown in the results already reported.

CONCLUSION

Explicitly accounting for the factors that influence a state's decision to adopt a nondiscretionary concealed-handgun law and that determine the arrest rate only serves to strengthen the earlier results: with this approach, both concealed-handgun laws and arrest rates explain much larger percentages of the changes in the crime rate than they did earlier. Several other facts are clear. Nondiscretionary laws have so far been adopted by relatively low-crime states in which the crime rate is rising. These states have also tended to vote Republican and to have high percentages of their populations enrolled in the National Rifle Association.

For studies that use the number of police officers as a proxy for the level of law enforcement, these results suggest some caution. Property-crime rates appear to have no systematic relationship to the number of police officers either with or without the power to make arrests. For violent crime, the presence of more police officers *with* arrest powers lowers the arrest rate, while a greater number of police officers *without* arrest powers raises the arrest rate.

Neither of these results alone is particularly troubling, because increasing the number of police officers could reduce the crime rate enough so that the arrest rate could fall even if the officers did not slack off. Theoretically, the relationship between the number of police officers and the arrest rate could go either way. Yet in the case of violent crimes, the drop in arrest rates associated with more police officers is too large to be explained by a drop in the crime rate. In fact, the direct relationship between the number of police officers and violent crime implies a positive relationship. There are many possible explanations for this. Quite plausibly, the presence of more police officers encourages people to come forward to report crime. Another possibility is that relatively large police forces tend to be unionized and have managed to require less work from their officers. The bottom line is that using the number of police officers directly as a proxy for the level of law enforcement is at best a risky proposition. We must control for many other factors before we know exactly what we are measuring.

Seven

The Political and Academic Debate

When my original study was released, many commentators were ready to attack it. Anyone who had shown any interest in looking at the article was given a copy while I was in the process of revising it for the *Journal of Legal Studies*, although I quickly learned that it was not common practice to circulate studies to groups on both sides of the gun debate. Few comments were offered privately, but once the paper began to receive national press coverage, the attacks came very quickly.

Before the press coverage started, it was extremely difficult to get even a proponent of gun control to provide critical comments on the paper when I presented it at the Cato Institute in early August 1996. I approached twenty-two pro-control people before Jens Ludwig, a young assistant professor at Georgetown University, accepted my request to comment on the paper.

One of the more interesting experiences occurred when I asked Susan Glick, of the Violence Policy Center, to participate.[1] Glick, whom I called during June 1996, was one of the last people that I approached. She was unwilling to comment on my talk at Cato because she didn't want to "help give any publicity to the paper." Glick said that her appearance might help bring media attention to the paper that it wouldn't otherwise have gotten. When I pointed out that C-SPAN was likely to cover the event, she said she didn't care because "we can get good media whenever we want." When I asked her if I could at least send her a copy of the paper because I would appreciate any comments that she might have, she said, "Forget it, there is no way that I am going to look at it. Don't send it."[2]

However, when the publicity broke on the story with an article in *USA Today* on August 2, she was among the many people who left telephone messages immediately asking for a copy of the paper. In her case, the media were calling, and she "need[ed] [my] paper to be able to criticize it." Because of all the commotion that day, I was unable to get back to her right away. ABC National Television News was doing a story on my study for that day, and when at around 3:00 P.M. the ABC reporter doing the story, Barry Serafin, called saying that certain objections had been raised about my paper, he mentioned that one of those who had criticized it was Ms. Glick. After talking to Mr. Serafin, I gave Glick a call to ask her if she still wanted a copy of my paper. She said that she wanted it sent to her right away and wondered if I could fax it to her. I then noted that her request seemed strange because I had just gotten off the telephone with Mr. Serafin at ABC News, who had told me that she had been very critical of the study, saying that it was "flawed." I asked how she could have said that there were flaws in the paper without even having looked at it yet. At that point Ms. Glick hung up the telephone.[3]

Many of the attacks from groups like Handgun Control, Inc. and the Violence Policy Center focused on claims that my study had been paid for by gun manufacturers or that the *Journal of Legal Studies* was not a peer-reviewed journal and that I had chosen to publish the study in a "student-edited journal" to avoid the close scrutiny that such a review would provide.[4] These attacks were completely false, and I believe that those making the charges knew them to be false. At least they had been told by all the relevant parties here at the University of Chicago and at the Olin Foundation that the funding issues were false, and the questions about publishing in a "student-edited journal" or one that was not peer-reviewed were well known to be false because of the prominence of the journal. Some statements involved claims that my work was inferior to an earlier study by three criminologists at the University of Maryland who had examined five counties.

Other statements, like those in the *Los Angeles Times,* tried to discredit the scholarliness of the study by claiming that "in academic circles, meanwhile, scholars found it curious that he would publicize his findings before they were subjected to peer review."[5] In fact, the paper was reviewed and accepted months before media stories started discussing it in August 1996.

The attacks claiming that this work had been paid for by gun manufacturers have been unrelenting. Congressman Charles Schumer (D–N.Y.) wrote as follows in the *Wall Street Journal:* "I'd like to point out one other 'association.' The Associated Press reports that Prof. Lott's fellowship at the University of Chicago is funded by the Olin Foundation, which is 'associated with the Olin Corporation,' one of the nation's largest gun manufacturers. Maybe that's a coincidence, too. But it's also a fact."[6] Others were even more direct. In a letter that the Violence Policy Center mass-mailed to newspapers around the country, M. Kristen Rand, the Center's federal policy director, wrote,

Lott's work was, in essence, funded by the firearms industry—the primary beneficiary of increased handgun sales. Lott is the John M. Olin fellow at the University of Chicago law school, a position founded by the Olin Foundation. The foundation was established by John Olin of the Olin Corp., manufacturer of Winchester ammunition and maker of the infamous "Black Talon" bullet. Lott's study of concealed handgun laws is the product of gun-industry funding.... (See, as one of many examples, "Gun Industry Paid," *Omaha World Herald,* March 10, 1997, p. 8.)[7]

Dan Kotowski, executive director of the Illinois Council Against Handgun Violence, said that "the study was biased because it was funded by the parent company of Winchester, Inc., a firearms manufacturer."[8] Kotowski is also quoted as saying that the claimed link between Winchester and my study's conclusions was "enough to call into question the study's legitimacy. It's more than a coincidence."[9] Similar claims have been made by employees of Handgun Control, Inc. and other gun-control organizations.

Indeed, gun-control groups that were unwilling to comment publicly on my study at the Cato Institute forum had time to arrange press conferences that were held exactly at the time that I was presenting my paper in Washington. Their claims were widely reported by the press in the initial news reports on my findings. A typical story stated that "Lott's academic position is funded by a grant from the Olin Foundation, which is associated with the Olin Corp. Olin's Winchester division manufactures rifles and bullets,"[10] and it was covered in newspapers from the *Chicago Tribune* to the *Houston Chronicle* and the *Des Moines Register,* as well as in "highbrow" publications like *The National Journal.* The Associated Press released a partial correction stating that the Olin Foundation and Olin Corporation are separate organizations and that the Winchester subsidiary of the Olin Corporation makes ammunition, not guns, but a Nexis search of news stories revealed that only one newspaper in the entire country that had published the original report carried the Associated Press correction.[11]

Congressman Schumer's letter did produce a strong response from William Simon, the Olin Foundation's president and former U.S. Secretary of the Treasury, in the *Wall Street Journal* for September 6, 1996:

An Insult to Our Foundation
As president of the John M. Olin Foundation, I take great umbrage at Rep. Charles Schumer's scurrilous charge (Letters to the Editor, Sept. 4) that our foundation underwrites bogus research to advance the interests of companies that manufacture guns and ammunition. He asserts (falsely) that the John M. Olin Foundation is "associated" with the Olin Corp. and (falsely again) that the Olin Corp. is one of the nation's largest gun manu-

facturers. Mr. Schumer then suggests on the basis of these premises that Prof. John Lott's article on gun-control legislation (editorial page, Aug. 28) must have been fabricated because his research fellowship at the University of Chicago was funded by the John M. Olin Foundation.

This is an outrageous slander against our foundation, the Olin Corp., and the scholarly integrity of Prof. Lott. Mr. Schumer would have known that his charges were false if he had taken a little time to check his facts before rushing into print. Others have taken the trouble to do so. For example, Stephen Chapman of the *Chicago Tribune* looked into the charges surrounding Mr. Lott's study, and published an informative story in the Aug. 15 issue of that paper, which concluded that, in conducting his research, Prof. Lott was not influenced either by the John M. Olin Foundation or by the Olin Corp. Anyone wishing to comment on this controversy ought first to consult Mr. Chapman's article and, more importantly, should follow his example of sifting the facts before reaching a conclusion. For readers of the Journal, here are the key facts.

The John M. Olin Foundation, of which I have been president for nearly 20 years, is an independent foundation whose purpose is to support individuals and institutions working to strengthen the free enterprise system. We support academic programs at the finest institutions in the nation, including the University of Chicago, Harvard, Yale, Stanford, Columbia, the University of Virginia, and many others. We do not tell scholars what to write or what to say.

The foundation was created by the personal fortune of the late John M. Olin, and is not associated with the Olin Corp. The Olin Corp. has never sought to influence our deliberations. Our trustees have never taken into account the corporate interests of the Olin Corp. or any other company when reviewing grant proposals. We are as independent of the Olin Corp. as the Ford Foundation is of the Ford Motor Co.

The John M. Olin Foundation has supported for many years a program in law and economics at the University of Chicago Law School. This program is administered and directed by a committee of faculty members in the law school. This committee, after reviewing many applications in a very competitive process, awarded a research fellowship to Mr. Lott. We at the foundation had no knowledge of who applied for these fellowships, nor did we ever suggest that Mr. Lott should be awarded one of them. We did not commission his study, nor, indeed, did we even know of it until last month, when Mr. Lott presented his findings at a conference sponsored by a Washington think tank.

As a general rule, criticism of research studies should be based on factual grounds rather than on careless and irresponsible charges about the motives of the researcher. Mr. Lott's study should be evaluated on its own merits without imputing motives to him that do not exist. I urge Mr. Schumer to check his facts more carefully in the future.

Finally, it was incorrectly reported in the *Journal* (Sept. 5) that the John M. Olin Foundation is 'headed by members of the family that founded the Olin Corp.' This is untrue. The trustees and officers of the foundation have been selected by virtue of their devotion to John Olin's principles, not by virtue of family connections. Of our seven board members, only one is a member of the Olin family. None of our officers is a member of the Olin family—neither myself as president, nor our secretary-treasurer, nor our executive director.

This letter, I think, clarifies the funding issue, and I would only like to add that while the faculty at the Law School chose to award me this fellowship, even they did not inquire into the specific research I planned to undertake.[12] The judgment was made solely on the quality and quantity of my past research, and while much of my work has dealt with crime, this was my first project involving gun control. No one other than myself had any idea what research I was planning to do. However, even if one somehow believed that Olin were trying to buy research, it must be getting a very poor return on its money. Given the hundreds of people at the different universities who have received the same type of fellowship, I have been the only one to work on the issue of gun control.

Unfortunately, as the quote from Ms. Rand's letter and statements by many other gun-control advocates—made long after Simon's explanation—indicates, the facts about funding did little to curtail the comments of those spreading the false rumors.[13]

After these attacks on my funding, the gun-control organizations brought up new issues. For example, during the spring of 1997 the Violence Policy Center sent out a press release entitled "Who Is John Lott?" that claimed, among other things, "Lott believes that some crime is good for society, that wealthy criminals should not be punished as harshly as poor convicts." I had in fact been arguing that "individuals guilty of the same crime should face the same expected level of punishment" and that with limited resources to fight crime, it is not possible to eliminate all of it.[14] I would have thought that most people would recognize these silly assertions for what they were, but they were picked up and republished by publications such as the *New Republic*.[15]

The aversion to honest public debate has been demonstrated to me over and over again since my study first received attention. Recently, for example, Randy Roth, a visiting colleague at the University of Chicago Law School, asked me to appear on a radio program that he does from the University of Hawaii on a public radio station. I had almost completely stopped doing radio interviews a few months before because they were too much of an interruption to my work, but Randy, whom I have known only very briefly from lunch-table conversation, seemed like a very interesting person, and I thought that it would be fun to do the show with him. I can only trust that he doesn't normally have as much trouble as he had this time in getting an opposing viewpoint for his program. In a note that Randy shared with me, he described a conversation that he had with Brandon Stone, of the Honolulu Police Department, whom he had been trying for a while to get to participate. Randy wrote as follows on March 3, 1997:

> Brandon called to say he had not changed his mind—he will not participate in any gun-control radio show involving John Lott. Furthermore, he said he had discussed this with all the others who are active in this area (the Hawaii Firearms Coalition, I think he called it), and that they have "banded together"—none will participate in such a show.
>
> He said he didn't want to "impugn" John's character . . . [and] then he went on to talk about all the money involved in this issue, the fact that [the] Olin Corp. is in the firearm business and financing John's chair, etc. He said John's study had been given to the media before experts first could discredit it, implying that this "tactic" was used because the study could not withstand the scrutiny of objective scholars.
>
> He said the ideas promoted by John's study are "fringe ideas" and that they are "dangerous." When I pointed out that such ideas not only have been publicly debated in other states, but that some of those states actually have enacted legislation, he basically just said that Hawaii is a special place and other states have sometimes been adversely affected by unfair tactics by the pro-gun lobby.
>
> I kept coming back to my belief that public debate is good and that my show would give him an opportunity to point out anything about John's study that he believes to be incorrect, irrelevant, distorted, or whatever. He kept saying that public debate does more harm than good when others misuse the forum. When he specifically mentions the firearm industry ("follow the money" was his suggestion, to understand what John's study is all about), I reminded him of John's association with the University of Chicago and his outstanding reputation, both for scholarship and integrity. He then said he realized John was "my friend," as though I couldn't be expected to be objective. He also said that John was "out of his field" in this area.
>
> My hunch is that it's going to be extremely difficult finding a studio guest with the credentials and ability to do a good job on the pro–gun-control side.

After talking with Randy and in an attempt to create a balanced program, I also telephoned Mr. Stone. While we did not get into the detail that he went into with Randy, I did try to address his concerns over my funding and my own background in criminal justice as chief economist at the U.S. Sentencing Commission during the late 1980s. Stone also expressed his concerns to me that Hawaiians would not be best served by our debating the issue and that Hawaiians had already made up their minds on this topic. I said that he seemed like an articulate person and that it would be good to have a lively discussion on the subject, but he said that the program "could only do more harm than good" and that any pro—gun-control participation would only lend "credibility" to the discussion.[16]

Before I did my original study, I would never have expected it to receive the attention that it did. None of the refereed journal articles that I have produced has received so much attention. Many people have told me that it was politically naive. That may be, but this much is clear: I never would have guessed how much people fear discussion of these issues. I never would have known how much effort goes into deliberately ignoring certain findings in order to deny them news coverage. Nor would I have seen, after news coverage did occur, how much energy goes into attacking the integrity of those who present such findings, with such slight reference—or no reference at all—to the actual merits of the research. I was also surprised by the absolute confidence shown by gun-control advocates that they could garner extensive news coverage whenever they wanted.

CRITICISMS OF THE ORIGINAL STUDY

A second line of attack came from academic, quasi-academic, and gun-control advocacy groups concerning the competence with which the study was conducted. Many of these objections were dealt with somewhere in the original study, which admittedly is very long. Yet it should have been easy enough for critics—especially academics—to check.

The attacks have been fairly harsh, especially by the standards of academic discourse. For example,

> "They highlight things that support their hypothesis while they ignore things contrary to their hypothesis," said Daniel Webster, an assistant professor at Johns Hopkins University Center for Gun Policy and Research.
>
> "We think the study falls far short of any reasonable standard of good social science research in making [their] case," said economist Daniel

Nagin of Carnegie-Mellon University, who has analyzed Lott's data with colleague Dan Black.[17]

I have made the data I used available to all academics who have requested them, and so far professors at twenty-four universities have taken advantage of that. Of those who have made the effort to use the extensive data set, Dan Black and Daniel Nagin have been the only ones to publicly criticize the study.

The response from some academics, particularly those at the Johns Hopkins Center for Gun Policy and Research, has been highly unusual in many ways. For instance, who has ever heard of academics mounting an attack on a scholarly study by engaging in a systematic letter-writing campaign to local newspapers around the country?[18] One letter from a citizen to the *Springfield (Illinois) State Journal-Register* noted, "Dear Editor: Golly, I'm impressed that the staff at Johns Hopkins University reads our local *State Journal-Register.* I wonder if they subscribe to it."[19]

The rest of this chapter briefly reviews the critiques and then provides my responses to their concerns. I discuss a number of issues below that represent criticisms raised in a variety of published or unpublished research papers as well as in the popular press:

1   *Is the scale of the effect realistic?*

Large reductions in violence are quite unlikely because they would be out of proportion to the small scale of the change in carrying firearms that the legislation produced. (Franklin Zimring and Gordon Hawkins, "Concealed-Handgun Permits: The Case of the Counterfeit Deterrent," *The Responsive Community* [Spring 1997]: 59, cited hereafter as Zimring and Hawkins, "Counterfeit Deterrent")

In some states, like Pennsylvania, almost 5 percent of the population has concealed-handgun permits. In others, like Florida, the portion is about 2 percent and growing quickly. The question here is whether these percentages of the population are sufficient to generate 8 percent reductions in murders or 5 percent reductions in rapes. One important point to take into account is that applicants for permits do not constitute a random sample of the population. Applicants are likely to be those most at risk. The relevant comparison is not between the percentage of the population being attacked and the percentage of the entire population holding permits, but between the percentage of the population most vulnerable to attack and the percentage of that population holding permits.

Let us consider some numbers from the sample to see how believable these results are. The yearly murder rate for the average county is 5.65 murders per 100,000 people, that is, .00565 percent of the people in the average county are murdered each year. An 8 percent change in this murder rate amounts to a reduction of 0.0005 percent. Obviously, even if only 2 percent of the population have handgun permits, that 2 percent is a huge number relative to the 0.0005 percent reduction in the murder rate. Even the largest category of violent crimes, aggravated assault, involves 180 cases per 100,000 people in the average county per year (that is, 0.18 percent of the people are victims of this crime in the typical year). A 7 percent change in this number implies that the assault rate declines from 0.18 percent of the population to 0.167 percent of the population. Again, this 0.013 percent change in the assault rate is quite small compared to the observed changes in the number of concealed-handgun permits.

Even if those who carry concealed handguns face exactly the same risk of being attacked as everyone else, a 2 percent increase in the portion of the population carrying concealed handguns seems comparable to the percentage-point reductions in crime. Bearing in mind that those carrying guns are most likely to be at risk, the drop in crime rates correlated with the presence of these guns even begins to seem relatively small. Assuming that just 2 percent of the population carries concealed handguns, the drop in the murder rate only requires that 0.025 percent of those with concealed-handgun permits successfully ward off a life-threatening attack to achieve the 0.0005 percent reduction in the murder rate. The analogous percentage for aggravated assaults is only 0.65 percent. In other words, if less than seven-tenths of one percent of those with concealed handguns successfully ward off an assault, that would account for the observed drop in the assault rate.

2 *The importance of "crime cycles"*

> Crime rates tend to be cyclical with somewhat predictable declines following several years of increases. . . . Shall-issue laws, as well as a number of other measures intended to reduce crime, tend to be enacted during periods of rising crime. Therefore, the reductions in violent crime . . . attribute[d] to the implementation of shall-issue laws may be due to the variety of other crime-fighting measures, or to a commonly observed downward drift in crime levels towards some long-term average. (Daniel W. Webster, "The Claims That Right-to-Carry Laws Reduce Violent Crime Are Unsubstantiated," The Johns Hopkins Center for Gun Policy and Research, copy obtained March 6, 1997, p. 1; cited hereafter as Webster, "Claims")

Despite claims to the contrary, the regressions do control for national and state crime trends in several different ways. At the national level, I use a separate variable for each year, a technique that allows me to account for the changes in average national crime rates from one year to another. Any national cycles in crime rates should be accounted for by this method. At the state level, some of the estimates use a separate time trend for each state, and the results with this method generally yielded even larger drops in violent-crime rates associated with nondiscretionary (shall-issue) laws.

To illustrate that the results are not merely due to the "normal" ups and downs for crime, we can look again at the diagrams in chapter 4 showing crime patterns before and after the adoption of the nondiscretionary laws. The declines not only begin right when the concealed-handgun laws pass, but the crime rates end up well below their levels prior to the law. Even if laws to combat crime are passed when crime is rising, why would one believe that they happened to be passed right at the peak of any crime cycle?

As to the concern that other changes in law enforcement may have been occurring at the same time, the estimates account for changes in other gun-control laws and changes in law enforcement as measured by arrest and conviction rates as well as by prison terms. No previous study of crime has attempted to control for as many different factors that might explain changes in the crime rate.

3 *Did I assume that there was an immediate and constant effect from these laws and that the effect should be the same everywhere?*

The "statistical models assumed: (1) an immediate and constant effect of shall-issue laws, and (2) similar effects across different states and counties." (Webster, "Claims," p. 2; see also Dan Black and Daniel Nagin, "Do 'Right-to-Carry' Laws Deter Violent Crime?" *Journal of Legal Studies* 27 [January 1998], p. 213.)

One of the central arguments both in the original paper and in this book is that the size of the deterrent effect is related to the number of permits issued, and it takes many years before states reach their long-run level of permits. Again, the figures in chapter 4 illustrate this quite clearly.

I did not expect the number of permits to change equally across either counties or states. A major reason for the larger effect on crime in the more urban counties was that in rural areas, permit requests already were being approved; hence it was in urban areas that the number of permitted concealed handguns increased the most.

A week later, in response to a column that I published in the *Omaha World-Herald*,[20] Mr. Webster modified this claim somewhat:

Lott claims that his analysis did not assume an immediate and constant effect, but that is contrary to his published article, in which the *vast majority* of the statistical models assume such an effect. (Daniel W. Webster, "Concealed-Gun Research Flawed," *Omaha World-Herald*, March 12, 1997; emphasis added.)

When one does research, it is most appropriate to take the simplest specifications first and then gradually make things more complicated. The simplest way of doing this is to examine the mean crime rates before and after the change in a law. Then one would examine the trends that existed before and after the law. This is the pattern that I followed in my earlier work, and I have followed the same pattern here. The bottom line should be, How did the different ways of examining the data affect the results? What occurs here is that (1) the average crime rate falls after the nondiscretionary concealed-handgun laws are adopted; (2) violent-crime rates were rising until these laws were adopted, and they fell dramatically after that; and (3) the magnitude of the drops, both across counties and states and over time, corresponds to the number of permits issued.

4   *When were these concealed-handgun laws adopted in different states?*

Lott and Mustard also use incorrect dates of shall-issue law implementation in their analyses. For example, they claim that Virginia adopted its shall-issue law in 1988. . . . Some populous counties in Virginia continued to issue very few permits until 1995 (after the study period), when the state eliminated this discretion. Lott and Mustard identify 1985 as the year in which Maine liberalized its concealed-carry policy. It is unclear why they chose 1985 as the year of policy intervention, because the state changed its concealed-carry law in 1981, 1983, 1985, 1989, and 1991. (Webster, "Claims," p. 3; see also Daniel W. Webster, "Concealed-Gun Research Flawed," *Omaha World-Herald*, March 12, 1997; cited hereafter as Webster, "Flawed.")

I do think that Virginia's 1988 law clearly attempted to take away local discretion in issuing permits, and, indeed, all but three counties clearly complied with the intent of the law. However, to satisfy any skeptics, I examined whether reclassifying Virginia affected the results: it did not. The 1988 law read as follows:

The court, after consulting the law-enforcement authorities of the county or city and receiving a report from the Central Criminal Records Exchange, *shall issue* such permit if the applicant is of good character, has demonstrated a need to carry such concealed weapon, which need may include but is not limited to lawful defense and security, is physically and mentally competent to carry such weapon, and is not prohibited by law from receiving, possessing, or transporting such weapon [emphasis added].[21]

As with Virginia, I relied on a study by Clayton Cramer and David Kopel to determine when Maine changed its law to a nondiscretionary law. Maine enacted a series of changes in its law in 1981, 1983, 1985, and 1991. The 1985 law did not completely eliminate discretion, but it provided the foundation for what they then considered to be a switch to a de facto shall-issue regime, which was upheld in a number of important state court decisions.[22] The bottom line, however (again, as with Virginia), is that reclassifying Maine (or even eliminating it from the data set) does not change the results much.

5 *Should robbery be the crime most affected by the adoption of the nondiscretionary law?*

Shall-issue laws were adopted principally to deter predatory street crime, the most common example of which is robbery by a stranger. But [the] results indicate that shall-issue laws had little or no effect on robbery rates. Instead the strongest deterrent effects estimated were for rape, aggravated assault, and murder. (Webster, "Claims," p. 3)

Is it credible that laws that allow citizens to carry guns in public appear to have almost no effect on robberies, most of which occur in public spaces, yet do reduce the number of rapes, most of which occur outside of public spaces within someone's home. (Jens Ludwig, speaking on *Morning Edition,* National Public Radio, 10:00 A.M. ET December 10, 1996.)

I have two responses. First, as anyone who has carefully read this book will know, it is simply not true that the results show "little or no effect on robbery rates." Whether the effect was greater for robbery or other violent crimes depends on whether one simply compares the mean crime rates before and after the laws (in which case the effect is relatively small for robbery) or compares the slopes before and after the law (in which case the effect for robbery is the largest).

Second, it is not clear that robbery should exhibit the largest impacts, primarily because the term *robbery* encompasses many crimes that are not street robberies. For instance, we do not expect bank or residential robberies to decrease; in fact, they could even rise. Allowing law-abiding citizens to carry concealed handguns makes street robberies more difficult, and thus may make other crimes like residential robbery *relatively* more attractive. Yet not only is it possible that these two different components of robbery could move in opposite directions, but to rank some of these different crimes, one requires information on how sensitive different types of criminals are to the increased threat.

Making claims about what will happen to different types of violent crimes is much more difficult than predicting the relative differences between, say, crimes that involve no contact with victims and crimes that do. Even here, however, some of these questions cannot be settled *a priori*. For example, when violent crimes decline, more people may feel free to walk around in neighborhoods, which implies that they are more likely to observe the illegal actions of strangers.[23] Criminals who commit violent crimes are also likely to commit some property crimes, and anything that can make an area unattractive to them will reduce both types of crime.

6 *Do concealed-handgun laws cause criminals to substitute property crimes for rape?*

> Lott and Mustard argue that criminals, in response to shall-issue laws, substitute property crimes unlikely to involve contact with victims. But their theory and findings do not comport with any credible criminological theory because theft is the motive for only a small fraction of the violent crimes for which Lott and Mustard find shall-issue effects. It is difficult to rationalize why a criminal would, for example, steal a car because he felt deterred from raping or assaulting someone. (Webster, "Claims," p. 4. See also Jens Ludwig, "Do Permissive Concealed-Carry Laws Reduce Violent Crime?" Georgetown University working paper, October 8, 1996, p. 19, hereafter cited as Ludwig, "Permissive Concealed-Carry Laws.")

No one believes that hard-core rapists who are committing their crimes only for sexual gratification will turn into auto thieves, though some thefts do also involve aggravated assault, rape, or murder.[24] Indeed, 16 percent of murders in Chicago from 1990 to 1995 occurred in the process of a robbery.[25] What is most likely to happen, however, is that robbers will try to obtain money by other means such as auto theft or larceny. Although it is not unusual for rape victims to be robbed, the decline in rape most likely reflects the would-be rapist's fear of being shot.

I am also not completely clear on what Webster means when he says that "theft is the motive for only a small fraction of violent crimes," since robbery accounted for as much as 34 percent of all violent crimes committed during the sample between 1977 and 1992 (and this excludes robberies that were committed when other more serious crimes like murder or rape occurred in connection with the robbery).

7 *Comparing crime rates for two to three years before nondiscretionary laws go into effect with crime rates for two to three years after the passage of such laws*

> If right-to-carry laws have an immediate, substantial impact on the crime rates, the coefficients on the right-to-carry laws immediately after the enactment of the law should be substantially different from those immediately preceding the law's enactment. To test formally for the impact of right-to-carry laws, we see if the sum of the coefficients for two to three years prior to adoption is significantly different from the sum for two and three years following adoption. . . . Only in the murder equation do our findings agree with Lott and Mustard. In contrast to Lott and Mustard, we find evidence that robberies and larcenies are reduced when right-to-carry laws are passed and no evidence of an impact on rape and aggravated assaults. (Dan Black and Daniel Nagin, "Do 'Right-to-Carry' Laws Deter Violent Crime?" Carnegie-Mellon University working paper, October 16, 1996, p. 7)

Instead of the approach used earlier in this book (a simple time trend and time trend squared for the number of years before and after the concealed-handgun laws) Black and Nagin use ten different variables to examine these trends. Separate variables were used for the first year after the law, the second year after the law, the third year after the law, the fourth year after the law, and five or more years after the law. Similarly, five different variables were used to measure the effects for the five years leading up to the adoption of the law. They then compare the average coefficient values for the variables measuring the effects two to three years before the law with the average effect for the variables two to three years after the law.

A quick glance at figures 7.1 to 7.5, which plot their results, will explain their findings. Generally, the pattern is very similar to what we reported earlier. In addition, as crime is rising right up until the law is adopted and falling thereafter, it is not surprising that some values when the crime rate is going down are equal to those when it was going up. It is the slopes of the lines and not simply their levels that matter. But more generally, why choose to compare only two to three years before and after to look for changes created by the law. Why not use all the data available?

Examining the entire period before the law versus the entire period after produces the significant results that I reported earlier in the book. Alternatively, one could have chosen to analyze the differences in crime rates between the year before the law went into effect and the year after, but one would hope that if deviations are made from any simple rule, some rationale for doing so would be given.

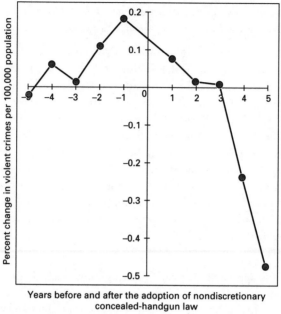

Figure 7.1. Average year-dummy effects for violent crimes, using Black's and Nagin's "full sample"

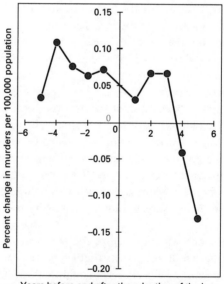

Figure 7.2. The effect of concealed-handgun laws on murder, using Black's and Nagin's "full sample"

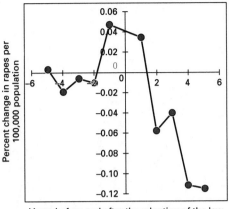

Figure 7.3. The effect of concealed-handgun laws on rapes, using Black's and Nagin's "full sample"

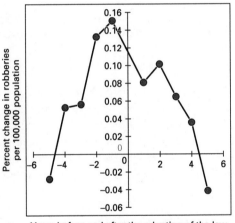

Figure 7.4. The effect of concealed-handgun laws on robbery, using Black's and Nagin's "full sample"

They claim that their results differ from ours because they find a statistically significant decline. This is puzzling; it is difficult to see why their results would be viewed as inconsistent with my argument. I had indeed also found some evidence that larcenies were reduced by nondiscretionary laws (for example, see the results using the state-level data or the results using two-stage least squares), but I chose to emphasize those results implying the smallest possible positive benefits from concealed-handgun laws.

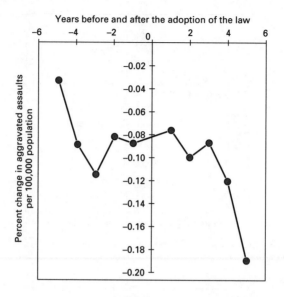

Figure 7.5. The effect of concealed-handgun laws on aggravated assaults, using Black's and Nagin's "full sample"

The bottom line—even using their choice of the dates that they deem most appropriate—is that murder and robbery rates fall after the passage of the laws and that none of the other violent-crime categories experienced an increase. Looking further at whether violent-crime rates were rising or falling before and after these laws, one finds that violent-crime rates were almost always rising prior to the passage of the law and always falling after it.

8 *The impact of including Florida in the sample*

Our concern is particularly severe for the state of Florida. With the Mariel boat lift of 1980 and the thriving drug trade, Florida's crime rates are quite volatile. Moreover, four years after the passage of the right-to-carry law in 1987, Florida passed several gun-related measures, including background checks of handgun buyers and a waiting period for handgun purchases. To test the sensitivity of the results to the inclusion of Florida, we reestimated the model . . . without Florida. Only in the robbery equation can we reject the hypothesis that the crime rate two and three years after adoptions is different than the crime rate two and three years prior to adoption. (Dan Black and Daniel Nagin, "Do 'Right-to-Carry' Laws Deter Violent Crime?" Carnegie-Mellon University working paper, October 16, 1996, p. 9)

In fact, Nagin and Black said they found that virtually all of the claimed benefits of carry laws were attributable to changes in the crime rate in just one state: Florida. (Richard Morin, "Unconventional Wisdom: New facts and Hot Stats from the Social Sciences," *Washington Post*, March 23, 1997, p. C5)

This particular suggestion—that we should throw out the data for Florida because the drop in violent crimes is so large that it affects the results—is very ironic. Handgun Control, Inc. and other gun-control groups continue, as of this writing, to cite the 1995 University of Maryland study, which claimed that if evidence existed of a detrimental impact of concealed handguns, it was for Florida.[26] If the Maryland study is to be believed, the inclusion of Florida must have biased my results in the opposite direction.[27]

More important, as we shall see below, the reasons given by Black and Nagin for dropping Florida from the sample are simply not valid. Furthermore, the impact of excluding Florida is different from what they claim. Figure 7.6 shows the murder rate in Florida from the early 1980s until 1992. The Mariel boat lift did dramatically raise violent-crime rates like murder, but these rates had returned to their pre-Mariel levels by 1982. For murder, the rate was extremely stable until the nondiscretionary concealed-handgun law passed there in 1987, when it began to drop dramatically.

The claim that Florida should be removed from the data because a

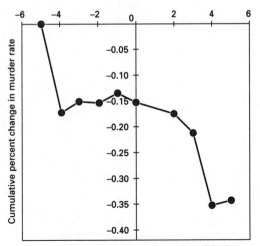

Years before and after implementation of the law

Figure 7.6. Florida's murder rates

waiting period and a background check went into effect in 1992 is even weaker. If this were a valid reason for exclusion, why not exclude other states with these laws as well? Why only remove Florida? Seventeen other states had waiting periods in 1992. A more valid response would be to try to account for the impact of these other laws—as I did in chapter 4. Indeed, accounting for these other laws slightly strengthens the evidence that concealed handguns deter crime.

The graph for Florida in figure 7.6 produces other interesting results. The murder rate declined in each consecutive year following the implementation of the concealed-handgun law until 1992, the first year that these other, much-touted, gun-control laws went into effect. I am not claiming that these laws caused murder rates to rise, but this graph surely makes it more difficult to argue that laws restricting the ability of law-abiding citizens to obtain guns would reduce crime.

While Black's and Nagin's explanations for dropping Florida from the data set are invalid, there is some justification for concern that results are being driven by a few unusual observations. Figure 7.7 shows the relationship between violent-crime rates and concealed-handgun laws when

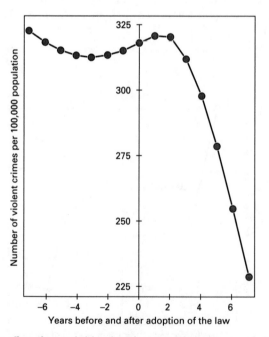

Figure 7.7. The effect of concealed-handgun laws on violent crimes, excluding Florida

Florida is excluded. A careful comparison of this graph with that of figure 4.5, which includes Florida, reveals only a few very small differences.

As a more systematic response to this concern, I excluded Florida and reestimated all the regressions shown in this book. Indeed, there were eight regressions out of the more than one thousand discussed in which the exclusion of Florida did cause the coefficient for the nondiscretionary variable to lose its statistical significance, although it remained negative. The rest of the regression estimates either remained unchanged or (especially for aggravated assault and robbery) became larger and more statistically significant.

Black and Nagin seem to feel that their role in this debate is to see if they can find some specification using any combination of the data that weakens the results.[28] But traditional statistical tests of significance are based on the assumption that the researcher is not deliberately choosing which results to present. Even if a result is statistically significant at the 1 percent level, one would expect that one out of every one hundred regressions would not yield a statistically significant result; in other words, out of one thousand regressions, one would expect to find at least ten for which the impact of nondiscretionary concealed-handgun laws was not statistically significant.

> Lott's claims that Florida's concealed-carry law was responsible for lower murder rates in that state is questionable. Florida did not experience reductions in murders and rapes until four or five years after the law was liberalized. Lott attributes this "delayed effect" to the cumulative influence of increases in carrying permits. Other research attributes Florida's declines in murders in the 1990s to laws requiring background checks and waiting periods for handgun purchases that were implemented several years after gun-carrying laws were liberalized. (Webster, "Flawed")

Much of Webster's comment echoes the issues raised previously by Black and Nagin—indeed, I assume that he is referring to their piece when he mentions "other research." However, while I have tested whether other gun-control laws might explain these declines in crime (see table 4.11), Black and Nagin did not do so, but merely appealed to "other research" to support their affirmation. The preceding quotation seems to imply that my argument involved some sort of "tipping" point: as the number of permits rose, the murder rate eventually declined. As figure 7.6 illustrates, however, Florida's decline in murder rates corresponded closely with the rise in concealed-handgun permits: no lag appears in the decline; rather, the decline begins as soon as the law goes into effect.

9 *The impact of including Maine in the sample*

> One should also be wary of the impact that Maine has on Lott's graphs. . . .
> When Maine was removed from the analyses, the suggested delayed
> [effects of the law] on robberies and aggravated assaults vanished. (Web-
> ster, "Flawed")

This comment is curious not only because Mr. Webster does not cite a
study to justify this claim but also because he has never asked for the
data to examine these questions himself. Thus it is difficult to know how
he arrived at this conclusion. A more direct response, however, is simply
to show how the graphs change when Maine is excluded from the
sample. As figures 7.8 and 7.9 show, the exclusion of Maine has very little
effect.

10 *How much does the impact of these laws vary across states?*

> [Dan Black and Dan Nagin] found the annual murder rate did go down in
> six of the ten states—but it went up in the other four, including a 100
> percent increase in West Virginia. Rape dropped in five states—but in-
> creased in the other five. And the robbery rate went down in six states—
> but went up in four. "That's curious," Black said. If concealed weapons
> laws were really so beneficial, their impact should not be so "wildly"
> different from state to state. (Richard Morin, "Unconventional Wisdom:
> New Facts and Hot Stats from the Social Sciences," *Washington Post*, March
> 23, 1997, p. C5)

Unfortunately, Black's and Nagin's evidence was not based on statewide
crime rates but on the crime rates for counties with over 100,000 people.

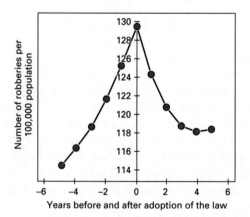

Figure 7.8. The effect of concealed-handgun laws on robbery rates, excluding Maine

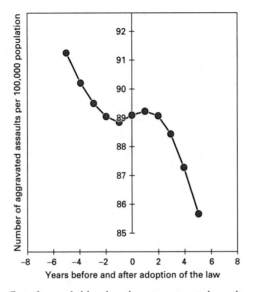

Figure 7.9. The effect of concealed-handgun laws on aggravated assaults, excluding Maine

This fact is important, for instance, in West Virginia, where it means that *only one single county*—Kanawha—was examined. The other fifty-four counties in West Virginia, which include 89 percent of the state's population, were excluded from their estimates. They used only one county for three of the ten states, and only three counties for another state. In fact, Black and Nagin managed to eliminate 85 percent of all counties in the nation in their analysis.

As shown in table 4.9 (see chapter 4), my estimates using all the counties certainly did not yield "wildly" different estimates across states. Violent-crime rates fell in nine of the ten states enacting new nondiscretionary concealed-handgun laws between 1977 and 1992. The differences that did exist across states can be explained by differences in the rates at which concealed-handgun permits were issued. Table 4.10 also provides evidence that the states that issued more permits experienced greater reductions in crime.

11 *Do the coefficient estimates for the demographic variables make sense?*

Perhaps even more surprising are the coefficient estimates for measures of a county's population that is black, female, and between the ages of 40 and 49 or over the age of 65. [Lott and Mustard find] evidence to suggest that these variables have a statistically significant, positive correlation with murder rates . . . and that black females ages 40 to 49 have a statistically significant positive correlation with the aggravated assault rate. . . . There remain two competing explanations for [these] findings. First, middle-aged and elderly African-American women could be actively [engaged] in the commission of car thefts, assaults, and murders across the United States. The more likely explanation is that [their results] are misspecified and, as a result, their coefficient estimates are biased. (Ludwig, "Permissive Concealed-Carry Laws," pp. 20–21. See also Albert W. Alschuler, "Two Guns, Four Guns, Six Guns, More: Does Arming the Pubic Reduce Crime?" *Valparaiso University Law Review* 31 (Spring 1997): 367.)

No, black females ages 40 to 49 are not responsible for a crime wave. Other results in the regressions that were not mentioned in this quotation indicate that the greater the percentage of women between the ages of 10 and 29, the greater the rape rate—but these estimates do not imply that young women are going out and committing rapes. To show that crime rates are higher where greater percentages of the population are of a certain demographic age group does not imply that the people in that group are committing the crimes. The positive relationship may exist because these people are relatively easy or attractive victims.

If such an objection were valid, it should also apply to my finding that in areas where personal incomes are high, auto-theft rates are also high. Should we infer from this that high-income individuals are more likely to steal cars? Presumably not. What is most likely is that wealthy individuals own cars that are attractive targets for auto thieves.

12 *Can we compare counties with discretionary and nondiscretionary concealed-handgun laws?*

Many counties with very permissive permit systems can be found in states with no shall-issue laws, such as Louisiana and California. For example, for example, in El Dorado county in California, 1,289 concealed-carry permits were issued in 1995. With a population of 148,600, this implies that 0.87 percent of this county's population received concealed-carry permits in one year alone. In contrast, a total of 186,000 people in Florida had concealed-carry permits in 1996 out of a total state population of 13,958,000; that is, 1.33 percent of the population was licensed to carry concealed [guns]. Yet under [the] classification scheme used in most of their results, El Dorado county would not be classified as shall-issue, while every county in Florida would be so classified. (Jens Ludwig, "Permissive Concealed-Carry Laws," pp. 20–21.)

The simplest question that we are asking is, What happens to the crime rate when nondiscretionary laws are passed allowing law-abiding citizens to carry concealed handguns? The key here is the *change* in the leniency of the laws. The regressions have individual variables for each county that allow us to account for differences in the mean crime rate. The purpose of all the other variables is to explain why crime rates differ from this average. Under discretionary laws some counties are extremely liberal in granting permits—essentially behaving as if they had nondiscretionary laws. In the regressions, differences between counties with discretionary laws (including differences in how liberally they issued concealed-handgun permits) are already being partly "picked up" by these individual county variables. For my test to work, it is only necessary for nondiscretionary laws *on average* to increase the number of concealed-handgun permits.

True, the amount of change in the number of permits does vary across counties. As this book has documented, law officials in discretionary states across the country have said that the more rural counties with relatively low populations were much more liberal in granting permits under discretionary laws. Since no usable statistics are available regarding how easily permits are granted, I tested whether nondiscretionary laws changed the crime rates the most in counties with the largest or densest populations. The results confirmed that this was the case (see figure 4.1).

We also tried another approach to deal with this question. A few states did keep good records on the number of concealed-handgun permits issued at either the county or the state level. We reported earlier the results for Pennsylvania and Oregon (see tables 5.4 and 5.5 in chapter 5). Despite the small samples, we accounted for all the variables controlled for in the larger regressions, and the results confirmed that murder rates decline as the number of a permits issued in a county rises.

13 *Should changes in the arrest rate be accounted for when explaining changes in the crime rate?*

The use of arrest rates as an explanatory variable is itself quite problematic. . . . Since the arrest rate is calculated as the number of arrests for a particular crime divided by the number of crimes committed, unobserved determinants of the crime rate will by construction also influence the arrest rate. When the arrest rate is included as an explanatory variable in a regression equation, this leads to the statistical problem known as "endogeneity," or "simultaneity bias." (Jens Ludwig, "Permissive Concealed-Carry Laws," pp. 7–8)

True, there is an endogeneity "problem." However, on theoretical grounds, the inclusion of the arrest rate is highly desirable. There is strong reason to believe that crime rates depend on the probability of punishment. In addition, to exclude variables that obviously should be included in the analysis would create even more important potential bias problems. Furthermore, the endogeneity problem was dealt with in the original paper: it was precisely our awareness of that problem that led us to use two-stage least squares to estimate the set of regressions, which is the recognized method of dealing with such a problem. As reported in chapter 6, the two-stage least-squares estimate provided even stronger evidence that concealed handguns deter crime.

The simplest point to make, however, is that excluding the arrest rate does not alter the findings regarding concealed handguns. Reestimating the regressions in tables 4.1 and 4.3 for the same samples and control variables produces virtually identical results. Ironically, two of my strongest critics, Dan Black and Dan Nagin, also tried excluding the arrest rates, and they admitted in early drafts of their paper that their results agreed with ours: "The inclusion of the arrest-rate variable has very little impact on the coefficient estimates of the right-to-carry laws."[29]

14 *Are the graphs in this book misleading?*

> Lott rebuts many of the criticisms of his study by pointing to his simple but misleading graphs. The graphs are visually compelling yet very deceptive. What is not obvious to the casual observer of the graphs is that each data point represents an aggregate average for states that liberalized their gun-carrying laws, but the states that make up the average are not the same each year. Lott examined 10 states he claims adopted "shall-issue" concealed-gun-carrying laws during his sample period. For many of the states studied, data were available for only one to three years after the laws were implemented. (Webster, "Flawed")

The graphs presented in the paper do indeed represent the average changes in crime rates before and after the implementation of these laws. The graphs consistently show that violent-crime rates are rising before these laws go into effect and falling afterward. Since some states only adopted nondiscretionary, "shall-issue" laws toward the end of the sample period, it was not possible to examine all the states for the same number of years after the laws were implemented. I disagree that this is "misleading" or "deceptive." The results were by no means generated by the aggregation itself, and anybody doubting the meaning of the graph can examine the regression results. Since the regressions already control for each county's average crime rate, any changes refer to deviations from that county's average crime rate.[30]

Ian Ayres and Steven Levitt use similar graphs and find similar results when they look at the deterrent effect of Lojack antitheft devices on cars (these are radio tracking devices that can be activated by police when a car is stolen).[31] In many ways, the theoretical deterrent effect of these devices is the same as that of concealed handguns: because the device is small and easy to hide, a criminal cannot easily know whether a car has the tracking device until the police arrive.

Future studies will be able to track these changes in crime over longer periods of time because more states will have had right-to-carry laws for longer periods of time. Such studies will ultimately help to test my findings. I have used all the data that was available at the time that David Mustard and I put this data set together. With 54,000 observations and hundreds of variables available over the 1977 to 1994 period, it is also by far the largest data set that has ever been put together for any study of crime, let alone for the study of gun control.[32] I find it ironic that my study is attacked for not having enough data when these same researchers have praised previous studies that relied on much shorter time periods for a single state or a few counties. For example, Mr. Webster expresses no such criticism when referring to a study conducted by the University of Maryland. Yet that study analyzed merely five counties and covered a shorter period of time after the law was enacted.[33]

15 *Should concealed-handgun laws have differential effects on the murder rates of youths and adults?*

Ludwig points out that in many states only adults may carry concealed weapons. So, according to Lott's deterrence theory, adults should be safer than young people. But this hasn't happened, Ludwig says. (Kathleen Schalch describing Jens Ludwig's arguments on *Morning Edition,* National Public Radio, 10:00 A.M. ET Tuesday, December 10, 1996.)

As noted in chapter 4, I tested the hypothesis that murder rates would be lower for adults than for adolescents under nondiscretionary concealed-handgun laws, and reported the results in the original paper. However, the results did not bear out this possibility. Concealed-handgun laws reduce murder rates for both adults and for adolescents. One explanation may simply be that young people also benefited from the carrying of concealed handguns by adults. Several plausible scenarios may explain this. First, criminals may well tend to leave an area where law-abiding adults carry concealed handguns, and since all age groups live in the same neighborhood, this lowers crime rates for all population groups. Second, when gun-carrying adults are physically present, they may able to protect some youngsters in threatening situations.

Could some other factor be lowering the juvenile murder rate—

something that is unrelated to concealed handguns? Certainly, the results of any research may be affected by unknown factors. But until such a factor has been found, it is premature to conclude, as Ludwig does, that "these findings are not consistent with the hypothesis that shall-issue laws decrease crime through a deterrence effect."[34]

16 *Are changes in the characteristics of victims consistent with the theory?*

> Lott and Mustard offer data on the character of victims in homicide cases. They report (astonishingly) that the proportion of stranger killings increases following the enactment of right-to-carry laws, while the proportion of intrafamily killings declines. That right-to-carry laws deter intrafamily homicides more than they deter stranger homicides is inconceivable. (Albert W. Alschuler, "Two Guns, Four Guns, Six Guns, More: Does Arming the Public Reduce Crime?" *Valparaiso University Law Review* 31 (1997): 369)

> Josh Sugarmann of the Violence Prevention Center noted that most murders are committed by people who know each other. "Concealed-weapons laws are not passed to protect people from people they know," Sugarmann said. (Doug Finke, "Sides Stick to Their Guns, Concealed-Carry Bill Set for Showdown in General Assembly," *Springfield State Journal-Register,* March 31, 1997, p. 1)

As noted in the first chapter, the category of acquaintance murder is extremely broad (encompassing shootings of cab drivers, gang members, drug dealers or buyers, and prostitutes or their clients). For the Chicago data that we discussed, the number of acquaintance murders involving friends was actually only a small percentage of the total number of acquaintance murders. If the breakdown found for Chicago provides even the remotest proxy for the national data, it is not particularly surprising that the relative share of acquaintance murders involving friends should rise, because we expect that many of the murders in this category are unlikely to be affected by law-abiding citizens carrying concealed handguns. Family members may also find that concealed handguns protect them from other estranged family members. A wife seeking a divorce may find that a concealed handgun provides her protection against a husband who is unwilling to let go of the relationship, and attacks by such people do not always take place in a home. Surely there are many cases of spousal abuse where women fear for their lives and find that a handgun provides them with a significant degree of protection.

A recent case involving a woman who used a handgun to protect herself from an abusive husband created an important new legal precedent in California: for the first time, women are now allowed to use self-defense before they suffer serious blows. The *San Francisco Examiner* reported as follows:

[Fay] Johnson, a 47-year-old mother of four, said that on July 2, 1995, she feared her 62-year-old husband, Clarence, would beat her as he always did after a weekend of drinking and hanging out with his motorcycle buddies.

She had overspent her budget on supplies for a Fourth of July barbecue and didn't have dinner ready, and the house was not clean—so when she heard her husband's motorcycle pull into the driveway, she decided to take matters into her own hands.

Johnson said she grabbed a loaded gun . . . [and fired,] hitting her husband five times. He survived and testified against her. She was arrested and spent 21 months in prison until her acquittal.

"I regret being in jail, but I just wouldn't tolerate it anymore," said Johnson, a friendly, articulate woman who is celebrating her freedom with her children and six grandchildren. "It would have been suicide."

Johnson said she had endured nearly 25 years of mental and physical abuse at the hands of her husband, whose usual form of punishment was slamming her head into a wall. The beatings got so bad, she said, that she had to be hospitalized twice and tried getting counseling until he found out and forced her to stop. She said the pressure of the abuse had culminated that fateful day.[35]

Pointing to women who use handguns to protect themselves from abusive husbands or boyfriends in no way proves that the primary effects of concealed-handgun laws will involve such uses of guns, but these cases should keep us from concluding that significant benefits for these women are "inconceivable."

With reference to Alschuler's discussion, however, two points must be made clear. First, the diverse breakdown of these groupings makes it difficult to predict on theoretical grounds how the number of murders among family members, acquaintances, strangers, or unknown cases should necessarily change relative to each other. Second, as Alschuler himself has noted, these estimates are suggestive; they are not statistically significant, in that we cannot say with much certainty how concealed-handgun laws have affected the proportions of victims across the categories mentioned above.

An additional response should be made to Sugarmann's claims. Even if one accepts the claim that nondiscretionary concealed-handgun laws do not reduce the number of murders against people who know each other (and I do not concede this), what about other types of murders, such as those arising from street robbery? For Chicago during the period from 1990 to 1995, 16 percent of all murders involved nonacquaintance robbery. Moreover, one must ask about nonfriend acquaintance murders (excluding prostitution, gang, and drug cases), murders by complete strangers, and at least some of those murders still classified as mysteries (an additional 22 to 46 percent of all murders). Since permitted handguns are virtually never used in crimes against others and they do not produce accidental deaths, should not the reduction of these other types of murders still be deemed important?[36]

17 *Do nondiscretionary concealed-handgun laws only affect crimes that occur in public places?*

> Handguns were freely available for home and business use in all the "shall-issue" jurisdictions prior to the new laws. The new carrying privilege would thus not affect home or business self-defense but should have most of its preventive impact on street crime and offenses occurring in other public places. But the study contains no qualitative analysis of different patterns within crime categories to corroborate the right-to-carry prevention hypothesis. (Zimring and Hawkins, "Counterfeit Deterrent," p. 54)

Contrary to the claim of Zimring and Hawkins, concealed handguns may very well affect crime in homes and businesses in several ways. First, being allowed to carry a concealed gun outside is likely to increase the number of guns owned by law-abiding citizens. Since these guns will be kept at least part of the time in the home, this should have a deterrent effect on crimes committed at home and also at one's business. Second, as some of the evidence suggests, nondiscretionary laws could even increase the number of crimes that occur in the home as criminals turn away from other crimes, like street robbery, for which the risks that criminals face have gone up. These two effects would thus work in opposite directions. Finally, to the extent that nondiscretionary handgun laws drive criminals out of a certain geographical area, rates for all types of crimes could fall.

Aggregation of the crime categories makes it difficult to separate all the different substitution effects. Still, the results presented here are very consistent with the two primary dimensions that we focused on: whether there is contact between the criminal and the victim, and whether the crime occurs where law-abiding citizens could already legally carry a gun.

18 *Is it reasonable to make comparisons across states?*

> The sort of state that passes a "shall-issue" law in the 1980s is apt to be the same kind of place where ordinary citizens carrying concealed firearms

might not be regarded as a major problem even before the law changed. . . . Idaho is not the same sort of place that New York is, and there seem to be systematic differences between states that change standards for concealed weapons and those that do not. (Zimring and Hawkins, "Counterfeit Deterrent," pp. 50–51)

The observed drop in crime rates in states that have enacted nondiscretionary concealed-handgun laws does not by itself imply that we will observe the same effect in other states that adopt such laws later. Several different issues arise here. First, the regressions used in this book have attempted to control for many differences that can explain the level of crime (for example, income, poverty, unemployment, population and population density, demographic characteristics, law enforcement, other gun laws). Admittedly, even my long list of variables does not pick up all the differences between states, which is the reason that a variable is added for each county or state to pick up the average differences in crime rates across places. Individual time trends are also allowed for each state.

Yet despite all these attempts to control for variables, some caution is still in order—especially when dealing with areas that are particularly extreme along dimensions that do not have obvious counterparts in areas with nondiscretionary laws. One obvious example would be New York City. While the regression results show that areas with the largest and most dense populations gain the most from nondiscretionary laws, there is always the possibility that the relationship changes for values of population and density that are different from those in places where we have been able to study the effects of these laws. To date, the fourth and fifth largest cities in the country have passed nondiscretionary laws (Houston and Philadelphia), and additional experience with large cities may help determine whether these laws would be equally useful in a city like New York. If one were skeptical about the effects in large cities, the laws should first be changed in Los Angeles and Chicago.

A second issue is whether there is something unique about states that have adopted nondiscretionary laws, and whether that characteristic caused them not only to adopt the laws but also reduced the potential problems resulting from adoption. For example, if local legislators in a few states had special information confirming that the citizens in their state were uniquely trustworthy with regard to concealed handguns, that might have led these few states to pass the laws and have little difficulty with them. It could then "falsely" appear that nondiscretionary laws are generally successful. Such an argument may have been plausible at one time, but its force has declined now that such large and varied areas are covered by these laws. Equally important is the fact that not all jurisdictions have willingly adopted these laws. Many urban areas, such as Atlanta and Philadelphia, fought strongly against them, but lost out to coalitions of rural and suburban representatives. Philadelphia's opposition was so strong that when Pennsylvania's nondiscretionary law was first passed, Philadelphia was partially exempted.

19 *Does my discussion provide a "theory" linking concealed-handgun ownership to reductions in crime? Do the data allow me to link the passage of these laws with the reduction in crime?*

Two idiosyncratic aspects of the Lott and Mustard analysis deserve special mention.... In the first place, there is very little in the way of explicit theory advanced to explain where and when right-to-carry laws should operate as deterrents to the types of crime that can be frustrated by citizens carrying concealed handguns.... They have no data to measure the critical intermediate steps between passing the legislation and reductions in crime rates. This is the second important failing ... that is not a recurrent feature in econometric studies. (Zimring and Hawkins, "Counterfeit Deterrent," pp. 52, 54)

This set of complaints is difficult to understand. The theory is obvious: A would-be criminal act is deterred by the risk of being shot. Many different tests described in this book support this theory. Not only does the drop in crime begin when nondiscretionary laws are adopted, but the extent of the decline is related to the number of permits issued in a state. Nondiscretionary laws reduce crime the most in areas with the greatest increases in the number of permits. As expected, crimes that involve criminals and victims in direct contact and crimes occurring in places where the victim was previously unable to carry a gun are the ones that consistently decrease the most.

20 *What can we infer about causality?*

Anyone who has taken a course in logical thinking has been exposed to the fallacy of arguing that because A happened (in this case, passage of a concealed-weapon law) and then B happened (the slowing of the rate of violent crime), A must surely have caused B. You can speculate that the passage of concealed-gun legislation caused a subsequent slowing of the rate of violent crime in various states, but you certainly can't prove it, despite the repeated claims that a University of Chicago law professor's "study" has offered "definitive scholarly proof." (Harold W. Andersen, "Gun Study Akin to Numbers Game," *Omaha World Herald,* April 3, 1997, p. 15)

An obvious danger arises in inferring causality because two events may coincide in time simply by chance, or some unknown factor may be the cause of both events. Random chance is a frequent concern with pure time-series data when there is just one change in a law. It is not hard to believe that when one is examining a single state, unrelated events A and B just happened to occur at the same time. Yet the data examined here involve many different states that changed their laws in many different years. The odds that one might falsely attribute the changes in the crime rate to changes in the concealed-handgun laws decline as one examines more experiences. The measures of statistical significance are in fact designed to tell us the likelihood that two events may have occurred randomly together.

The more serious possibility is that some other factor may have caused both the reduction in crime rates and the passage of the law to occur at the same time. For example, concern over crime might result in the passage of both concealed-handgun laws and tougher law-enforcement measures. Thus, if the arrest rate rose at the same time that the concealed-handgun law passed, not accounting for changes in the arrest rate might result in falsely attributing some of the reduction in crime rates to the concealed-handgun law. For a critic to attack the paper, the correct approach would have been to state what variables were not included in the analysis. Indeed, it is possible that the regressions do not control for some important factor. However, this study uses the most comprehensive set of control variables yet used in a study of crime, let alone any previous study on gun control. As noted in the introduction, the vast majority of gun-control studies do not take any other factors that may influence crime into account, and no previous study has included such variables as the arrest or conviction rate or sentence length.

Other pieces of evidence also help to tie together cause and effect. For example, the adoption of nondiscretionary concealed-handgun laws has not produced equal effects in all counties in a state. Since counties with easily identifiable characteristics (such as rural location and small population) tended to be much more liberal in granting permits prior to the change in the law, we would expect them to experience the smallest changes in crime rates, and this is in fact what we observe. States that were expected to issue the greatest number of new permits and did so after passing nondiscretionary laws observed the largest declines in crime. We know that the number of concealed-handgun permits in a state rises over time, so we expect to see a greater reduction in crime after a nondiscretionary law has been in effect for several years than right after it has passed. Again, this is what we observe. Finally, where data on the actual number of permits at the county level are available, we find that the number of murders declines as the number of permits increases.

The notion of statistical significance and the number of different specifications examined in this book are also important. Even if a relationship is false, it might be possible to find a few specifications out of a hundred that show a statistically significant relationship. Here we have presented over a thousand specifications that together provide an extremely consistent and statistically significant pattern about the relationship between nondiscretionary concealed-handgun laws and crime.

21 Concerns about the arrest rates due to missing observations

To control for variation in the probability of apprehension, the [Lott and Mustard] model specification includes the arrest ratio, which is the number of arrests per reported crime. Our replication analysis shows that the inclusion of this variable materially affects the size and composition of the estimation data set. Specifically, division by zero forces all counties with no reported crimes of a particular type in a given year to be dropped from the sample for that year. [Lott's and Mustard's] sample contains all counties, regardless of size, and this problem of dropping counties with no reported crimes is particularly severe in small counties with few crimes. The frequencies of missing data are 46.6% for homicide, 30.5% for rape, 12.2% for aggravated assault, and 29.5% for robbery. Thus, the [Lott and Mustard] model excludes observations based on the realization of the dependent variable, potentially creating a substantial selection bias. Our strategy for finessing the missing data problem is to analyze only counties maintaining populations of at least 100,000 during the period 1977 to 1992. . . . Compared to the sample [comprising] all counties, the missing data rate in the large-county sample is low: 3.82% for homicide, 1.08% for rape, 1.18% for assault, and 1.09% for robberies. (Dan Black and Daniel Nagin, "Do 'Right-to-Carry' Laws Deter Violent Crime?" *Journal of Legal Studies* 27 [January 1998], forthcoming)

The arguments made by Black and Nagin have changed over time, and some of their statements are not consistent.[37] In part because of the public nature of their attacks, I have tried to deal with all of the different attacks, so that those who have heard them may hear my responses. The problem described immediately above by Black and Nagin is indeed something one should be concerned about, but I had already dealt with the problem of missing observations in the original paper, and I discuss it again here at the end of chapter 6. My original paper and chapter 4 also reported the results when the arrest rate was removed entirely from the regressions. The discussion by Black and Nagin exaggerates the extent of the problem and, depending on the crime category being examined, quite amazingly proposes to solve the missing data problem by throwing out data for between 77 and 87 percent of the counties.

Black and Nagin present a very misleading picture of the trade-offs involved with the solution that examined the more populous counties.[38] The relevant comparison is between weighted numbers of missing observations, not the total number of missing observations, since the regressions are weighted by county population and the missing observations tend to be from relatively small counties, which are given a smaller weight.[39] When this is done, the benefits obtained by excluding all counties with fewer than 100,000 people become much more questionable. The most extreme case is for aggravated assault, where Black and Nagin eliminate 86 percent of the sample (a 29 percent drop in the weighted frequency) in order to reduce weighted missing values from 2.8 to 1.5 percent. Even for murder, 77 percent of the sample is dropped, so that the weighted missing data declines from 11.7 to 1.9 percent. The rape and robbery categories lie between these two cases, both in terms of the number of counties with fewer than 100,000 people and in terms of the change in the amount of weighted missing data.[40]

Why they choose to emphasize the cut-off that they did is neither explained nor obvious. The current cost-benefit ratio is rather lopsided. For example, eliminating counties with fewer than 20,000 people would have removed 70 percent of the missing arrest ratios for murder and lost only 20 percent of the observations (the weighted frequencies are 23 and 6 percent respectively). There is nothing wrong with seeing whether the estimates provide the same results over counties of various sizes, but if that is their true motivation for excluding portions of the data, it should be clearly stated.

Despite ignoring all these observations, it is only when they *also* remove the data for Florida that they weaken my results for murder and rape (though the results for aggravated assault and robbery are even larger and more statistically significant). Only eighty-six counties with more than 100,000 people adopted nondiscretionary concealed-handgun laws between 1977 and 1992, and twenty of these counties are in Florida. Yet after all this exclusion of data, Black and Nagin still find no evidence that allowing law-abiding citizens to carry concealed handguns increases crime, and two violent-crime categories show a statistically significant drop in crime. The difference between their approach and mine is rather stark: I did not select which observations to include; I used all the data for all the counties over the entire period for which observations were available.

22 *What can we learn about the deterrent effect of concealed handguns from this study?*

> The regression study [that Lott and Mustard] report is an all-or-nothing proposition as far as knowledge of legal impact is concerned. If the model is wrong, if their bottom-line estimates of impact cannot withstand scrutiny, there is no intermediate knowledge of the law's effects on behavior that can help us sort out the manifold effects of such legislation. As soon as we find flaws in the major conclusions, the regression analyses tell us nothing. What we know from this study about the effects of "shall-carry" laws is, therefore, nothing at all. (Zimring and Hawkins, "Counterfeit Deterrent," p. 59)

Academics can reasonably differ about what factors account for changes in crime. Sociologists and criminologists, for example, have examined gun control without trying to control for changes in arrest or conviction rates. Others might be particularly concerned about the impact of drugs on crime. Economists such as myself try to include measures of deterrence, though I am also sympathetic to other concerns. In this book and my other research, my approach has not been to say that only one set of variables or even one specification can explain the crime rate. My attitude has been that if someone believes that a variable is important and has any plausible reason for including it, I have made an effort to include it. This book reports many different approaches and specifications—all of which support the conclusion that allowing law-abiding citizens to carry concealed handguns reduces crime. I believe that no other study on crime has used as extensive a data set as was used here, and no previous study has attempted to control for as many different specifications.

23 *Summarizing the concerns about the evidence that concealed-handgun laws deter crime*

> The gun lobby claims to have a new weapon in its arsenal this year—a study by economist John Lott. But the Lott study shoots blanks. In reviewing Lott's research and methodology, Carnegie-Mellon University Profs. Daniel Nagin and Dan Black, and Georgetown University's Prof. Jens Ludwig corrected for the many fatal flaws in Lott's original analysis and found no evidence of his claim that easing restrictions on carrying concealed handguns leads to a decrease in violent crime. Nagin, Black, and Ludwig recently concluded in a televised debate with Lott that "there is absolutely no credible evidence to support the idea that permissive concealed-carry laws reduce violent crime," and that "it would be a mistake to formulate policy based on the findings from Dr. Lott's study." (James Brady, "Concealed Handguns; Putting More Guns on Streets Won't Make America Safer," *Minneapolis Star Tribune*, March 21, 1997, p. 21A)

Unlike the authors of past papers on gun control such as Arthur Kellermann and the authors of the 1995 University of Maryland study, I immediately made my data available to all academics who requested it.[41] To date, my data have been supplied to academics at twenty-four universities, including Harvard, Stanford, the University of Pennsylvania, Emory, Vanderbilt, Louisiana State, Michigan State, Florida State, the University of Texas, the University of Houston, the University of Maryland, Georgetown, and William and Mary College.

James Brady's op-ed piece ignores the fact that some of these academics from Vanderbilt, Emory, and Texas paid their own way to attend the December 9, 1996, debate sponsored by his organization—Handgun Control. While Handgun Control insisted on rules that did not allow these academics to participate, I am sure that they would have spoken out to support the integrity of my original study.

Those who have attempted to replicate the findings in the original *Journal of Legal Studies* paper have been able to do so, and many have gone beyond this to provide additional support for the basic findings. For example, economists at Vanderbilt University have estimated over 10,000 regressions attempting to see whether the deterrent effects of nondiscretionary laws are at all sensitive to all possible combinations of the various data sets on demographics, income, population, arrest rates, and so on. Their results are quite consistent with those reported in this book.[42]

I have tried in this chapter to examine the critiques leveled against my work. In many cases, the concerns they describe were addressed in the original paper. In others, I believe that relatively simple responses exist to the complaints. However, even taking these critics at their worst, I still believe that a comment that I made at the December 9 discussion sponsored by Handgun Control still holds:

> Six months ago, who would have thought that Handgun Control would be rushing out studies to argue that allowing law-abiding citizens to carry concealed handguns would have no effect, or might have a delayed impact, in terms of dropping crimes? (*Morning Edition,* National Public Radio, 10:00 A.M. ET, December 10, 1996.

Eight

Some Final Thoughts

As more than 30 diners sat in Sam's St. John's Sea-
food [in Jacksonville, Florida] about 7:20 P.M., a
masked man entered the eatery and ordered everyone to the floor, said co-owner Sam Bajalia. The
man grabbed waitress Amy Norton from where she
and another waitress were huddled on the floor
and tried to get her to open the cash register.
   At that point, [Oscar] Moore stood up and shot
him. Another diner . . . pulled out a .22-caliber der-
ringer and fired at the man as he ran out of the
restaurant. At least one shot hit the fleeing robber.
   [The robber was later arrested when he sought
medical care for his wound.] . . .
   "I'm glad they were here because if that girl
couldn't open the register, and he didn't get [any]
money, he might have started shooting," Bajalia
said.[1]

[It was] 1:30 A.M. when Angelic Nichole Hite, 26, the
night manager, and Victoria Elizabeth Shaver, 20,
the assistant manager at the Pizza Hut at 4450
Creedmoor Road, were leaving the restaurant with
Marty Lee Hite, 39, the manager's husband. He had
come to pick her up after work.
   They saw a man wearing a ski mask, dark
clothes, gloves, and holding a pistol walking toward
them, and the Hites ran back inside the restaurant.
Shaver apparently had reached her car already. . . .
The couple couldn't close the door behind them because the robber ran up and wedged the barrel of
his handgun in the opening. As they struggled to
get the door closed, . . . the masked man twice said
he would kill them if they didn't open it.
   Marty Hite, who carried a .38-caliber handgun,
pulled out his weapon and fired three times
through the opening, striking the robber in the ab-
domen and upper chest. The would-be bandit

staggered away, and the Hites locked the door and called police.

The Wake County district attorney will review the shooting, but Raleigh police did not file charges against the manager's husband. Police said it appeared the couple retreated as far as they could and feared for their lives, which would make it a justified shooting.[2]

Many factors influence crime, with arrest and conviction rates being the most important. However, nondiscretionary concealed-handgun laws are also important, and they are the most cost-effective means of reducing crime. The cost of hiring more police in order to change arrest and conviction rates is much higher, and the net benefits per dollar spent are only at most a quarter as large as the benefits from concealed-handgun laws.[3] Even private, medium-security prisons cost state governments about $34 a day per prisoner ($12,267 per year).[4] For concealed handguns, the permit fees are usually the largest costs borne by private citizens. The durability of guns allows owners to recoup their investments over many years. Using my yearly cost estimate of $43 per concealed handgun for Pennsylvanians, concealed handguns pay for themselves if they have only $\frac{1}{285}$ of the deterrent impact of an additional year in prison. This calculation even ignores the other costs of the legal system, such as prosecution and defense costs—criminals will expend greater effort to fight longer prison sentences in court. No other government policy appears to have anywhere near the same cost-benefit ratio as concealed-handgun laws.

Allowing citizens without criminal records or histories of significant mental illness to carry concealed handguns deters violent crimes and appears to produce an extremely small and statistically insignificant change in accidental deaths. If the rest of the country had adopted right-to-carry concealed-handgun provisions in 1992, about 1,500 murders and 4,000 rapes would have been avoided. On the other hand, consistent with the notion that criminals respond to incentives, county-level data provide some evidence that concealed-handgun laws are associated with increases in property crimes involving stealth and in crimes that involve minimal probability of contact between the criminal and the victim. Even though both the state-level data and the estimates that attempt to explain why the law and the arrest rates change indicate that crime in all the categories declines, the deterrent effect of nondiscretionary handgun laws is largest for violent crimes. Counties with the largest populations, where the deterrence of violent crimes is the greatest, are also the counties where the substitution of property crimes for violent crimes by criminals is the highest. The estimated annual gain in 1992 from allowing concealed handguns was over $5.74 billion.

Many commonly accepted notions are challenged by these findings. Urban areas tend to have the most restrictive gun-control rules and have fought the hardest against nondiscretionary concealed-handgun laws, yet they are the very places that benefit the most from nondiscretionary concealed-handgun laws. Not only do urban areas tend to gain in their fight against crime, but reductions in crime rates are greatest precisely in those urban areas that have the highest crime rates, largest and most dense populations, and greatest concentrations of minorities. To some this might not be too surprising. After all, law-abiding citizens in these areas must depend on themselves to a great extent for protection. Even if self-protection were accepted, concerns would still arise over whether these law-abiding citizens would use guns properly. This study provides a very strong answer: a few people do and will use permitted concealed handguns improperly, but the gains completely overwhelm these concerns.

Another surprise involves women and blacks. Both tend to be the strongest supporters of gun control, yet both obtain the largest benefits from nondiscretionary concealed-handgun laws in terms of reduced rates of murder and other crimes. Concealed handguns also appear to be the great equalizer among the sexes. Murder rates decline when either more women or more men carry concealed handguns, but the effect is especially pronounced for women. An additional woman carrying a concealed handgun reduces the murder rate for women by about three to four times more than an additional man carrying a concealed handgun reduces the murder rate for men. Providing a woman with a concealed handgun represents a much larger change in her ability to defend herself than it does for a man.

The benefits of concealed handguns are not limited to those who use them in self-defense. Because the guns may be concealed, criminals are unable to tell whether potential victims are carrying guns until they attack, thus making it less attractive for criminals to commit crimes that involve direct contact with victims. Citizens who have no intention of ever carrying concealed handguns in a sense get a "free ride" from the crime-fighting efforts of their fellow citizens. However, the "halo" effect created by these laws is apparently not limited to people who share the characteristics of those who carry the guns. The most obvious example is the drop in murders of children following the adoption of nondiscretionary laws. Arming older people not only may provide direct protection to these children, but also causes criminals to leave the area.

Nor is the "halo" effect limited to those who live in areas where people are allowed to carry guns. The violent-crime reduction from one's own state's adopting the law is in fact greatest when neighboring states also allow law-abiding citizens to carry concealed handguns. The evidence also indicates that the states with the most guns have the lowest crime rates. Urban areas may experience the most violent crime, but they also have the smallest number of guns. Blacks may be the racial group most vulnerable to violent crime, but they are also much less likely than whites to own guns.

These estimates make one wonder about all the attention given to other types of gun legislation. My estimates indicate that waiting periods and background checks appear to produce little if any crime deterrence. Yet President Clinton credits the Brady law with lowering crime because it has, according to him, been "taking guns out of the hands of criminals."[5] During the 1996 Democratic National Convention, Sarah Brady, after whose husband the bill was named, boasted that it "has helped keep more than 100,000 felons and other prohibited purchasers from buying handguns."[6] From 1994 until the Supreme Court's decision in 1997, backers of the Brady law focused almost exclusively on the value of background checks, the one part of the law that the Supreme Court specifically struck down.[7]

Actually, the downward crime trend started in 1991, well before the Brady law became effective in March 1994. With a national law that goes into effect only once, it is difficult to prove empirically that the law was what altered crime rates, because so many other events are likely to have occurred at that same time. One of the major advantages of the large data set examined in this book is that it includes data from many different states that have adopted nondiscretionary laws in many different years.

Others estimate a much smaller effect of the Brady law on gun sales. In 1996 the General Accounting Office reported that initial rejections based on background checks numbered about 60,000, of which over half were for purely technical reasons, mostly paperwork errors that were eventually corrected.[8] A much smaller number of rejections, 3,000, was due to convictions for violent crimes, and undoubtedly many of the people rejected proceeded to buy guns on the street. By the time the background-check provision was found unconstitutional, in June 1997, only four people had gone to jail for violations.

Presumably, no one would argue that rejected permits are meaningful by themselves. They merely proxy for what might happen to crime rates, provided that the law really stops criminals from getting guns. Do criminals simply get them from other sources? Or do the restrictions primarily inconvenience law-abiding citizens who want guns for self-defense? The results presented in this book are the first systematic national look at such gun laws, and if the national Uniform Crime Report data through 1994 or state waiting periods and background checks are any indication, the empirical evidence does not bode well for the Brady law. No statistically significant evidence has appeared that the Brady law has reduced crime, and there is some statistically significant evidence that rates for rape and aggravated assault have actually risen by about 4 percent relative to what they would have been without the law.

Yet research does not convince everybody. Perhaps the Supreme Court's June 1997 decision on the constitutionality of the Brady law's national background checks will shed light on how effective the Brady law was. The point of making the scope of the background check *national* was that without it, criminals would buy guns from jurisdictions without the checks and use them to commit crimes in the rest of the country. As these national standards are eliminated, and states and local jurisdictions discontinue their background checks,[9] will crime rates rise as quickly without this provision of the law as gun-control advocates claimed they fell because of it? My bet is no, they will not. If President Clinton and gun-control advocates are correct, a new crime wave should be evident by the time this book is published.

Since 1994, aside from required waiting periods, many new rules making gun ownership by law-abiding citizens more difficult have come into existence. There were 279,401 active, federal gun-dealer licenses in the nation when the new licensing regulations went fully into effect in April 1994. By the beginning of 1997 there were 124,286, a decline of 56 percent, and their number continues to fall.[10] This has undoubtedly made purchasing guns less convenient. Besides increasing licensing fees from $30 to $200 for first-time licenses and imposing renewal fees of $90, the 1994 Violent Crime Control and Law Enforcement Act imposed significant new regulatory requirements that were probably much more important in reducing the number of licensees.[11]

The Bureau of Alcohol, Tobacco, and Firearms (BATF) supports this decrease largely because it believes that it affects federal license holders who are illegally selling guns. The BATF's own (undoubtedly high) estimate is that about 1 percent of federal license holders illegally sell guns, and that this percentage has remained constant with the decline in licensed dealers.[12] If so, 155,115 licensees have lost their licenses in order to eliminate 1,551 illegal traffickers. Whether this lopsided trade-off justifies stiffer federal regulation is unclear, but other than simply pointing to the fact that crime continued on its downward course nationally during this period, no evidence has been offered. No attempt has been made to isolate this effect from many other changes that occurred over the same period of time.[13]

Changes in the law will also continue to have an impact. Proposals are being made by the U.S. Department of Justice to "require owners of firearms 'arsenals' to provide notice to law enforcement," where the definition of what constitutes an "arsenal" seems to be fairly subjective, and to "require gun owners to record the make, model, and serial number of their firearms as a condition of obtaining gun insurance." Other proposals would essentially make it impossible for private individuals to transfer firearms among themselves.

It is too early to conclude what overall impact these federal rules have had on gun ownership. Surely the adoption of the Brady law dramatically increased gun ownership as people rushed out to buy guns before the law went into effect,[14] and the evidence discussed in chapter 3 also indicates that gun ownership increased dramatically between 1988 and 1996. But without annual gun-ownership data, we cannot separate all the different factors that have altered the costs and benefits of gun ownership.

Other changes are in store during the next couple of years that could affect some of the discussion in this book. The Clinton administration has been encouraging the development of devices for determining at a distance what items a person is carrying.[15] Such devices will enable police to see whether individuals are carrying guns and can help disarm criminals,[16] but criminals who managed to acquire them could also use them to determine whether a potential victim would offer armed resistance. The ability to target unarmed citizens would lower the risks of committing crime and reduce the external benefits produced by concealed handguns. Since both police and criminals might use them, the net effect on crime rates of their use is not immediately clear.

Yet governmental use of these detection devices is not a foregone conclusion. Before granting the government the right to use such long-range devices, we must answer some novel questions regarding constitutional rights. For example, would the ability to take a picture of all the objects that a person is carrying amount to an invasion of privacy? Would it constitute an illegal search?[17]

What implications does this study have for banning guns altogether? This book has not examined evidence on what the crime rate would be if all guns could be eliminated from society—no data were present in the data set for areas where guns were completely absent for any period of time, but the findings do suggest how costly the transition to that gun-free goal would be. If outlawing guns would primarily affect their ownership by law-abiding citizens, this research indicates that at least in the short run, we would expect crime rates to rise. The discussion is very similar to the debate over nuclear disarmament. A world without nuclear weapons might be better off, but unilateral disarmament may not be the best way to accomplish that goal. The large stock of guns in the United States, as well as the ease with which illegal items such as drugs find their way across borders implies that not only might the transition to a gun-free world be costly (if not impossible), but the transition might also take a long time.

Further, not everyone will benefit equally from the abolition of guns. For example, criminals will still maintain a large strength advantage over many of their victims (such as women and the elderly). To the extent that guns are an equalizer, their elimination will strengthen criminals relative to physically weak victims. As we have seen in discussing international crime data, eliminating guns alters criminals' behavior in other ways, such as reducing their fear of breaking into homes while the residents are there.

All these discussions, of course, ignore the issues that led the founding fathers to put the Second Amendment in the Constitution in the first place—important issues that are beyond the scope of this book.[18] They believed that an armed citizenry is the ultimate bulwark against tyrannical government. Possibly our trust in government has risen so much that we no longer fear what future governments might do. Having just fought a war for their independence against a government that had tried to confiscate their guns, the founding fathers felt very strongly about this issue.

WHAT CAN WE CONCLUDE?

How much confidence do I have in these results? The largest previous study on gun control produced findings similar to those reported here but examined only 170 cities within a single year. This book has examined over 54,000 observations (across 3,000 counties for eighteen years) and has controlled for a range of other factors never accounted for in previous crime studies. I have attempted to answer numerous questions. For example, do higher arrest or conviction rates reduce crime? What about changes in other handgun laws, such as penalizing the use of a gun in the commission of a crime, or the well-known waiting periods? Do income, poverty, unemployment, drug prices, or demographic changes matter? All these factors were found to influence crime rates, but no previous gun study had accounted for changing criminal penalties, and this study is the first to look at more than a few of any of these other considerations.

Preventing law-abiding citizens from carrying handguns does not end violence; it merely makes victims more vulnerable to attack. While people have strong views on either side of this debate, and one study is unlikely to end this discussion, the size and strength of my deterrence results and the lack of evidence that holders of permits for concealed handguns commit crimes should at least give pause to those who oppose concealed handguns. In the final analysis, one concern unites us all: Will allowing law-abiding citizens to carry concealed handguns save lives? The answer is yes, it will.

Appendix One

The following research relies on what is known as *regression analysis,* a statistical technique that essentially lets us "fit a line" to a data set. Take a two-variable case involving arrest rates and crime rates. One could simply plot the data and draw the line somewhere in the middle, so that the deviations from the line would be small, but each person would probably draw the line a little differently. Regression analysis is largely a set of conventions for determining exactly how the line should be drawn. In the simplest and most common approach—ordinary least squares (OLS)—the line chosen minimizes the sum of the squared differences between the observations and the regression line. Where the relationship between only two variables is being examined, regression analysis is not much more sophisticated than determining the correlation.

The regression *coefficients* tell us the relationship between the two variables. The diagram in figure A1.1 indicates that increasing arrest rates decreases crime rates, and the slope of the line tells us how much crime rates will fall if we increase arrest rates by a certain amount. For example, in terms of figure A1, if the regression coefficient were equal to -1, lowering the arrest rate by one percentage point would produce a similar percentage-point increase in the crime rate. Obviously, many factors account for how crime changes over time. To deal with these, we use what is called *multiple regression analysis.* In such an analysis, as the name suggests, many explanatory (or exogenous) variables are used to explain how the endogenous (or dependent) variable moves. This allows us to determine whether a relationship exits between different variables after other effects have already been taken into consideration. Instead of merely drawing a line that best fits a two-dimensional plot of data points, as shown in figure A1.1, multiple regression analysis fits the best line through an

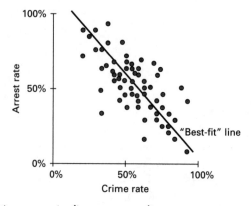

Figure A1.1. Fitting a regression line to a scatter diagram

n-dimensional data plot, where n is the number of variables being examined.

A more complicated regression technique is called *two-stage least squares.* We use this technique when two variables are both dependent on each other and we want to try to separate the influence of one variable from the influence of the other. In our case, this arises because crime rates influence whether the nondiscretionary concealed-handgun laws are adopted at the same time as the laws affect crime rates. Similar issues arise with arrest rates. Not only are crime rates influenced by arrest rates, but since an arrest rate is the number of arrests divided by the number of crimes, the reverse also holds true. As is evident from its name, the method of two-stage least squares is similar to the method of ordinary least squares in how it determines the line of best fit—by minimizing the sum of the squared differences from that line. Mathematically, however, the calculations are more complicated, and the computer has to go through the estimation in two stages.

The following is an awkward phrase used for presenting regression results: "a one-standard-deviation change in an explanatory variable explains a certain percentage of a one-standard-deviation change in the various crime rates." This is a typical way of evaluating the importance of statistical results. In the text I have adopted a less stilted, though less precise formulation: for example, "variations in the probability of arrest account for 3 to 11 percent of the variation in the various crime rates." As I will explain below, standard deviations are a measure of how much variation a given variable displays. While it is possible to say that a one-percentage-point change in an explanatory variable will affect the crime rate by a certain amount (and, for simplicity, many tables use such phrasing whenever possible), this approach has its limitations. The reason is that a 1 percent change in the explanatory variable may sometimes be very unlikely: some variables may typically change by only a fraction of a percent, so assuming a one-percentage-point change would imply a much larger impact than could possibly be accounted for by that factor. Likewise, if the typical change in an explanatory variable is much greater than 1 percent, assuming a one-percentage-point change would make its impact appear too small.

The convention described above—that is, measuring the percent of a one-standard-deviation change in the endogenous variable explained by a one-standard-deviation change in the explanatory variable—solves the problem by essentially normalizing both variables so that they are in the same units. Standard deviations are a way of measuring the typical change that occurs in a variable. For example, for symmetric distributions, 68 percent of the data is within one standard deviation of either side of the mean, and 95 percent of the data is within two standard deviations of the mean. Thus, by comparing a one-standard-deviation change in both variables, we are comparing equal percentages of the typical changes in both variables.[1]

The regressions in this book are also "weighted by the population" in the counties or states being studied. This is necessitated by the very high level of "noise" in a particular year's measure of crime rates for low-population areas. A county with only one thousand people may go through many years with no murders, but when even one murder occurs, the murder rate (the number of murders divided by the county's population) is extremely high. Presumably, no one would believe that this small county has suddenly become as dangerous as New York City. More populous areas experience much more stable crime rates over time. Because of this difficulty in consistently measuring the risk of murder in low-population counties, we do not want to put as much emphasis on any one year's observed murder rate, and this is exactly what weighting the regressions by county population does.

Several other general concerns may be anticipated in setting up the regression specification. What happens if concealed-handgun laws just happen to be adopted at the same time that there is a downward national trend in crime rates? The solution is to use separate variables for the different years in the sample: one variable equals 1 for all observations during 1978 and zero for all other times, another equals 1 for all observations during 1979 and zero otherwise, and so on. These "year-dummy" variables thus capture the change in crime from one year to another that can only be attributed to time itself. Thus if the murder rate declines nationally from 1991 to 1992, the year-dummy variables will measure the average decline in murder rates between those two years and allow us to ask if there was an additional drop, even after accounting for this national decline, in states that adopted nondiscretionary concealed-handgun laws.

A similar set of "dummy" variables is used for each county in the United States, and they measure deviations in the average crime rate across counties. Thus we avoid the possibility that our findings may show that nondiscretionary concealed-handgun laws appear to reduce crime rates simply because the counties with these laws happened to have low crime rates to begin with. Instead, our findings should show whether there is an additional drop in crime rates after the adoption of these laws.

The only way to properly account for these year and county effects, as well as the influences on crime from factors like arrest rates, poverty, and demographic changes, is to use a multiple-regression framework that allows us to directly control for these influences.

Unless we specifically state otherwise, the regressions reported in the tables attempt to explain the natural logarithms of the crime rates for the different categories of crime. Converting into "logs" is a conventional method of rescaling a variable so that a given absolute numerical change represents a given percentage change. (The familiar Richter scale for measuring earthquakes is an example of a base-10 logarithmic scale, where a tremor that registers 8 on the scale is ten times as powerful as one that registers 7, and one that registers 7 is ten times as powerful as one that registers 6.) The reason for using logarithms of the endogenous variable rather than their simple values is twofold. First, using logs avoids giving undue importance to a few, very large, "outlying" observations. Second, the regression coefficient can easily be interpreted as the percent change in the endogenous variable for every one-point change in the particular explanatory variable examined.

Finally, there is the issue of *statistical significance*. When we estimate coefficients in a regression, they take on some value, positive or negative. Even if we were to take two completely unrelated variables—say, sunspot activity and the number of gun permits—a regression would almost certainly yield a coefficient estimate other than zero. However, we cannot conclude that any positive or negative regression coefficient really implies a true relationship between the variables. We must have some measure of how certain the coefficient estimate is. The size of the coefficient does not really help here—even a large coefficient could have been generated by chance.

This is where statistical significance enters in. The measure of statistical significance is the conventional way of reporting how certain we can be that the impact is different from zero. If we say that the reported number is "positive and statistically significant at the 5 percent level," we mean that there is only a 5 percent chance that the coefficient happened to take on a positive value when the true relationship in fact was zero or negative.[2] To say that a number is statistically significant at the 1 percent level represents even greater certainty. The convention among many social scientists is usually not to affirm conclusions unless the level of significance reaches 10 percent or lower; thus, someone who says that a result is "not significant" most likely means that the level of significance failed to be as low as 10 percent.

These simple conventions are, however, fairly arbitrary, and it would be wrong to think that we learn nothing from a value that is significant at "only" the 11 percent level, while attaching a great deal of weight to one that is significant at the 10 percent level. The true connection between the significance level and what we learn involves a much more continuous relationship. We are more certain of a result when it is significant at the 10 percent level rather than at the 15 percent level, and we are more certain of a result at the 1 percent level than at the 5 percent level.

Appendix Two

Arrest rate: The number of arrests per crime.

Crime rate: The number of crimes per 100,000 people.

Cross-sectional data: Data that provide information across geographic areas (cities, counties, or states) within a single period of time.

Discretionary concealed-handgun law: Also known as a "may-issue" law; the term *discretionary* means that whether a person is ultimately allowed to obtain a concealed-handgun permit is up to the discretion of either the sheriff or judge who has the authority to grant the permit. The person applying for the permit must frequently show a "need" to carry the gun, though many rural jurisdictions automatically grant these requests.

Endogenous: A variable is endogenous when changes in the variable are assumed to caused by changes in other variables.

Exogenous: A variable is exogenous when its values are as given, and no attempt is made to explain how that variable's values change over time.

Externality: The costs of or benefits from one's actions may accrue to other people. External benefits occur when people cannot capture the beneficial effects that their actions produce. External costs arise when people are not made to bear the costs that their actions impose on others.

Nondiscretionary concealed-handgun law: Also known as a "shall-issue" or "do-issue" law; the term *nondiscretionary* means that once a person meets certain well-specified criteria for obtaining a concealed-handgun permit, no discretion is involved in granting the permit—it must be issued.

Pooled, cross-sectional, time-series data: Data that allow the researcher not only to compare differences across geographic areas, but also to see how these differences change across geographic areas over time.

Regression: A statistical technique that essentially lets us fit a line to a data set to determine the relationship between variables.

Statistical significance: A measure used to indicate how certain we can be that the impact of a variable is different from some value (usually whether it is different from zero).

Time-series data: Data that provide information about a particular place over time. For example, time-series data might examine the change in the crime rate for a city over many years.

Appendix Three

DESCRIPTION OF THE DATA

This appendix provides a detailed discussion of the variables used in this study and their sources. The number of arrests and offenses for each crime in every county from 1977 to 1992 were provided by the FBI's *Uniform Crime Reports (UCR)*. The UCR program is a nation-wide, cooperative statistical effort by over 16,000 city, county, and state law-enforcement agencies to compile data on crimes that are reported to them. During 1993, law-enforcement agencies active in the UCR program represented over 245 million U.S. inhabitants, or 95 percent of the total population. The coverage amounted to 97 percent of the U.S. population living in Metropolitan Statistical Areas (MSAs) and 86 percent of the population in non-MSA cities and in rural counties.[1] The *Supplementary Homicide Reports* of the *UCR* supplied the data on the sex and race of victims and on whatever relationship might have existed between victim and offender.[2]

The regressions report results from a subset of the *UCR* data set, though we also ran the regressions with the entire data set. The main differences were that the effect of concealed-handgun laws on murder was greater than what is reported in this study, and the effects on rape and aggravated assault were smaller. Observations were eliminated because of changes in reporting practices or definitions of crimes; see *Crime in the United States* for the years 1977 to 1992. For example, from 1985 to 1994, Illinois operated under a unique, "gender-neutral" definition of sex offenses. Another example involves Cook County, Illinois, from 1981 to 1984, which experienced a large jump in reported crime because of a change in the way officers were trained to report crime.

The additional observations that were either never provided or were dropped from the data set include those from Arizona (1980), Florida (1988), Georgia (1980), Kentucky (1988), and Iowa (1991). Data for counties containing the following cities were also eliminated for the crime rates listed: violent crime and aggravated assault for Steubenville, Ohio (1977–89); violent crime and aggravated assault for Youngstown, Ohio (1977–87); violent crime, aggravated assault, and burglary for Mobile, Alabama

(1977–85); violent crime and aggravated assault for Oakland, California (1977–90); violent crime and aggravated assault for Milwaukee, Wisconsin (1977–85); all crime categories for Glendale, Arizona (1977–84); violent crime and aggravated assault for Jackson, Mississippi (1977 and 1982); violent crime and aggravated assault for Aurora, Colorado (1977 and 1982); violent crime and aggravated assault for Beaumont, Texas (1977 and 1982); violent crime and aggravated assault for Corpus Christi, Texas (1977 and 1982); violent crime and rape for Macon, Georgia (1977–81); violent crime, property crime, robbery, and larceny for Cleveland, Ohio (1977–81); violent crime and aggravated assault for Omaha, Nebraska (1977–81); all crime categories for Eau Claire, Wisconsin (1977–78); all crime categories for Green Bay, Wisconsin (1977); and all crime categories for Little Rock, Arkansas (1977–79).

The original *Uniform Crime Report* data set did not have arrest data for Hawaii in 1982. These missing observations were supplied to us by the Hawaii UCR program. In the original data set several observations included two observations for the same county and year identifiers. The incorrect observations were deleted from the data.

For all of the different crime rates, if the true rate was zero, we added 0.1 before we took the natural log of those values. It is not possible to take the natural log of zero, because any change from zero is an infinite percentage change. For the accident rates and the supplementary homicide data, if the true rate was zero, we added 0.01 before we took the natural logs of those values.[3]

The number of police in a state, the number of officers who have the power to make arrests, and police payrolls for each state by type of officer are available for 1982 to 1992 from the U.S. Department of Justice's *Expenditure and Employment Data for the Criminal Justice System.*

The data on age, sex, and racial distributions estimate the population in each county on July 1 of the respective years. The population is divided into five-year age segments, and race is categorized as white, black, and neither white nor black. The population data, with the exception of 1990 and 1992, were obtained from the U.S. Bureau of the Census.[4] The estimates use modified census data as anchor points and then employ an iterative proportional-fitting technique to estimate intercensal populations. The process ensures that the county-level estimates are consistent with estimates of July 1 national and state populations by age, sex, and race. The age distributions of large military installations, colleges, and institutions were estimated by a separate procedure. The counties for which special adjustments were made are listed in the report.[5] The 1990 and 1992 estimates have not yet been completed by the Bureau of the

Census and made available for distribution. We estimated the 1990 data by taking an average of the 1989 and 1991 data. We estimated the 1992 data by multiplying the 1991 populations by the 1990–91 growth rate of each county's population.

Data on income, unemployment, income maintenance, and retirement were obtained by the Regional Economic Information System (REIS). Income maintenance includes Supplemental Security Insurance (SSI), Aid to Families with Dependent Children (AFDC), and food stamps. Unemployment benefits include state unemployment insurance compensation, Unemployment for federal employees, unemployment for railroad employees, and unemployment for veterans. Retirement payments include old-age survivor and disability payments, federal civil employee retirement payments, military retirement payments, state and local government employee retirement payments, and workers compensation payments (both federal and state). Nominal values were converted to real values by using the consumer price index.[6] The index uses the average consumer price index for July 1983 as the base period. County codes for twenty-five observations did not match any of the county codes listed in the ICPSR codebook. Those observations were deleted from the sample.

Data concerning the number of concealed-weapons permits for each county were obtained from a variety of sources. Mike Woodward, of the Oregon Law Enforcement and Data System, provided the Oregon data for 1991 and after. The number of permits available for Oregon by county in 1989 was provided by the sheriff's departments of the individual counties. Cari Gerchick, Deputy County Attorney for Maricopa County in Arizona, provided us with the Arizona county-level conviction rates, prison-sentence lengths, and concealed-handgun permits from 1990 to 1995. The Pennsylvania data were obtained from Alan Krug. The National Rifle Association provided data on NRA membership by state from 1977 to 1992. The dates on which states enacted enhanced-sentencing provisions for crimes committed with deadly weapons were obtained from a study by Marvell and Moody.[7] The first year for which the enhanced-sentencing variable equals 1 is weighted by the portion of that first year during which the law was in effect.

For the Arizona regressions, the Brady-law variable is weighted for 1994 by the percentage of the year for which it was in effect (83 percent).

The Bureau of the Census provided data on the area in square miles of each county. Both the total number of unintentional-injury deaths and the number of those involving firearms were obtained from annual issues of *Accident Facts* and *The Vital Statistics of the United States.* The classification of types of weapons is from *International Statistical Classification of Diseases and Related Health Problems,* vol. 1, 10th ed. The handgun category includes guns for single-hand use, pistols, and revolvers. The total includes all other types of firearms.

The means and standard deviations of the variables are reported in appendix 4.

Appendix Four

Table A4.1 National Sample Means and Standard Deviations

Variable	Observations	Mean	Standard deviation
Gun ownership information:			
Nondiscretionary law dummy	50,056	0.16	0.368
Arrests rates (ratio of arrests to offenses)			
Index crimes[a]	45,108	27.43	126.73
Violent crimes	43,479	71.31	327.25
Property crimes	45,978	24.03	120.87
Murder	26,472	98.05	109.78
Rape	33,887	57.83	132.80
Aggravated assault	43,472	71.37	187.35
Robbery	34,966	61.62	189.50
Burglary	45,801	21.51	47.299
Larceny	45,776	25.57	263.71
Auto theft	43,616	44.82	307.54
Crime rates (per 100,000 people)			
Index crimes	46,999	2,984.99	3,368.85
Violent crimes	47,001	249.08	388.72
Property crimes	46,999	2,736.59	3,178.41
Murder	47,001	5.65	10.63
Murder rate with guns (from 1982 to 1991 in counties with more than 100,000 people)	12,759	3.92	6.48
Rape	47,001	18.78	32.39
Robbery	47,001	44.69	149.21
Aggravated assault	47,001	180.05	243.26
Burglary	47,001	811.8642	1,190.23
Larceny	47,000	1,764.37	2,036.03
Auto theft	47,000	160.42	284.60
Causes of accidental deaths and murders (per 100,000 people)			
Rate of accidental deaths from guns	23,278	0.151	1.216175

Table A4.1 Continued

Variable	Observations	Mean	Standard deviation
Rate of accidental deaths from causes other than guns	23,278	1.165152	4.342401
Rate of total accidental deaths	23,278	51.95	32.13482
Rate of murders (handguns)	23,278	0.44	1.930975
Rate of murders (other guns)	23,278	3.478	6.115275
Income data (all values in real 1983 dollars)			
Real per-capita personal income	50,011	10,554.21	2,498.07
Real per-capita unemployment insurance	50,011	67.58	53.10
Real per-capita income maintenance	50,011	157.23	97.61
Real per-capita retirement (over age 65)	49,998	12,328.5	4,397.49
Population characteristics			
County population	50,023	75,772.78	250,350.4
County population per square mile	50,023	214.33	1421.25
State population	50,056	6,199,949	5,342,068
State NRA membership (per 100,000 people)	50,056	1098.11	516.0701
Percent voting Republican in presidential election	50,056	52.89	8.41

ᵃIndex crimes represent the total of all violent and property crimes.

Table A4.2 Average percent of the total population in U.S. counties in each age, sex, and race cohort from 1977 to 1992 (50,023 observations)

	10–19 years of age	20–29 years of age	30–39 years of age	40–49 years of age	50–64 years of age	Over 65 years of age
Black male	0.9%	0.8%	0.5%	0.4%	0.4%	0.4%
Black female	0.9%	0.8%	0.6%	0.4%	0.5%	0.6%
White male	7.3%	6.8%	6.4%	4.9%	6.5%	5.4%
White female	6.8%	6.6%	6.3%	5.0%	6.9%	7.5%
Other male	0.2%	0.2%	0.2%	0.1%	0.1%	0.1%
Other female	0.2%	0.2%	0.2%	0.1%	0.1%	0.1%

Appendix Five

CONTINUATION OF THE RESULTS FROM
TABLE 4.2: THE EFFECT OF
DEMOGRAPHIC CHARACTERISTICS
ON CRIME

Table A5.1 The effect of demographic characteristics on crime

The following assume a 1 percent change in the portion of the population in each category	Violent-crime rate	Murder rate	Rape rate	Aggravated assault rate	Robbery rate	Property-crime rate	Burglary rate	Larceny rate	Auto-theft rate
Percent of population that is black, male, and in the following age ranges:									
10–19	6%	11%	4%	9%***	11%***	13%*	7%**	17%*	5%
	(5%)	(8%)	(3%)	(7%)	(6%)	(22%)	(7%)	(25%)	(6%)
20–29	0%	7%	8%**	-5%*	-1%	-1%	-2%	-1%	1%
	(0%)	(4%)	(4%)	(3%)	(0%)	(2%)	(2%)	(1%)	(1%)
30–39	4%	11%**	-8%*	20%*	1%	4%	-1%	0%	15%*
	(2%)	(4%)	(3%)	(9%)	(0%)	(4%)	(0%)	(0%)	(11%)
40–49	-2%	-34%*	90%*	-37%*	-1%	-2%	-3%	19%*	-68%*
	(1%)	(9%)	(22%)	(11%)	(0%)	(1%)	(1%)	(10%)	(32%)
50–64	18%**	-35%*	-15%	29%*	-1%	-5%	9%	-13%***	6%
	(7%)	(11%)	(4%)	(10%)	(0%)	(4%)	(4%)	(9%)	(3%)
65 and over	12%	-14%	44%*	11%	17%	-4%	6%	-10%	-34%*
	(5%)	(4%)	(12%)	(4%)	(4%)	(3%)	(3%)	(6%)	(18%)
Percent of population that is black, female, and in the following age ranges:									
10–19	0%	4%	4%	-7%	-18%*	8%*	2%	16%*	-18%*
	(0%)	(3%)	(2%)	(6%)	(11%)	(14%)	(2%)	(23%)	(22%)
20–29	-10%*	-22%*	18%*	-19%*	-22%*	-10%*	-17%*	-1%	-25%*
	(7%)	(13%)	(9%)	(13%)	(11%)	(14%)	(13%)	(1%)	(26%)

Table A5.1 Continued

The following assume a 1 percent change in the portion of the population in each category	Violent-crime rate	Murder rate	Rape rate	Aggravated assault rate	Robbery rate	Property-crime rate	Burglary rate	Larceny rate	Auto-theft rate
30–39	12%*	-8%	15%*	9%*	38%*	13%*	27%*	9%*	17%*
	(7%)	(4%)	(6%)	(5%)	(14%)	(14%)	(16%)	(9%)	(14%)
40–49	1%	59%*	-74%*	27%*	-7%	6%	-5%	-3%	48%*
	(0%)	(19%)	(21%)	(10%)	(2%)	(4%)	(2%)	(2%)	(27%)
50–64	-21%*	20%***	10%	-5%	7%	-2%	-22%*	1%	12%
	(11%)	(9%)	(4%)	(3%)	(2%)	(2%)	(12%)	(1%)	(9%)
65 and older	-20%*	31%*	-52%*	-16%**	-37%*	-20%*	-39%*	-12%**	24%*
	(11%)	(14%)	(21%)	(8%)	(14%)	(22%)	(23%)	(12%)	(19%)
Percent of population that is white, male, and in the following age ranges:									
10–19	-1%	-3%	1%	4%**	0%	-1%	1%	0%	-6%*
	(1%)	(2%)	(0%)	(4%)	(0%)	(1%)	(1%)	(0%)	(8%)
20–29	1%	6%*	4%*	2%	4%*	0%	2%**	0%	-2%
	(1%)	(2%)	(3%)	(2%)	(3%)	(1%)	(2%)	(1%)	(3%)
30–39	-1%	-1%	-4%	7%*	-7%*	-5%*	-3%***	-6%*	-6%*
	(0%)	(5%)	(2%)	(6%)	(4%)	(8%)	(2%)	(8%)	(7%)
40–49	-1%	-2%	9%*	-4%	-11%*	-15%*	-10%*	-13%*	-10%*
	(1%)	(1%)	(4%)	(2%)	(5%)	(17%)	(7%)	(13%)	(8%)
50–64	-1%	-5%	4%	-9%*	-14%*	-13%*	7%*	-11%*	-27%*
	(0%)	(3%)	(2%)	(7%)	(8%)	(20%)	(6%)	(14%)	(31%)

65 and over	-11%* (19%)	-14%* (28%)	-12%* (15%)	-14%* (33%)	4% (3%)	-17%* (18%)	4% (4%)	2% (2%)	-13%* (15%)

Percent of population that is white, female, and in the following age ranges:

10–19	9%* (12%)	9%* (14%)	8%* (8%)	8%* (15%)	6%** (4%)	-1% (1%)	7%* (5%)	5% (3%)	2% (2%)
20–29	-3%*** (4%)	3%** (5%)	-4%* (5%)	-1% (2%)	1% (1%)	4%** (4%)	6%* (4%)	-4%*** (3%)	1% (1%)
30–39	-10%* (12%)	7%* (9%)	2% (1%)	4%* (6%)	-1% (1%)	3% (4%)	14%* (8%)	4% (3%)	2% (1%)
40–49	-2% (1%)	7%* (7%)	-4%* (2%)	6%* (7%)	-2% (1%)	0% (0%)	-7%** (3%)	0% (0%)	-9%* (5%)
50–64	11%* (13%)	11%* (7%)	6%* (6%)	10%* (7%)	3% (1%)	8%* (6%)	2% (3%)	1% (1%)	0% (0%)
65 and over	-5%* (10%)	4%* (9%)	5%* (8%)	2%** (6%)	-9%* (9%)	8%* (12%)	6%* (7%)	-7%* (8%)	6%* (9%)

Percent of population that is other males in the following age ranges:

10–19	60%* (38%)	15% (11%)	27%* (13%)	16%*** (13%)	54%* (16%)	19% (7%)	56%* (18%)	66%* (23%)	25%** (11%)
20–29	-41% (18%)	20%* (11%)	0% (0%)	8%* (5%)	1% (0%)	-6% (2%)	-17%** (4%)	14% (4%)	-12%** (4%)
30–39	65%* (24%)	-4% (2%)	-43%* (12%)	-18%** (9%)	-10% (2%)	40%* (9%)	-19% (4%)	-30% (6%)	23%** (6%)
40–49	46%* (11%)	-23%*** (7%)	24%** (4%)	3% (1%)	78%* (9%)	-19% (3%)	-24% (4%)	-36% (5%)	13% (6%)
50–64	-42%** (13%)	-20% (7%)	27%** (6%)	-2% (1%)	-40%** (6%)	-28% (5%)	24% (4%)	-16% (3%)	-9% (2%)

Table A5.1 Continued

The following assume a 1 percent change in the portion of the population in each category	Violent-crime rate	Murder rate	Rape rate	Aggravated assault rate	Robbery rate	Property-crime rate	Burlgary rate	Larceny rate	Auto-theft rate
65 and over	35%**	−26%	87%*	102%*	−27%	−8%	19%	−23%***	−18%
	(6%)	(3%)	(10%)	(15%)	(3%)	(2%)	(3%)	(6%)	(4%)
Percent of population that is other females in the following age ranges:									
10–19	−3%	−73%	−11%	12%	−35%**	−18%**	−29%*	−23%**	−27%**
	(1%)	(25%)	(3%)	(5%)	(10%)	(14%)	(13%)	(16%)	(17%)
20–29	−13%	−33%**	21%*	9%	−30%	−15%*	−32%**	−33%***	−56%*
	(4%)	(8%)	(5%)	(3%)	(6%)	(9%)	(11%)	(18%)	(26%)
30–39	−22%*	−11%	16%	−17%	−22%	−9%	27%	−28%*	−75%*
	(6%)	(2%)	(3%)	(4%)	(4%)	(4%)	(8%)	(12%)	(28%)
40–49	−14%	57%**	8%	18%	−48%**	25%**	28%*	70%	−15%
	(2%)	(8%)	(1%)	(3%)	(6%)	(8%)	(5%)	(20%)	(4%)
50–64	−10%	44%	−66%*	−27%	37%	−5%	−49%*	16%	31%***
	(2%)	(7%)	(10%)	(5%)	(5%)	(2%)	(11%)	(6%)	(9%)
65 and over	44%*	6%	−37%**	−44%*	−36%**	−11%	−14%	−5%	−59%*
	(7%)	(1%)	(4%)	(6%)	(4%)	(3%)	(2%)	(1%)	(13%)

*The result is statistically significant at the 1 percent level for a two-tailed t-test.
**The result is statistically significant at the 5 percent level for a two-tailed t-test.
***The result is statistically significant at the 10 percent level for a two-tailed t-test.

Notes

CHAPTER ONE

1. Gary Kleck, *Targeting Guns* (Hawthorne, NY: Aldine de Gruyter Publishers, 1997), and David B. Kopel, *Guns: Who Should Have Them?* (Amherst, NY: Prometheus Books, 1995), pp. 260–61, 300–1. The estimates on the number of guns are very sensitive to the rate at which guns are assumed to wear out. Higher depreciation rates produce a lower estimated current stock. About a third of all guns are handguns.

A recent poll by the *Dallas Morning News* indicated that "52 percent of the respondents said they or a member of their household own a gun. That response is consistent with Texas Polls dating to 1985 that found more than half of Texans surveyed own guns.

"In the latest poll, of those who said they owned a gun, 43 percent said they had two to five guns; 28 percent said they had one; and 19 percent said they had more than five guns. And of the gun owners polled, 65 percent said they had some type of shooting instruction." See Sylvia Moreno, "Concealed-Gun Law Alters Habits of Some Texans, Poll Finds Supporters, Foes Disagree About What That Means," *Dallas Morning News,* Nov. 3, 1996, p. 45A. The number of people owning guns is examined in more detail in chapter 3.

2. For example, in Chicago 59 percent of police officers report never having had to fire their guns. See Andrew Martin, "73% of Chicago Cops Have Been Attacked While Doing Their Job," *Chicago Tribune,* June 17, 1997, p. A3.

3. Dawn Lewis of Texans Against Gun Violence provided a typical reaction from gun-control advocates to the grand jury decision not to charge Gordon Hale. She said, "We are appalled. This law is doing what we expected, causing senseless death." Mark Potok, a Texan, said that the concealed-gun law saved his life. "I did what I thought I had to do," (*USA Today,* Mar. 22, 1996, p. 3A). For a more recent evaluation of the Texas experience, see "Few Problems Reported After Allowing Concealed Handguns, Officers Say," *Fort Worth Star-Telegram,* July 16, 1996. By the end of December 1996, more than 120,000 permits had been issued in Texas.

4. Japan Economic Newswire, "U.S. Jury Clears Man Who Shot Japanese Student," *Kyodo News Service,* May 24, 1993; and Lori Sharn, "Violence Shoots Holes in USA's Tourist Image," *USA Today,* Sept. 9, 1993, p. 2A.

5. Gary Kleck, *Point Blank: Guns and Violence in America* (Hawthorne, NY: Aldine de Gruyter Publishers, 1991).

6. John R. Lott, Jr., "Now That the Brady Law Is Law, You Are Not Any Safer Than Before," *Philadelphia Inquirer,* Feb. 1, 1994, p. A9. For a more detailed breakdown of police shootings in the larger U.S. cities, see William A. Geller and Michael S. Scott, *Deadly Force: What We Know* (Washington, DC: Police Executive Research Forum, 1992).

7. "Mexican Woman Who Killed Would-Be Rapist to Turn to Activism," *Associated Press Newswire,* Feb. 12, 1997, dateline Mexico City.

8. For many examples of how guns have prevented rapes from occurring, see Paxton Quigley, *Armed and Female* (New York: St. Martin's, 1989).

9. Newspaper stories abound. Examples of pizza deliverymen defending themselves can be found in the *Chicago Tribune,* May 22, 1997, p. 1; *Baltimore Sun,* Aug. 9, 1996, p. B1; *Tampa*

Tribune, Dec. 27, 1996, p. A1; and *Los Angeles Times,* Jan. 28, 1997, p. B1. Another recent example involved a pizza deliveryman in New Paltz, NY (*Middletown (New York) Times Herald Record,* Jan. 25, 1997). Examples of thwarted carjackings (*Little Rock Democrat-Gazette,* Aug. 3, 1996) and robberies at automatic teller machines (*York (Pennsylvania) Daily Record,* April 25, 1996) are also common.

For a case in which a gun was merely brandished to stop an armed street robbery, see the *Annapolis Capitol,* Aug. 7, 1996. Other examples of street robberies that were foiled by law-abiding citizens using concealed handguns include the case of Francisco Castellano, who was shot in the chest during an attempted street robbery by two perpetrators but was able to draw his own handgun and fire back. Castellano's actions caused the robbers to flee the scene (Corey Dada and Ivonne Perez, "Armed Robbery Botched as Restaurateur Shoots Back," *Miami Herald,* Aug. 3, 1996, p. B6.) The following story gives another example: "Curtis Smalls was standing outside the USF&G building when he was attacked by two thugs. They knocked him down, robbed, and stabbed him. Mr. Smalls pulled a .38-caliber revolver and shot both attackers, who were later charged with this attack and two other robberies and are suspects in at least 15 more robberies." This story was described in "Gun Laws Render Us Self-Defenseless," *Baltimore Sun,* Sept. 27, 1996. See also Charles Strouse, "Attacker Killed by His Victim," *Fort Lauderdale (Florida) Sun-Sentinel,* Sept. 16, 1997, p. 4B; Henry Pierson Curtis, "Bicyclist Kills Man Who Tried to Rob Him," *Orlando Sentinel,* Sept. 19, 1997, p. D3; and *Florence (Alabama) Times Daily,* Dec. 27, 1996, for other examples. Examples of foiled carjackings can be found in "Guns and Carjacking: This Is My Car," *Economist,* Sept. 20, 1997. Many other types of robberies have been foiled by people carrying concealed handguns. In at least one case, citizens carrying concealed handguns in Jacksonville, Florida may have saved a restaurant waitress from being shot ("Pistol-Packing Seniors in Florida Wound Robber," Reuter Information Service, Sept. 24, 1997, 6:15 P.M. EDT). For another example, see Clea Benson, "Wounded Barmaid Kills Gunman in Holdup," *Philadelphia Inquirer,* Jan. 23, 1997, p. R1.

10. Stories involving defensive uses of guns in the home are featured even more prominently. For example, four intruders forced their way into the home of two elderly women, struggled with them, and demanded their car keys. The attack stopped only after one of the women brandished her handgun ("Pistol-Packing Grandmas Honored by Sheriff," *Associated Press Newswire,* Feb. 16, 1997 2:30 P.M. EST, dateline Moses Lake, WA). In another case a twenty-three-year-old burglar "pummeled" a 92-year-old man and "ransack[ed]" his house. The burglar left only after the elderly man reached his gun ("Burglar Puts 92-Year-Old in the Gun Closet and Is Shot," *New York Times,* Sept. 7, 1995, p. A16). Although the defensive use of guns in the home is interesting, my focus in this book is on the effects of allowing citizens to carry concealed handguns.

11. Not all news stories of defensive uses involve shots being fired. For example, the *Arizona Republic* reported the following: "In January 1995, a permit-holder who lives in Scottsdale pulled a handgun from a shoulder holster and scared off two men armed with aluminum baseball bats who attempted to rob him near 77th Street and East McDowell Road. No shots were fired." ("In Arizona, High Numbers of Concealed-Weapon Permit Holders Are Found in the Suburbs," *Arizona Republic,* Mar. 17, 1996.)

12. "Mom Saves Self and Child with Handgun," *Atlanta Constitution,* Nov. 12, 1996, p. E2.

13. See *Los Angeles Times,* Jan. 28, 1997, p. B1. Similarly, Pete Shields, Handgun Control, Inc.'s founder, wrote that "the best defense against injury is to put up no defense—give them what they want or run. This may not be macho, but it can keep you alive." See Pete Shields, *Guns Don't Die, People Do* (New York: Arbor, 1981).

14. Problems exist with the National Crime Victimization Survey both because of its nonrepresentative sample (for example, it weights urban and minority populations too heavily) and because it fails to adjust for the fact that many people do not admit to a law-enforcement agency that they used a gun, even defensively; such problems make it

difficult to rely too heavily on these estimates. Unfortunately, this survey is the only source of evidence on the way the probability of significant injury varies with the level and type of resistance.

15. Lawrence Southwick, Jr., "Self-Defense with Guns: The Consequences," *Managerial and Decision Economics* (forthcoming), tables 5 and 6; see also Kleck, *Point Blank.*

16. For example, see David B. Kopel, *The Samurai, the Mountie, and the Cowboy* (Amherst, NY: Prometheus, 1992), p. 155; and John R. Lott, Jr., "Now That the Brady Law Is Law, You Are Not Any Safer Than Before," *Philadelphia Inquirer,* Feb. 1, 1994, p. A9.

17. James D. Wright and Peter Rossi, *Armed and Considered Dangerous: A Survey of Felons and Their Firearms* (Hawthorne, NY: Aldine de Gruyter Publishers, 1986).

Examples of anecdotes in which people successfully defend themselves from burglaries with guns are quite common. For example, see "Burglar Puts 92-Year-Old in the Gun Closet and Is Shot," *New York Times,* Sept. 7, 1995, p. A16. George F. Will, in "Are We 'a Nation of Cowards'?" *Newsweek,* Nov. 15, 1993, discusses more generally the benefits produced from an armed citizenry.

18. See Wright and Rossi, *Armed and Considered Dangerous,* p. 150.

19. Ibid., p. 151.

20. *Baltimore Sun,* Oct. 26, 1991; referred to in Don Kates and Dan Polsby, "Of Genocide and Disarmament," *Journal of Criminal Law and Criminology* 86 (Fall 1995): 252.

21. Rebecca Trounson, "Anxiety, Anger Surround Return of Young Survivors," *Los Angeles Times,* Mar. 14, 1997, p. A1.

22. It is possible that both terrorists and citizens are worse off because of the switch to bombings if shootings would have involved targeted attacks against fewer citizens.

23. David Firestone, "Political Memo: Gun Issue Gives Mayor Self-Defense on Crime," *New York Times,* Mar. 7, 1997, p. B1.

24. Using an on-line retrieval search, it is easy to find many news articles and letters to the editor that repeat this common claim. For example, one letter to the *Newark Star-Ledger* (Oct. 12, 1996) stated that "over half the firearm homicides are committed not by criminals but by friends, family members, and lovers—people with no criminal record."

25. The sum of these percentages does not equal precisely 100 percent because fractions of a percent were rounded to the nearest whole percent.

26. Captain James Mulvihill recently testified before the U.S. Senate that "the greater L. A. area suffers under the weight of more than 1,250 known street gangs, whose membership numbers approximately 150,000. These gangs are responsible for nearly 7,000 homicides over the last 10 years, and injury to thousands of other people." (Prepared testimony of Captain James Mulvihill, commander of the Safe Streets Bureau for Sheriff Block of Los Angeles County before the Senate Judiciary Committee, Apr. 23, 1997.)

27. I would like to thank Kathy O'Connell of the Illinois Criminal Justice Information Authority for taking the time to provide me with such a detailed breakdown of these data.

28. Many such murders also end up in the "undetermined relationship" category.

Probably the best known study of who kills whom is by Daly and Wilson. They examined nonaccidental homicide data for Detroit in 1972. In contrast to my emphasis here, however, they focused exclusively on trying to explain the composition of murders when relatives killed relatives. Of the total of 690 murders committed in Detroit in 1972, 243 (47.8 percent) involved unrelated acquaintances, 138 (27.2 percent) involved strangers, and 127 (25 percent) involved relatives. Of this last category, 32 (4.6 percent) involved blood relatives, and 80 (11.6 percent) victims were spouses (36 women killed by their husbands, and 44 men killed by their wives). The percentage of Chicago's murders involving relatives in 1972 was very similar (25.2 percent), though by the 1990–95 period the percentage of murders involving relatives had fallen to 12.6 percent (7.2 percent involving spouses). For the information about Detroit, see Martin Daly and Margo Wilson, *Homicide* (Hawthorne, NY: Aldine de Gruyter Publishers, 1988).

29. Kathy O'Connell of the Illinois Criminal Justice Information Authority provided these data.

30. See also Daniel D. Polsby, "From the Hip: The Intellectual Argument in Favor of Restrictive Gun Control Is Collapsing. So How Come the Political Strength of Its Advocates Is Increasing?" *National Review* (Mar. 24, 1997): 35–36.

31. In these seventy-five largest counties in 1988, 77 percent of murder arrestees and 78 percent of defendants in murder prosecutions had criminal histories, with over 13 percent of murders being committed by minors, who by definition cannot have criminal records. This implies that 89 percent of those arrested for murders must be adults with criminal records, with 90 percent of those being prosecuted. See Bureau of Justice Statistics Special Reports, "Murder in Large Urban Counties, 1988," (Washington, DC: U.S. Department of Justice, 1993), and "Murder in Families" (Washington, DC: U.S. Department of Justice, 1994); see also Don B. Kates and Dan Polsby, "The Background of Murders," Northwestern University Law School working paper (1997).

32. The average victim had 9.5 prior arraignments, while the average offender had 9.7. David M. Kennedy, Anne M. Piehl, and Anthony A. Braga, "Youth Violence in Boston: Gun Markets, Serious Youth Offenders, and a Use-Reduction Strategy," *Law and Contemporary Problems* 59 (Winter 1996): 147–96.

33. The relationship between age and sex and who commits murders holds across other countries such as Canada; see Daly and Wilson, *Homicide*, pp. 168–70.

34. James Q. Wilson and Richard J. Herrnstein, *Crime and Human Nature*, (New York: Simon and Schuster, 1985), p. 177. Wilson and Herrnstein also discuss in chapter 3 evidence linking criminality to physical characteristics. The surveys that they summarize find evidence that criminality is more likely among those who are shorter and more muscular.

35. Ibid., pp. 204–7; see also Michael K. Block and Vernon E. Gerety, "Some Experimental Evidence on the Differences between Student and Prisoner Reactions to Monetary Penalties," *Journal of Legal Studies* 24 (Jan. 1995): 123–138.

36. John J. DiIulio, Jr., "The Question of Black Crime," *The Public Interest* 117 (Fall 1994): 3–24; and "White Lies About Black Crime," *The Public Interest* 118 (Winter 1995): 30–44.

37. While there are many sources of misinformation on the deaths that arise from handguns, some stories attempt to clarify claims. For example, a *Nando Times* (www.nando.com) news story (Oct. 26, 1996) reported that "during a campaign visit here this week, President Clinton met with the widow of a police officer killed in the line of duty and later during a political rally cited his death as a reason to outlaw armor-piercing bullets. What he did not tell his audience, however, was that the officer died in an auto accident, not from gunfire. . . . Neither a bulletproof vest nor a ban on 'cop-killer bullets,' however, would have saved Officer Jerome Harrison Seaberry Sr., 35. He was responding to a radio call for backup on Christmas night last year when 'he lost control of his vehicle, going too fast . . . hit a tree head-on, and the vehicle burst into flames,' said Lake Charles Police Chief Sam Ivey. Armor-piercing bullets, Ivey said, 'had nothing to do with it.'"

38. National Safety Council, *Accident Facts* (Washington, DC: National Safety Council, 1996).

39. Editorial, "The Story of a Gun and a Kid," *Washington Times*, May 22, 1997, p. A18.

40. Joyce Price, "Heston Attacks Trigger-Lock Proposal: Actor Begins Role as NRA Executive," *Washington Times*, May 19, 1997, p. A4.

41. Currently, the impact of gun locks is difficult to test simply because no state requires them. Seven states (California, Connecticut, Florida, Hawaii, Minnesota, New Jersey, and North Carolina) and the District of Columbia have laws regarding proper storage, but these laws do not mandate a particular method of storage.

42. W. Kip Viscusi, "The Lulling Effect: The Impact of Child-Resistant Packaging on Aspirin and Analgesic Ingestions," *American Economic Review* (May, 1984): 324–27.

43. The Department of Justice's National Institute of Justice recently released a

government-funded study entitled "Guns in America: National Survey on Private Ownership and Use of Firearms," by Philip Cook and Jens Ludwig. The study used poll evidence
from 2,568 adults in 1994 to claim that "20 percent of all gun-owning households had an
unlocked, loaded gun at the time of the survey. The report cited the accidental deaths of
185 children under the age of 14, and many times that number of accidental shootings.
For each death, there are several accidental shootings that cause serious injuries." Fifty
percent of respondents were said to have stored an unloaded gun that was unlocked. The
Justice Department's press release quoted Attorney General Janet Reno as claiming that
"these results show how dangerous unlocked guns are to children. That's why we must
pass the child-safety-lock provision in the President's Anti-Gang and Youth Violence Act
of 1997, now before Congress. A locked gun can avoid a family tragedy." Ignoring problems with the survey itself, several problems exist with these conclusions. First, the report
does not show that those 20 percent of gun-owning households with "unlocked, loaded"
guns were responsible for the 185 firearm deaths of children. We would be interested to
know if the 20 percent of households included children. Second, the report only concen-
trates on the costs, while ignoring any possible benefits. One question that might be
useful in considering benefits is this: Where did those with unlocked, loaded guns tend
to live? For example, were they more likely to live in urban, high-crime areas? (See Department of Justice, *PR Newswire*, May 5, 1997.)

Unfortunately, despite issuing press releases and talking to the press about their findings, neither the Department of Justice, nor professors Cook or Ludwig, nor the Police
Foundation, which oversaw the government grant, have made any attempt to release
their data at least by August 1997.

44. U.S. Department of Commerce, Bureau of the Census, *Statistical Abstract of the United
States* (Washington, DC: U.S. Government Printing Office, 1995). A common claim I will
discuss later is that "more than half of all firearm deaths occur in the home where the
firearm is kept." As noted in the text, since one-half of all firearm deaths are suicides, this
should come as no surprise.

45. Editorial, *Cincinnati Enquirer*, Jan. 23, 1996, p. A8. Others share this belief. "It's common sense," says Doug Weil, research director at the Center to Prevent Handgun Violence, in Washington. "The more guns people are carrying, the more likely it is that
ordinary confrontations will escalate into violent confrontations" (William Tucker,
"Maybe You Should Carry a Handgun," the *Weekly Standard*, Dec. 16, 1996, p. 30).

46. For these arguments, see P. J. Cook, "The Role of Firearms in Violent Crime," in
M. E. Wolfgang and N. A. Werner, eds., *Criminal Violence* (Newbury, NJ: Sage Publishers,
1982); and Franklin Zimring, "The Medium Is the Message: Firearm Caliber as a Determinant of Death from Assault," *Journal of Legal Studies* 1 (1972): 97–124.

47. P. J. Cook, "The Technology of Personal Violence," *Crime and Justice: Annual Review of
Research* 14 (1991): 57, 56 n. 4. The irony of Cook's position here is that his earlier work
argued that the National Crime Victimization Survey radically underreports other
violence-related events, including domestic violence, rapes, and gunshot woundings
linked to criminal acts; see Gary Kleck, *Targeting Guns* (Hawthorne, NY: Aldine de Gruyter
Publishers, 1997).

It is easy to find people who argue that concealed handguns will have no deterrent
effect. H. Richard Uviller writes that "more handguns lawfully in civilian hands will not
reduce deaths from bullets and cannot stop the predators from enforcing their criminal
demands and expressing their lethal purposes with the most effective tool they can get
their hands on." See H. Richard Uviller, *Virtual Justice: The Flawed Prosecution of Crime in America*
(New Haven: Yale University Press, 1996), p. 95.

48. For instance, the University of Chicago's National Opinion Research Center states
that reported gun-ownership rates are much lower in urban areas. In the nation's twelve
largest cities, just 18 percent of all households report owning a gun. Women in rural areas

appear to own guns at about three times the rate that women in the twelve largest cities do. For a discussion about how these numbers vary between urban and rural areas generally or for women across areas, see James A. Davis and Tom W. Smith, *General Social Surveys, 1972–1993: Cumulative Codebook* (Chicago: National Opinion Research Center, 1993); and Tom W. Smith and Robert J. Smith, "Changes in Firearm Ownership Among Women, 1980–1994," *Journal of Criminal Law and Criminology* 86 (Fall 1995): 133–49. This issue is discussed further in chapter 3.

49. Gary Kleck provides an excellent discussion of the methodological weaknesses in the National Crime Victimization Survey. As an example, he writes, "Unfortunately, 88 percent of the violent crimes reported to the [National Crime Victimization Survey] in 1992 were committed away from the victim's home. Thus, by the time the self-protection question is asked, almost all the [respondents] who in fact had used a gun for self-protection know that they had already admitted that the incident occurred in a place where it would be a crime for them to have possessed a gun" (see Kleck, *Targeting Guns*).

50. Still another survey deals more directly with the number of lives potentially saved by defensive gun uses. It reports that potential victims believe that each year, 400,000 people "almost certainly" saved a life by using a gun, though even the researchers providing this estimate believe that the number is too high. See Gary Kleck and Marc Gertz, "Armed Resistance to Crime: The Prevalence and Nature of Self-Defense with a Gun," *Journal of Criminal Law and Criminology* 86 (Fall 1995): 150, 153, 180, 180–2; see also Gary Kleck, "Critique of Cook/Ludwig Paper," undated manuscript, Dept. of Criminology, Florida State University). Recent evidence confirms other numbers from Kleck's and Gertz's study. For example, Annest et al. estimate that 99,025 people sought medical treatment for nonfatal firearm woundings. When one considers that many criminals will not seek treatment for wounds and that not all wounds require medical treatment, Kleck's and Gertz's estimate of 200,000 woundings seems somewhat plausible, though even Kleck and Gertz believe that this is undoubtedly too high, given the very high level of marksmanship that this implies for those firing the guns. Even if the true number of times that criminals are wounded is much smaller, however, this still implies that criminals face a very real expected cost when they attack armed civilians. For discussions of the defensive use of guns, see J. L. Annest et al., "National Estimates of Nonfatal, Firearm-Related Injuries: Beyond the Tip of the Iceberg," *Journal of the American Medical Association* (June 14, 1995): 1749–54; and Lawrence Southwick, Jr., "Self-Defense with Guns: The Consequences," *Managerial and Decision Economics* (forthcoming).

51. Information from telephone call to Susan Harrell, Administrator, Bureau of License Issuance for the state of Florida in Tallahassee. David Kopel writes that "in Florida as a whole, 315,000 permits had been issued by December 31, 1995. Only five had been revoked because the permit holder committed a violent crime with a gun." See David Kopel, "The Untold Triumph of Concealed-Carry Permits," *Policy Review* 78 (July–Aug. 1996); see also Stan Schellpeper, "Case for a Handgun-Carry Law," *Omaha World-Herald,* Feb. 6, 1997, p. 27; and Clayton E. Cramer and David B. Kopel, "'Shall Issue': The New Wave of Concealed-Handgun Permit Laws," *Tennessee Law Review* 62 (Spring 1995): 679, 691. An expanded version of this last article is available from the Independence Institute, 14142 Denver West Parkway, Suite 185, Golden, Colorado, 80401-3134.

52. Cramer and Kopel, "New Wave of Concealed-Handgun Permit Laws," pp. 691–92.

53. Bob Barnhart, "Concealed-Handgun Licensing in Multnomah County," mimeo (Intelligence/Concealed Handgun Unit: Multnomah County, Oct. 1994).

54. See *Richmond Times Dispatch,* Jan. 16, 1997.

55. Schellpeper, "Case for a Handgun-Carry Law," p. 27.

56. "Packin' and More Peaceful," *Las Vegas Review-Journal,* Aug. 5, 1996, p. 6B.

57. Kentucky State Police Trooper Jan Wuchner is also quoted as saying that he has "heard nothing around the state related to crime with a gun committed by permit hold-

ers. There has been nothing like that that I've been informed of." See Terry Flynn, "Gun-Toting Kentuckians Hold Their Fire," *Cincinnati Enquirer,* June 16, 1997, p. A1.

58. Lee Anderson, "North Carolina's Guns," *Chattanooga Free Press,* May 31, 1997, p. A4.

59. Lawrence Messina, "Gun-Permit Seekers Not the Criminal Type," *Charleston Gazette,* July 28, 1997, p. C1.

60. This is the incident discussed in note 3 that occurred during the beginning of 1996 in Texas. As for citizens with concealed handgun permits coming to the aid of police officers see the end of note 68.

61. Peter Hermann, "Unarmed Resident Slain by Intruder; Victim's Rifle Taken by Authorities," *Baltimore Sun,* Sept. 19, 1996, p. B1.

62. Christi Parsons and Andrew Martin, "Bead Drawn on Gun Law," *Chicago Tribune,* May 22, 1997, p. 1; the article includes a long list of such cases, not all of which ended with the charges being dropped. For example,

> In Chicago, two motorists, both U.S. Marine Recruiters, were charged with felonies for allegedly having guns in their car when stopped by police for a minor traffic violation. State Rep. Joel Brunsvold (D–Milan) said a downstate woman who kept an assembled rifle in her car to shoot rodents on her farm was pulled over and charged with a felony, as if she had been planning a drive-by shooting. And in March, Chicago Bears defensive end Alonzo Spellman was charged with a felony after volunteering to a police officer during a traffic stop that he had a handgun inside his car.

63. Stephen Singular, *Talked to Death* (New York: Beech Tree Books, 1987), p. 142. In several other tragic cases people have carried concealed handguns because of death threats, only to be arrested by the police for carrying them; see, for example, Kristi Wright, "Executive Decision," *Omaha World-Herald,* June 8, 1997, p. 1E.

64. A recent case in Oklahoma illustrates how a gun allowed an elderly woman to defend herself:

> An 83-year-old woman proved her aim was good Tuesday morning as she shot a burglar trying to get inside her home. Della Mae Wiggins's home has been burglarized four times. She was beaten by a burglar in November. And she wasn't going to let it happen again. When she heard someone trying to break into her home at about 5 A.M., Wiggins said she grabbed a gun that had been loaded for nine years but never fired. She told police an intruder removed her window-unit air conditioner to enter her home. She said she warned the intruder she was armed. Then she pulled the trigger, hitting the intruder in the thigh. The man backed out the window and fled. (Robert Medley, "83-Year-Old Woman Shoots Fifth Burglar to Try to Victimize Her," *Oklahoma City Daily Oklahoman,* May 21, 1997.

This case also illustrates another point, because it involves a crime where the perpetrator would have been classified as knowing the intended victim. The attacker had just a few days earlier "mowed a lawn at a rental property for her."

65. Kristi O'Brien, "Concealed-Gun Legislation Bottled Up Again," *Copley News Service* (Apr. 15, 1997).

66. As Lon Cripps, the police chief in Langsberg, Montcalm County, Michigan, said in discussing concealed handguns, "There comes a time when you have to take responsibility for your own life. Police officers just aren't always going to be there" (*Detroit News,* June 14, 1996).

67. States where less than 10 percent of the members responded to the poll were excluded from the polling numbers reported by the National Association of Chiefs of Police.

68. Recent legislative testimony during 1997 provides similar evidence. In testifying before the Kansas House of Representatives on behalf of the Kansas State Lodge of the

Fraternal Order of Police, Joseph T. Gimar said, "We ... continue our support of the [right-to-carry] legislation with the belief that the citizens of Kansas will use it responsibly. ... I have gone to great lengths to speak to as many national [Fraternal Order of Police] members as possible, many in jurisdictions that have concealed-carry statutes, but [I] have been unable to find any that were in opposition to their statutes." (For this and other quotations by law-enforcement officers, see Gary K. Hayzlett, "Kansans Should Get to Carry and Conceal Arms," *Kansas City Star,* Mar. 21, 1997.)

Many stories involve armed citizens, some with licensed concealed handguns, who have come to the aid of police officers who are being attacked. For example,

> Shapiro was arrested April 9 after punching and kicking Howey police Officer David Kiss in the face and mouth during a State Road 48 traffic stop, which also involved his wife, Susan Jane Shapiro.
>
> The melee didn't break up until a Mission Inn employee who was passing by shot Mark Shapiro in the back of his left knee.
>
> The passer-by, Vincent McCarthy, 46, of Eustis, had a permit to carry his .25-caliber automatic pistol and will not be charged, Lake sheriff's authorities said.
>
> The Howey Town Council earlier this week commended McCarthy for coming to the aid of Kiss. (Linda Chong, "Man Gets House Arrest in Law Officer's Beating," *Orlando Sentinel Tribune,* May 16, 1992, p. 8)

69. Related stories can be found in the *Alva (Oklahoma) Review Courier,* Jan. 8, 1995; the *Tuscaloosa News,* Jan. 12, 1995; and the *Houston Post,* Jan. 22, 1994; see "Gun-Control Survey," *Law Enforcement Technology* (July–Aug. 1991), pp. 14–15.

Police officers are well aware that off-duty officers have often been able to thwart crimes because they were armed. News stories on such cases are easy to find; see, for example, Deborah Hastings, "Girl Killed in California During Stop for Ice Cream on Parents' Anniversary," *Associated Press,* June 18, 1997, dateline Los Angeles, 02:50 A.M. EDT).

70. See Richard Connelly, "Handgun Law's First Year Belies Fears of 'Blood in the Streets,'" *Texas Lawyer,* Dec. 9, 1996, p. 2.

71. See the *Florida Times-Union,* May 9, 1988, and *Palm Beach Post,* July 26, 1988.

72. Flynn, "Gun-Toting Kentuckians Hold Their Fire," p. A1.

73. However, other polls, such as one done by the Johns Hopkins Center for Gun Policy and Research, a group that I will discuss again in chapter 7, argue that people favor more restrictions on gun ownership and claim that 82 percent favored mandatory registration of all handguns (Larry Bivens, "Most Want Child-Proof Handguns, Poll Shows," *Detroit News,* Mar. 14, 1997, p. A5).

74. Tom Smith, "1996 National Gun-Policy Survey of the National Opinion Research Center: Research Findings," (Chicago: National Opinion Research Center, Mar. 1997), p. 21.

75. Ibid., pp. 8–9. The survey did include overwhelmingly positive responses to many questions on additional safety regulations for guns. I believe that many of these responses would have been significantly altered if the questions had been posed in terms of the trade-off between safety benefits and estimates of their costs, or if terms describing dangers to children had been eliminated (especially, as already noted in the text, since the number of children harmed by gun accidents is probably much smaller than most people believe).

76. Ibid., p. 13. The other major deciding factor for people's views on gun control appears to be whether they trust government. Those who do trust government are much more in favor of gun control.

77. Erika Schwarz (the first runner-up in the 1997 Miss America Pageant) decided to obtain a gun after a gunman stole her car when she pulled into her driveway. "It's about time they allow citizens to protect themselves. I don't advocate taking the law in your

own hand. But in a situation where you're cooped up in a car or house and somebody wants to harm you, this is a good law" (Guy Coates, "Beauty Gets Ready to Shoot Carjackers," *Chattanooga Free Press,* Aug. 14, 1997, p. B7). Similar stories are told by others who were motivated to obtain firearms training. A recent *Wall Street Journal* story discussed the reasons given by fourteen people who enrolled in a self-defense class run by Smith & Wesson: "The budget analyst had a knife held to her throat in a crowded Manhattan bar. Ms. Denman awoke 18 months ago in her rural home to find a masked, armed burglar at the foot of her bed. He'd kicked in her deadbolted door, and shot at her several times before fleeing. She dialed 911, and then waited 45 minutes for help to arrive." See Caitlin Kelly, "Gun Control," *Wall Street Journal,* Sept. 12, 1997, p. A20.

78. "Georgia Lawmakers Quietly Vote Themselves the Right to Carry Weapons," *Associated Press,* dateline Atlanta, Mar. 19, 1996, 11:09 P.M. EST.

79. According to Larry Mason of the Association of California Deputy District Attorneys, "The association is . . . glad prosecutors have been permitted to protect themselves and that they can continue to do so for their own peace of mind and well-being" (quoted in Greg Krikorian, "Lungren Rules Prosecutors Can Carry Guns to Offices," *Los Angeles Times,* July 25, 1997, p. B1).

The Fraternal Order of Police has also strongly supported legislation that would allow current or retired police officers to carry concealed handguns with them wherever they travel within the United States. (Prepared testimony of Bernard H. Teodorski, National Vice President, Fraternal Order of Police, before the House Committee on the Judiciary, Subcommittee on Crime (*Federal News Service,* July 22, 1997.)

80. *Los Angeles Times,* Jan. 4, 1996, p. E1; Louis Graham, "Officials, Celebs Become Gun-Toting Sheriff's Deputies in Long Tradition," *Memphis Commercial Appeal,* Oct. 3, 1994, pp. 1A, B7; and Clayton B. Cramer and David B. Kopel, "'Shall Issue': New Wave of Concealed-Handgun Permit Laws" (Independence Institute: Golden Colorado, Oct. 17, 1994).

81. See note 77 above.

82. See Adriel Bettelheim, "Campbell Gunning for Concealed-Weapon Proposal," *Denver Post,* June 8, 1997, p. A31.

83. Gary Marx and Janan Hanna, "Boy Called Unfit for Murder Trial," *Chicago Tribune,* Jan. 18, 1995, p. 3; and Joan Beck, "The Murder of Children," *St. Louis Post-Dispatch,* Oct. 24, 1994, p. B19.

84. Maggi Martin, "Symphony of Life Ended Too Quickly for Musician: Grieving Friends Say Man Stabbed in Lakewood Had Much to Give," *Cleveland Plain Dealer,* July 12, 1995, p. 1A.

85. John Stevenson, "Jurors Begin Deliberating Stroud's Fate," *Durham (North Carolina) Herald-Sun,* Feb. 9, 1995, p. C1.

86. In 1992, only three states did not allow insanity as a defense (Idaho, Montana, and Utah), but even in these states, insanity can be used in determining whether a person had intent.

87. See Dan Kahan and Martha Nussbaum, "Two Conceptions of Emotion in Criminal Law," *Columbia Law Review* 96 (Mar. 1996): 269–374.

88. *Model Penal Code* § 2100.3(1)(b) (1980).

89. See Kahan and Nussbaum, "Emotion in Criminal Law," *Columbia Law Review:* 315–17.

90. *Bullock v United States,* 122 F2d 214 (DC Cir 1941).

91. Kahan and Nussbaum, "Emotion in Criminal Law," *Columbia Law Review:* 325.

92. Anne Lamoy, "Murder Rate in KCK Lowest Since 1991," *Kansas City Star,* Jan. 1, 1997, p. C1.

93. John H. Kagel, Raymond C. Battalio, Howard Rachlin, and Leonard Green, "Demand Curves for Animal Consumers," *Quarterly Journal of Economics* 96 (Feb. 1981): 1–16; John H. Kagel, Raymond C. Battalio, Howard Rachlin, and Leonard Green, "Experimental Studies of Consumer Demand Behavior Using Laboratory Animals," *Economic Inquiry* 13

(Jan. 1975): 22–38; Raymond C. Battalio, John H. Kagel, and Owen R. Phillips, "Optimal Prices and Animal Consumers in Congested Markets," *Economic Inquiry* 24 (Apr. 1986): 181–93; Todd Sandler, "Optimal Prices and Animal Consumers in Congested Markets: A Comment," *Economic Inquiry* 25 (Oct. 1987): 715–20; Raymond C. Battalio, John H. Kagel, and Owen R. Phillips, "Optimal Prices and Animal Consumers in Congested Markets: A Reply," *Economic Inquiry* 25 (Oct. 1987): 721–22; and Raymond C. Battalio, John H. Kagel, Howard Rachlin, and Leonard Green, "Commodity Choice Behavior with Pigeons as Subjects," *Journal of Political Economy* 84 (Feb. 1981): 116–51.

94. William M. Landes, "An Economic Study of U.S. Aircraft Hijacking, 1961–1976," *Journal of Law and Economics* 21 (Apr. 1978): 1–29.

95. Alfred Blumstein and Daniel Nagin, "The Deterrent Effect of Legal Sanctions on Draft Evasion," *Stanford University Law Review* 28 (1977): 241–76.

96. For a particularly well-done piece that uses data from another country, see Kenneth Wolpin, "An Economic Analysis of Crime and Punishment in England and Wales, 1894–1967," *Journal of Political Economy* 86 (1978): 815–40. For a recent survey of papers in this area, see Isaac Ehrlich, "Crime, Punishment, and the Market for Offenses," *Journal of Economic Perspectives* 10 (Winter 1996): 43–67.

97. Alfred Blumstein, Jacqueline Cohen, and Daniel Nagin, eds., *Deterrence and Incapacitation: Estimating the Effects of Criminal Sanctions on Crime Rates* (Washington, DC: National Academy of Sciences, 1978), pp. 4, 7. Economists have responded to this report; see Isaac Ehrlich and Randall Mark, "Fear of Deterrence: A Critical Evaluation of the 'Report of the Panel on Research on Deterrent and Incapacitation Effects,'" *Journal of Legal Studies* 6 (June 1977): 293–316.

98. Wallace P. Mullin, "Will Gun Buyback Programs Increase the Quantity of Guns?" Michigan State University working paper (Mar. 1997), and Martha R. Plotkin, ed., *Under Fire: Gun Buy-Backs, Exchanges, and Amnesty Programs* (Washington, DC: Police Executive Research Forum, 1996).

CHAPTER TWO

1. The Supreme Court Justices would not uphold broad protections for gun ownership "if they thought blood would flow in the streets." This point was made by Professor Daniel Polsby in a talk given at the University of Chicago, February 20, 1997. As he points out, the Supreme Court would not have allowed the publication of the Pentagon Papers, despite the arguments about the freedom of the press, if it had posed a severe military risk to the United States. It is not the role of this book to debate the purpose of the Second Amendment. However, the argument that the Second Amendment implies broad protection of gun ownership seems quite strong. William Van Alstyne argues that the reference to a "well-regulated Militia" refers to the "ordinary citizen" and that it was emphatically not an allusion to "regular armed soldiers." It was ordinary citizens who were to bring their own arms to form an army when the Republic was in danger. The amendment was viewed as the ultimate limit on a government's turning against the will of the people. See William Van Alstyne, "The Second Amendment Right to Arms," *Duke Law Review* 43 (Apr. 1994): 1236–55.

2. The opposite of endogenous is exogenous. An exogenous change in something is an independent change, not a response to something else. In reality, almost everything is to some extent related to something else, so the distinction between exogenous and endogenous is a matter of degree. Since models and statistical methods must put a limit on how much to include, some variables will always be treated as "exogenously given" rather than dependent on other variables. For the social sciences, this is a constant headache. Virtually any study is open to the criticism that "if variable X depends upon variable

Y, your results are not necessarily valid." In general, larger studies that rely on more data have better chances of reliably incorporating more relationships. Part of the process of doing research is determining which relationships may raise important concerns for readers and then attempting to test for those concerns.

3. With purely cross-sectional data, if one recognizes that differences may exist in crime rates even after all the demographic and criminal-punishment variables are accounted for, there are simply not enough observations to take these regional differences into account. One cannot control for more variables than one has observations to explain.

The problem with time-series data is the same. Time-series studies typically assume that crime follows a particular type of time trend (for example, they may simply assume that crime rises at a constant rate over time, or they may assume more complicated growth rates involving squared or cubic relationships). Yet almost any crime pattern over time is possible, and, as with cross-sectional data, unexplained differences over time will persist even after all the demographic and criminal-punishment variables are accounted for. Ideally, one could allow each year to have a different effect, but with time-series data we would again find that we had more variables with which to explain changes than we had observations to explain.

4. Gary Kleck and E. Britt Patterson, "The Impact of Gun Control and Gun-Ownership Levels on Violence Rates," *Journal of Quantitative Criminology* 9 (1993): 249–87.

5. David McDowall, Colin Loftin, and Brian Wiersema, "Easing Concealed Firearm Laws: Effects on Homicide in Three States," *Journal of Criminal Law and Criminology* 86 (Fall 1995): 193–206.

6. Arthur L. Kellermann, et al., "Gun Ownership as a Risk Factor for Homicide in the Home," *New England Journal of Medicine* (Oct. 7, 1993): 1084–91.

7. Ibid., p. 1084.

8. The interesting letter that provoked this response from Kellermann et al. was written by students in a graduate statistics class at St. Louis University. See the *New England Journal of Medicine* (Feb. 3, 1994): 366, 368.

9. Recent attempts to relate the crime rate to the prison population concern me. Besides difficulties in relating the total prison population to any particular type of crime, I think it is problematic to compare a stock (the prison population) with a flow (the crime rate). See, for example, Steven Levitt, "The Effect of Prison Population Size on Crime Rates: Evidence from Prison Overcrowding Litigation," *Quarterly Journal of Economics* 111 (1996): 144–67.

10. Gary S. Becker, "Crime and Punishment: An Economic Approach," *Journal of Political Economy* 76 (Mar./Apr. 1968): 169–217. See also, for example, Isaac Ehrlich, "Participation in Illegitimate Activities: A Theoretical and Empirical Investigation," *Journal of Political Economy* 81 (1973): 521–65; Michael K. Block and John Heineke, "A Labor Theoretical Analysis of Criminal Choice," *American Economic Review* 65 (June 1975): 314–25; William M. Landes, "An Economic Study of U.S. Aircraft Hijacking, 1961–1976," *Journal of Law and Economics* 21 (Apr. 1978): 1–29.; John R. Lott, Jr., "Juvenile Delinquency and Education: A Comparison of Public and Private Provision," *International Review of Law and Economics* 7 (Dec. 1987): 163–75; James Andreoni, "Criminal Deterrence in the Reduce Form: A New Perspective on Ehrlich's Seminal Study," *Economic Inquiry* 33 (July 1995): 476–83; Morgan O. Reynolds, "Crime and Punishment in America," (Dallas: National Center for Policy Analysis, June 1995); and Levitt, "Effect of Prison Population Size on Crime Rates."

11. John R. Lott, Jr., "Do We Punish High-Income Criminals Too Heavily?" *Economic Inquiry* 30 (Oct. 1992): 583–608.

12. John R. Lott, Jr., "The Effect of Conviction on the Legitimate Income of Criminals," *Economics Letters* 34 (Dec. 1990): 381–85 ; John R. Lott, Jr., "An Attempt at Measuring the Total Monetary Penalty from Drug Convictions: The Importance of an Individual's Reputation," *Journal of Legal Studies* 21 (Jan. 1992): 159–87.

13. This approach is also known as controlling for "fixed effects," where a separate dummy variable is used to account for each county.

14. James Q. Wilson and George L. Kelling, "Making Neighborhoods Safe," *Atlantic Monthly*, Feb. 1989, and "Broken Windows," *Atlantic Monthly*, Mar. 1982.

15. Arson was excluded because of a large number of inconsistencies in the data and the small number of counties reporting this measure.

16. Robbery includes street robbery, commercial robbery, service station robbery, convenience store robbery, residence robbery, and bank robbery. (See also the discussion of burglary regarding why the inclusion of residence robbery creates difficulty with this broad measure.) After I wrote the original paper, two different commentators attempted to argue that "If 'shall-issue' [a synonym for "nondiscretionary"] concealed-carrying laws really deter criminals from undertaking street crimes, then it is only reasonable to expect the laws to have an impact on robberies. Robbery takes place between strangers on the street. A high percentage of homicide and rape, on the other hand, occurs inside a home—where concealed-weapons laws should have no impact. These findings strongly suggest that something else—not new concealed-carry laws—is responsible for the reduction in crime observed by the authors." See, for example, Doug Weil, "Response to John Lott's Study on the Impact of 'Carry-Concealed' Laws on Crime Rates," *U.S. Newswire*, Aug. 8, 1996. The curious aspect of the emphasis on robbery over other crimes like murder and rape is that if robbery is the most obvious crime to be affected by gun-control laws, why have virtually no gun-control studies examined robberies? In fact, Kleck's literature survey only notes one previous gun-control study that examined the issue of robberies ("Guns and Violence: An Interpretive Review of the Field," Social Pathology 1 [Jan. 1995]: 12–47). More important, given that the FBI includes many categories of robberies besides those that "take place between strangers on the street," it is not obvious why this category should exhibit the greatest sensitivity to concealed-handgun laws.

17. "NRA poll: Salespeople No. 1 for Permit Applications," *Dallas Morning News*, Apr. 19, 1996, p. 32A.

18. For example, see Arnold S. Linsky, Murray A. Strauss, and Ronet Bachman-Prehn, "Social Stress, Legitimate Violence, and Gun Availability," Paper presented at the annual meetings of the Society for the Study of Social Problems, 1988; and Clayton E. Cramer and David B. Kopel, "'Shall Issue': The New Wave of Concealed-Handgun Permit Laws," *Tennessee Law Review* 62 (Spring 1995): 680–91.

19. Among those who made this comment to David Mustard and me were Bob Barnhart, Manager of the Intelligence/Concealed Handgun United of Multnomah County, Oregon; Mike Woodward, of the Oregon Law Enforcement Data System; Joe Vincent of the Washington Department of Licensing Firearms Unit; Alan Krug, who provided us with the Pennsylvania Permit data; and Susan Harrell of the Florida Department of State Concealed Weapons Division. Evidence for this point with respect to Virginia was obtained from Eric Lipton, "Virginians Get Ready to Conceal Arms: State's New Weapon Law Brings a Flood of Inquiries," *Washington Post*, June 28, 1995, p. A1, who notes that "analysts say the new law, which drops the requirement that prospective gun carriers show a 'demonstrated need' to be armed, likely won't make much of a difference in rural areas, where judges have long issued permits to most people who applied for them. But in urban areas such as Northern Virginia—where judges granted few permits because few residents could justify a need for them—the number of concealed weapon permits issued is expected to soar. In Fairfax, for example, a county of more than 850,000 people, only 10 now have permits." See also Cramer and Kopel, "New Wave of Concealed-Handgun Permit Laws," pp. 679–758.

20. For example, see Kleck and Patterson, "Impact of Gun Control and Gun-Ownership Levels on Violence Rates."

21. The sex ratios in Alaska are quite large. For example, white males outnumber

white females in the 20–29 age range by 19 percent, while the difference for the United States as a whole is 3 percent. The same ratio for the 30–39 age range is 12 percent in Alaska and 1 percent nationally. Yet the greatest differences occur for blacks. In Alaska black males outnumber black females in the 20–29 age range by 40 percent, while in the rest of the United States the reverse is true, with black females outnumbering (nonincarcerated) black males by 7 percent.

22. While no reliable data are available on this question, a couple of polls indicate that the number of otherwise law-abiding citizens who carry concealed handguns may be substantial. The results of a recent Oklahoma poll showed that up to 6 percent of Oklahoma residents already carry concealed handguns either on their persons or in their cars; see Michael Smith, "Many Permits to Go to Lawbreakers," *Tulsa World,* May 5, 1996, p. A15. The margin of error in the poll was 3.5 percent, which is substantial, given the small value with which this error is compared.

23. Sam Peltzman, "The Effects of Automobile Safety Regulation," *Journal of Political Economy* 83 (Aug. 1975): 677–725.

24. Steven Peterson, George Hoffer, and Edward Millner, "Are Drivers of Air-Bag-Equipped Cars More Aggressive? A Test of the Offsetting-Behavior Hypothesis," *Journal of Law and Economics* 38 (Oct. 1995): 251–64.

25. Kieran Murray, "NRA Taps into Anger of Mid-American Gunlovers," *Reuters Newswire,* dateline Dallas, Apr. 21, 1996.

26. At least since the work of Isaac Ehrlich, economists have also realized that potential biases exist from using the offense rate as both the variable that one is seeking to explain and as the denominator in determining the arrest rate. To see this, suppose that mistakes are made in measuring the crime rate (and mistakes are certainly made) because of recording inaccuracies or simply because citizens may change the rates at which they report crime over time. Accidentally recording a crime rate that is too high will result in our recording an arrest rate that is too low, since the arrest rate is the total number of arrests divided by the total number of crimes. The converse is also true: When too low a crime rate is recorded, the arrest rate that we observe will be too high. Obviously, this problem will make it appear that a negative relationship exists between arrest rates and crime even if no relationship exists. There is also the concern that increasing crime rates may lower arrest rates if the same resources are being asked to do more work. See Isaac Ehrlich, "Participation in Illegitimate Activities: A Theoretical and Empirical Investigation," *Journal of Political Economy* 81 (1973): 548–53.

CHAPTER THREE

1. The 1988 poll's margin of error was 1.1 percent, while that of the 1996 poll was 2.2 percent.

2. In order to obtain the rate at which people in the general population owned guns, I weighted the respondents' answers to give less weight to groups that were overrepresented among voters compared to their share in the overall population, and to give greater weight to those groups that were underrepresented. Twenty-four categories of personal characteristics were used to compute these weightings: white males and females, and black males and females, aged 18–29; neither black nor white males and females 18–29; white males and females, and black males and females 30–44; neither black nor white males and females 30–44; white males and females, and black males and females 45–59; neither black nor white males and females 45–59; white males and females, and black males and females over 59; neither black nor white males and females over 59.

3. This argument has been made explicitly in the press many times. See, for example, Scott Baldauf, "As Crime Shrinks, Security Is Still Growth Industry," *Christian Science Monitor,* Oct. 2, 1996, p. 1.

4. Alix M. Freedman, "Tinier, Deadlier Pocket Pistols Are in Vogue," *Wall Street Journal*, Sept. 12, 1996, P. B1.

5. The primary concern here is that letting people check those parts of a list that apply will result in fewer positive responses than asking people to answer individual questions about each item. As one way of checking the importance of this concern, I examined whether other questions that changed in a similar way between the two polls experienced a change in the same direction as that shown for gun ownership. The two questions that I looked at—regarding marriage and whether children less than 18 lived with the respondent—moved in the opposite direction. Relatively more people indicated these responses in the 1988 poll when the questions were presented in a list than did so when they were presented with separate questions about these characteristics. I have also done extensive research using other questions involving marriage and children under 18 living with the respondent that were part of a "check as many as apply" question. That research provides extremely strong evidence that these questions were answered consistently between 1988 and 1996. See John R. Lott, Jr. and Larry W. Kenny, "How Dramatically Did Women's Suffrage Change the Size and Scope of Government?" University of Chicago School of Law working paper (1997). The relative differences in gun ownership across groups is also consistent with recent work using other polls by Edward Glaeser and Spencer Glendon, "Who Owns Guns?" *American Economic Review* 88 (May 1998).

The empirical work that will be done later will allow us to adjust for the changes in the reported level of gun ownership that might result from the change in this question.

6. I appreciate Tom Smith's taking the time to talk to me about these issues on May 30, 1997.

7. Gun owners within each of the twenty-four categories listed in note 2 above may have particular characteristics that cause them to vote at rates that differ from the rates at which other people vote. One would hope that some of that difference would be accounted for in the detailed demographic characteristics, but there is a good chance that this may not occur. Several attempts were made to see how large this effect might be by asking, for example, whether gun owners were more or less likely not to have voted in previous elections. This question has also been broken down to account for those who are old enough to have voted previously. For 1988, the difference in gun ownership between those who were voting for the first time and those who had voted previously was 3 percent (23.2 percent of those voting for the first time and 26.2 percent of those who were not owned guns). Limiting this question to people who were 30 years of age or older produced an even smaller difference: 28.9 percent of first-time voters owned guns versus 27.5 percent of those who had voted previously. Similarly, for the question of whether voters in 1988 had also voted in 1984, the difference was also 3 percent (23 percent of those who did not vote in 1984 and 26.4 percent of those who did owned guns).

Because most people voted, a 13 percent increase in the proportion of the general population owning guns would require an even greater drop in gun ownership among those who didn't vote in order for gun ownership to have remained constant. For some groups, such as women, for whom gun ownership among voters increased by over 70 percent, the increase is so large and the percent of women voting so high that an 80 percent drop in gun ownership among nonvoting women would have been required for gun ownership among women to have remained constant.

8. Indeed, making this adjustment produces a number that is much closer to that found in other polls of the general population, such as the National Opinion Research Center's 1996 National Gun-Policy Survey, which finds that 42 percent of the general adult population owns guns.

9. The previous peak in murder rates occurred at the end of Prohibition in the early 1930s, with the peak of 9.7 murders per 100,000 people being reached in 1933. The 1996 murder rate of 7.3 murders per 100,000 people seems tame by comparison. Indeed many people, such as Milton Friedman, have argued that much of the change in murder rates

over time has been driven by the country's war on drugs and its earlier war on alcohol. Even the gradual increase in murder rates leading up to the Nineteenth Amendment's adoption in 1991 corresponds with passage of individual state laws. Kansas, Maine, and North Dakota enacted prohibition laws between 1880 and 1890. Five states enacted prohibition in 1907–1909, followed by twelve more between 1912 and 1915 and another twelve between 1916 and 1918. Obviously, all this points to the importance of other factors in the murder rate, and that is part of the reason why I include a measure of drug prices in my estimates to explain why crime rates change over time. See Ernest H. Cherrington, *The Evolution of Prohibition in the United States of America* (Westerville, OH: Tem-Press, 1920); Edward B. Dunford, *The History of the Temperance Movement* (Washington, DC: Tem-Press, 1943); D. Leigh Colvin, *Prohibition in the United States,* (New York: George H. Doran, 1926); as well as state statutes (as a check).

10. While I will follow Cramer and Kopel's definition of what constitutes a "shall-issue" or a "do-issue" state (see "'Shall Issue': The New Wave of Concealed-Handgun Permit Laws," *Tennessee Law Review* 62 [Spring 1995]), one commentator has suggested that it is not appropriate to include Maine in these categories (Stephen P. Teret, "Critical Comments on a Paper by Lott and Mustard," School of Hygiene and Public Health, Johns Hopkins University, mimeo, Aug. 7, 1996). Neither defining Maine so that the "shall-issue" dummy equals zero nor removing Maine from the data set alters the findings shown in this book.

11. While the intent of the 1988 legislation in Virginia was clearly to institute a "shall-issue" law, the law was not equally implemented in all counties in the state. To deal with this problem, I reran the regressions reported in this paper with the "shall-issue" dummy equal to both 1 and 0 for Virginia.

12. I rely on Cramer and Kopel for this list of states. Some states, known as "do-issue" states, are also included in Cramer and Kopel's list of "shall-issue" states, though these authors argue that for all practical purposes these two groups of states are identical. See Cramer and Kopel, "New Wave of Concealed-Handgun Permit Laws," pp. 679–91.

13. The Oregon counties providing permit data were Benton, Clackamas, Columbia, Coos, Curry, Deschutes, Douglas, Gilliam, Hood River, Jackson, Jefferson, Josephine, Klamath, Lane, Lincoln, Linn, Malheur, Marion, Morrow, Multnomah, Polk, Tillamook, Umatilla, Washington and Yamhill.

14. In economics jargon I would say that I am interacting the sentence length with year-dummy variables.

15. These variables are referred to as county fixed-effects, where a separate dummy variable is set equal to 1 for each individual county.

16. See appendix 4 for the list and summary statistics.

17. For example, see James Q. Wilson and Richard J. Herrnstein, *Crime and Human Nature* (New York: Simon and Schuster, 1985), pp. 126–47.

18. However, the effect of an unusually large percentage of young males in the population may be mitigated because those most vulnerable to crime may be more likely to take actions to protect themselves. Depending upon how responsive victims are to these threats, the coefficient for a variable like the percent of young males in the population could be zero even when the group in question poses a large criminal threat.

19. Edward L. Glaeser and Bruce Sacerdote, "Why Is There More Crime in Cities?" Harvard University working paper, Nov. 14, 1995.

20. For a discussion of the relationship between income and crime, see John R. Lott, Jr., "A Transaction-Costs Explanation for Why the Poor Are More Likely to Commit Crime," *Journal of Legal Studies* 19 (Jan. 1990): 243–45.

21. A brief survey of the laws, excluding the changes in the rules regarding permits, reveals the following: Alabama made no significant changes in these laws during the period. Connecticut law gradually changed its wording from "criminal use" to "criminal possession" from 1986 to 1994. Florida has the most extensive description of penalties; the

same basic law (790.161) persists throughout the years. An additional law (790.07) appeared only in 1986. In Georgia, a law (16-11-106) that does not appear in the 1986 edition appears in the 1989 and 1994 editions. The law involves possession of a firearm during commission of a crime and specifies the associated penalties. Because this legal change might have occurred at the same time as the 1989 changes in the rules regarding permits, I used a Lexis search to check the legislative history of 16-11-106 and found that the laws were last changed in 1987, two years before the permit rules were changed (*Official Code of Georgia, Annotated*, at 16-11-106 [1996]). Idaho has made no significant changes over time. In Indiana and Maine no significant changes occurred in these laws during the period. In Mississippi, Law 97-37-1 talks explicitly about penalties. It appears in the 1986 version but not in the 1989 or the 1994 versions. Montana enacted some changes in punishments related to unauthorized carrying of concealed weapons, but no changes in the punishment for using a weapon in a crime. New Hampshire, North Dakota, Oregon, Pennsylvania, and Washington made no significant changes in these laws during period. In South Dakota, Law 22-14-13, which specifies penalties for commission of a felony while armed, appears in 1986 but not 1989. In Vermont, Section 4005, which outlines the penalties for carrying a gun when committing a felony, appears in 1986 but not in 1989 or 1994. Virginia and Washington made no significant changes in these laws during the period. West Virginia had Law 67-7-12 on the books in 1994, but not in the earlier versions. It involves punishment for endangerment with firearms. Removing Georgia from the sample, which was the only state that enacted changes in its gun laws near the year that the "shall-issue" law went into affect, eliminates the chance that the other changes in gun laws might affect my results and does not appreciably alter those results.

22. Thomas B. Marvell and Carlisle E. Moody, "The Impact of Enhanced Prison Terms for Felonies Committed with Guns," *Criminology* 33 (May 1995): 247, 258–61.

23. Marvell and Moody's findings (see note 22 above) show that the shortest time period between these sentencing enhancements and changes in concealed-weapon laws is seven years (Pennsylvania). Twenty-six states passed their enhancement laws prior to the beginning of my sample period, and only four states passed such laws after 1981. Maine, which implemented its concealed-handgun law in 1985, passed its sentencing-enhancement laws in 1971.

24. The states that had waiting periods prior to the beginning of the sample are Alabama, California, Connecticut, Illinois, Maryland, Minnesota, New Jersey, North Carolina, Pennsylvania, Rhode Island, South Dakota, Washington, and Wisconsin. The District of Columbia also had a waiting period prior to the beginning of my sample. The states that adopted this rule during the sample period are Hawaii, Indiana, Iowa, Missouri, Oregon, and Virginia.

CHAPTER FOUR

1. More precisely, it is the percentage of a one-standard-deviation change in the crime rate that can be explained by a one-standard-deviation change in the endogenous variable.

2. All the results are reported for the higher threshold required with a two-tailed t-test.

3. One possible concern with these initial results arises from my use of an aggregate public-policy variable (state right-to-carry laws) on county-level data. See Bruce C. Greenwald, "A General Analysis of the Bias in the Estimated Standard Errors of Least Squares Coefficients," *Journal of Econometrics* 22 (Aug. 1983): 323–38; and Brent R. Moulton, "An Illustration of a Pitfall in Estimating the Effects of Aggregate Variables on Micro Units," *Review of Economics and Statistics* 72 (1990): 334. Moulton writes, "If disturbances are correlated within the groupings that are used to merge aggregate with micro data, however, then even small levels of correlation can cause the standard errors from the ordinary

least squares (OLS) to be seriously biased downward." Yet this should not really be a concern here because of my use of dummy variables for all the counties, which is equivalent to using state dummies as well as county dummies for all but one of the counties within each state. Using these dummy variables thus allows us to control for any disturbances that are correlated within any individual state. The regressions discussed in table 4.2 reestimate the specifications shown in table 4.1 but also include state dummies that are interacted with a time trend. This should thus not only control for any disturbances that are correlated with the states, but also for any disturbances that are correlated within a state over time. Finally, while right-to-carry laws are almost always statewide laws, there is one exception. Pennsylvania partially exempted its largest county (Philadelphia) from the law when it was passed in 1989, and it remained exempt from the law during the rest of the sample period. However, permits granted in the counties surrounding Philadelphia were valid for use in the city.

4. However, the increase in the number of property crimes is larger than the decrease in the number of robberies.

5. While I adopt the classifications used by Cramer and Kopel in "'Shall Issue': The New Wave of Concealed-Handgun Permit Laws," Tennessee Law Review 62 (Spring 1995), some are more convinced by other classifications of states (for example, see Doug Weil, "Response to John Lott's Study on the Impact of 'Carry-Concealed' Laws on Crime Rates," *U.S. Newswire*, Aug. 8, 1996; and Stephen P. Teret, "Critical Comments on a Paper by Lott and Mustard," School of Hygiene and Public Health, Johns Hopkins University, mimeo, Aug. 7, 1996). Setting the "shall-issue" dummy for Maine to zero and rerunning the regressions shown in table 4.1 results in the "shall-issue" coefficient equaling –3% for violent crimes, –8% for murder, –6% for rape, –4.5 for aggravated assault, –1% for robbery, 3% for property crimes, 8.1% for automobile theft, 0.4% for burglary, and 3% for larceny. Similarly, setting the "shall-issue" dummy for Virginia to zero results in the "shall-issue" coefficient equaling –4% for violent crimes, –9% for murder, –5% for rape, –5% for aggravated assault, –0.11% for robbery, 3% for property crimes, 9% for automobile theft, 2% for burglary, and 3% for larceny. As a final test, dropping both Maine and Virginia from the data set results in the "shall-issue" coefficient equaling –2% for violent crimes, –10% for murder, –6% for rape, –3% for aggravated assault, 0.6% for robbery, 3.6% for property crimes, 10% for automobile theft, 2% for burglary, and 4% for larceny.

6. This information is obtained from Mortality Detail Records provided by the U.S. Department of Health and Human Services.

7. This assumption is implausible for many reasons. One reason is that accidental handgun deaths occur in states without concealed-handgun laws.

8. Given the possible relationship between drug prices and crime, I reran the regressions in table 4.1 and included an additional variable for cocaine prices. One argument linking drug prices and crime is that if the demand for drugs is inelastic and if people commit crimes in order to finance their habits, higher drug prices might lead to increased levels of crime. Using the Drug Enforcement Administration's STRIDE data set from 1977 to 1992 (with the exceptions of 1988 and 1989), Michael Grossman, Frank J. Chaloupka, and Charles C. Brown, ("The Demand for Cocaine by Young Adults: A Rational Addiction Approach," NBER working paper, July 1996), estimate the price of cocaine as a function of its purity, weight, year dummies, year dummies interacted with eight regional dummies, and individual city dummies. There are two problems with this measure of predicted prices: (1) it removes observations during a couple of important years during which changes were occurring in concealed-handgun laws, and (2) the predicted values that I obtained ignored the city-level observations. The reduced number of observations provides an important reason why I do not include this variable in the regressions shown in table 4. 1. However, the primary impact of including this new variable is to make the "shall-issue" coefficients in the violent-crime regressions even more negative and more

significant (for example, the coefficient for the violent-crime regression becomes –7.5%, –10% for the murder regression, –7.7% for rape, and –11% for aggravated assault, with all of them significant at more than the 0.01 level). Only for the burglary regression does the "shall-issue" coefficient change appreciably: it becomes negative and insignificant. The variable for drug prices itself is negatively related to murders and rapes and positively and significantly related, at least at the 0.01 level for a one-tailed t-test, to all the other categories of crime. I would like to thank Michael Grossman for providing me with the original regressions on drug prices from his paper.

9. In contrast, if we had instead inquired what difference it would make in crime rates if either all states or no states adopted right-to-carry concealed-handgun laws, the case of all states adopting concealed-handgun laws would have produced 2,000 fewer murders; 5,700 fewer rapes; 79,000 fewer aggravated assaults; and 14,900 fewer robberies. In contrast, property crimes would have risen by 336,410.

10. Ted R. Miller, Mark A. Cohen, and Brian Wiersema, *Victim Costs and Consequences: A New Look* (Washington, DC: National Institute of Justice, Feb. 1996).

11. See Sam Peltzman, "The Effects of Automobile Safety Regulation," *Journal of Political Economy* 83 (Aug. 1975): 677–725.

12. To be more precise, a one-standard-deviation change in the probability of arrest accounts for 3 to 11 percent of a one-standard-deviation change in the various crime rates.

13. Translating this into statistical terms, a one-standard-deviation change in the percentage of the population that is black, male, and between 10 and 19 years of age explains 22 percent of the ups and downs in the crime rate.

14. This is particularly observed when there are more black females between the ages of 20 and 39, more white females between the ages of 10 and 39 and over 65, and females of other races between 20 and 29.

15. In other words, the second number shows how a one-standard-deviation change in an explanatory variable explains a certain percent of a one-standard-deviation change in the various crime rates.

16. While I believe that such variables as the arrest rate should be included in any regressions on crime, one concern with the results reported in the various tables is over whether the relationship between the "shall-issue" variable and the crime rates occurs even when all the other variables are not controlled for. Using weighted least squares and reporting only the "shall-issue" coefficients, I estimated the following regression coefficients.

How do average crime rates differ among states with and without nondiscretionary laws?

Crime rates	Crime rates in states with nondiscretionary concealed-handgun laws compared to those without the law (regressing the crime rate only on the variable for the law)	Crime rates in states with nondiscretionary concealed-handgun laws compared to those without the law after adjusting for national trends (regressing the crime rate on the variable for the law and year-dummy variables)
Violent crimes	–40%	–57%
Murder	–48	–52
Rape	–16	–28
Aggravated assault	–38	–57

Crime rates	Crime rates in states with nondiscretionary concealed-handgun laws compared to those without the law (regressing the crime rate the law)	Crime rates in states with nondiscretionary concealed-handgun laws compared to those without the law after adjusting for national trends (regressing the crime rate on the variable for the law and year-dummy variables)
Robbery	−62	−75
Property crime	−17	−20
Auto theft	−31	−43
Burglary	−28	−24
Larceny	−11	−15

Note: The only factors included are the presence of the law and/or year-specific effects. All these differences are statistically significant at least at the 1 percent level for a two-tailed t-test. To calculate these percentages, I used the approximation $100 [\exp(\text{coefficient}) - 1]$.

17. The time-trend variable ranges from 1 to 16: for the first year in the sample, it equals 1; for the last year, it is 16.

18. Other differences arise in the other control variables, such as those relating to the portion of the population of a certain race, sex, and age. For example, the percent of black males in the population between 10 and 19 is no longer statistically significant.

19. If the task instead had been to determine the difference in crime rates when either all states or no states adopt the right-to-carry handgun laws, the case of all states adopting concealed-handgun laws would have produced 2,048 fewer murders, 6,618 fewer rapes, 129,114 fewer aggravated assaults, and 86,459 fewer robberies. Non-arson property crimes also would have fallen by 511,940.

20. Generally, aggregation is frowned on in statistics anyway, as it reduces the amount of information yielded by the data set. Lumping data together into a group cannot yield any new information that did not exist before; it only reduces the richness of the data.

21. Eric Rasmusen, "Stigma and Self-Fulfilling Expectations of Criminality," *Journal of Law and Economics* 39 (Oct. 1996): 519–44.

22. In January 1996, women held 118,728 permits in Washington and 17,930 permits in Oregon. The time-series data available for Oregon during the sample period even indicate that 17.6 percent of all permit holders were women in 1991. The Washington state data were obtained from Joe Vincent of the Department of Licensing Firearms Unit in Olympia, Washington. The Oregon state data were obtained from Mike Woodward of the Law Enforcement Data System, Department of State Police, Salem, Oregon. Recent evidence from Texas indicates that about 28 percent of applicants were women ("NRA poll: Salespeople No. 1 for Permit Applications," *Dallas Morning News*, Apr. 19, 1996, p. 32A).

23. For an interesting discussion of the benefits to women of owning guns, see Paxton Quigley, *Armed and Female* (New York: E. P. Dutton, 1989).

24. Unpublished information obtained by Kleck and Gertz in their 1995 National Self-Defense Survey implies that women were as likely as men to use handguns in self-defense in or near their homes (defined as in the yard, carport, apartment hall, street adjacent to home, detached garage, etc.), but that women were less than half as likely to use a gun in self-defense away from home. See Gary Kleck and Marc Gertz, "Armed Resistance to Crime: The Prevalence and Nature of Self-Defense with a Gun," *Journal of Criminal Law and Criminology* 86 (Fall 1995): 249–87.

25. Counties with real personal income of about $15,000 in real 1983 dollars experienced 8 percent drops in murder, while mean-income counties experienced a 5.5 percent drop.

26. Lori Montgomery, "More Blacks Say Guns Are Answer to Urban Violence," *Houston Chronicle,* July 9, 1995, p. A1. This article argues that while the opposition to guns in the black community is strong, more people are coming to understand the benefits of self-protection.

27. For an excellent overview of the role of race in gun control, see Robert J. Cottrol and Raymond T. Diamond, "The Second Amendment: Toward an Afro-Americanist Reconsideration," *Georgetown Law Review* 80 (Dec. 1991): 309.

28. See William Van Alstyne, "The Second Amendment Right to Arms," *Duke Law Review* 43 (Apr. 1994): 1236–55. In slave states prior to the Civil War, the freedoms guaranteed under the Bill of Rights were regularly restricted by states because of the fear that free reign might lead to an insurrection. As Akhil Reed Amar writes, "In a society that saw itself under siege after Nat Turner's rebellion, access to firearms had to be strictly restricted, especially to free blacks." See Akhil Reed Amar, "The Bill of Rights and the Fourteenth Amendment," *Yale Law Journal* 101 (Apr. 1992): 1193.

29. *Associated Press Newswire,* May 9, 1997, 4:37 P.M. EDT. As the *Washington Times* recently noted, this story "comes at an awkward time for the administration, since President Clinton has spent the last week or two berating Republicans for failing to include in anticrime legislation a provision requiring that child safety locks be sold with guns to keep children from hurting themselves" (Editorial, "The Story of a Gun and a Kid," *Washington Times,* May 22, 1997, p. A18).

30. The conversation took place on March 18, 1997, though regrettably I have misplaced the note containing the representative's name.

31. John Carpenter, "Six Other States Have Same Law," *Chicago Sun-Times,* Mar. 11, 1997, p. 8.

32. John J. DiIulio, Jr., "The Question of Black Crime," *The Public Interest* 117 (Fall 1994): 3–24. Similar concerns about the inability of minorities to rely on the police was also expressed to me by Assemblyman Rod Wright (D–Los Angeles) during testimony before the California Assembly's Public Safety Committee on November 18, 1997.

33. One additional minor change is made in two of the earlier specifications. In order to avoid any artificial collinearity either between violent crime and robbery or between property crimes and burglary, violent crimes net of robbery and property crimes net of burglary are used as the endogenous variables when robbery or burglary are controlled for.

34. The Pearson correlation coefficient between robbery and the other crime categories ranges between .49 and .80, and all are so statistically significant that a negative correlation would only appear randomly once out of every ten thousand times. For burglary, the correlations range from 0.45 to 0.68, and they are also equally statistically significant.

35. All the results in tables 4.1 and 4.4 as well as the regressions related to both parts of figure 4.1 were reestimated to deal with the concerns raised in chapter 3 over the "noise" in arrest rates arising from the timing of offenses and arrests and the possibility of multiple offenders. I reran all the regressions in this section by limiting the sample to those counties with populations over 10,000, over 100,000, and then over 200,000 people. The more the sample was restricted to larger-population counties, the stronger and more statistically significant was the relationship between concealed-handgun laws and the previously reported effects on crime. This is consistent with the evidence reported in figure 4.1. The arrest-rate results also tended to be stronger and more significant. I further reestimated all the regressions by redefining the arrest rate as the number of arrests over the last three years divided by the total number of offenses over the last three years. Despite the reduced sample size, the results remained similar to those already reported.

36. More formally, by using restricted least squares, we can test whether constraining

the coefficients for the period before the law produces results that yield the same pattern after the passage of the law. Using both the time-trend and the time-trend-squared relationships, the F-tests reject the hypothesis that the before and after relationships are the same, at least at the 10 percent level, for all the crime categories except aggravated assault and larceny, for which the F-tests are only significant at the 20 percent level. Using only the time-trend relationship, the F-tests reject the hypothesis in all the cases.

37. The main exception was West Virginia, which showed large drops in murder but not in other crime categories.

38. See Thomas B. Marvell and Carlisle E. Moody, "The Impact of Enhanced Prison Terms for Felonies Committed with Guns," *Criminology* 33 (May 1995): 259–60.

39. I should note, however, that the "nondiscretionary" coefficients for robbery in the county-level regressions and for property crimes using the state levels are no longer statistically significant.

40. Toni Heinzl, "Police Groups Oppose Concealed-Weapons Bill," *Omaha World-Herald,* Mar. 18, 1997, p. 9SF.

41. A simple dummy variable is used for whether the limit was 18 or 21 years of age.

42. Here is one example: "Mrs. Elmasri, a Wisconsin woman whose estranged husband had threatened her and her children, called a firearms instructor for advice on how to buy a gun for self-defense. She was advised that, under Wisconsin's progressive handgun law, she would have to wait 48 hours so that the police could perform the required background check.

"Twenty-four hours later, . . . Mrs. Elmasri's husband murdered the defenseless woman and her two children" (William P. Cheshire, "Gun Laws No Answer for Crime," *Arizona Republic,* Jan. 10, 1993, p. C1.) Other examples can be found in David B. Kopel, "Background Checks and Waiting Periods," in *Guns: Who Should Have Them,* ed. David B. Kopel (Amherst, NY: Prometheus Books, 1995.) Other examples tell of women who successfully evaded these restrictions to obtain guns.

> In September 1990, mail carrier Catherine Latta of Charlotte, N. C., went to the police to obtain permission to buy a handgun. Her ex-boyfriend had previously robbed her, assaulted her several times, and raped her. The clerk at the sheriff's office informed her that processing a gun permit would take two to four weeks. "I told her I'd be dead by then," Latta recalled.
>
> That afternoon, Latta bought an illegal $20 semiautomatic pistol on the street. Five hours later, her ex-boyfriend attacked her outside her house. She shot him dead. The county prosecutor decided not to prosecute Latta for either the self-defense homicide or the illegal gun. (Quoted from David B. Kopel, "Guns and Crime: Does Restricting Firearms Really Reduce Violence?" *San Diego Union-Tribune,* May 9, 1993, p. G4.)

For another example where a woman's ability to defend herself would have been impaired by a waiting period, see "Waiting Period Law Might Have Cost Mother's Life," *USA Today,* May 27, 1994, p. 10A.

43. Quoted in David Armstrong, "Cities' Crime Moves to Suburbs," *Boston Globe,* May 19, 1997, pp. 1 and B6.

CHAPTER FIVE

1. While county-level data were provided in the *Supplementary Homicide Reports,* matching these county observations with those used in the *Uniform Crime Reports* proved unusually difficult. A unique county identifier was used in the *Supplementary Homicide Reports* that was not consistent across years. In addition, some caution is necessary in using both the Mortality Detail Records and the *Supplementary Homicide Reports,* since the murder rates reported

in both sources have relatively low correlations of less than .7 with the murder rates reported in the *Uniform Crime Reports*. This is especially surprising for the supplementary reports, which are derived from the *Uniform Crime Reports*. See U.S. Department of Justice, FBI staff, *Uniform Crime Reports* (Washington, DC: U.S. Govt. Printing Office) for the years 1977 to 1992.

2. Indeed, the average age of permit holders is frequently in the mid- to late forties (see, for example, "NRA poll: Salespeople No. 1 for Permit Applications," *Dallas Morning News*, Apr. 19, 1996, p. 32A.) In Kentucky the average age of permit holders is about fifty (see Terry Flynn, "Gun-Toting Kentuckians Hold Their Fire," *Cincinnati Enquirer*, June 16, 1997, p. A1).

3. This is the significance for a two-tailed t-test.

4. Similar breakdowns for deaths and injuries are explored in much more depth in a paper that I have written with William Landes; see William Landes and John R. Lott, Jr., "Mass Public Shootings, Bombings, and Right-to-Carry Concealed-Handgun Laws," University of Chicago working paper, 1997.

5. A second change was also made. Because of the large number of observations noting no deaths or injuries from mass public shootings in a given year, I used a statistical technique known as Tobit that is particularly well suited to this situation.

6. The results shown below provide the estimates for the simple linear time trends before and after the adoption of the law. They demonstrate that for each year leading up to the passage of the law, total deaths or injuries from mass public shootings rose by 1.5 more per 10 million people and that after the passage of the law, total deaths or injuries fell by 4 more per 10 million people. The difference in these two trends is statistically significant at the 1 percent level for a two-tailed t-test. It is interesting to note that higher murder arrest rates, although they deter murderers, do not seem to deter perpetrators of mass public shootings.

Linear time trends for deaths and injuries from mass public shootings before and after adoption of concealed-handgun law

	Total deaths and injuries per 100,000 population
Average annual change for years after adoption of the law	−0.04*
Average annual change for years before adoption of the law	0.015*
Arrest rate for Murder	−0.0003

*Statistically significant at least at the 10 percent level for a two-tailed t-test
Note: numbers are negative; years furthest beyond adoption are the largest

7. See appendix 4 for the means and standard deviations of the variables used in these regressions.

8. Again, this is stating that a one-standard-deviation change in arrest rates explains more than 15 percent of a one-standard-deviation change in crime rates.

9. Running the regressions for all Pennsylvania counties (not just those with more than 200,000 people) produced similar signs for the coefficient for the change in concealed-handgun permits, though the coefficients were no longer statistically significant for violent crimes, rape, and aggravated assault. Alan Krug, who provided us with the Pennsylvania handgun-permit data, told us that one reason for the large increase in concealed-handgun permits in some rural counties was that people used the guns for

hunting. He told us that the number of permits issued in these low-population, rural counties tended to increase most sharply in the fall around hunting season. If people were in fact getting large numbers of permits in low-population counties (which already have extremely low crime rates) for some reason other than crime, it would be more difficult to pick up the deterrent effect of concealed handguns on crime that was occurring in the larger counties.

10. A one-standard-deviation change in conviction rates explains 4 to 20 percent of a one-standard-deviation change in the corresponding crime rates.

11. I reran these regressions using the natural logs of the arrest and conviction rates, and I consistently found statistically larger and even economically more important effects for the arrest rates than for the conviction rates.

12. For example, see Dan M. Kahan, "What Do Alternative Sanctions Mean?" *University of Chicago Law Review* 63 (1996): 591–653.

13. See John R. Lott, Jr., "The Effect of Conviction on the Legitimate Income of Criminals," *Economics Letters* 34 (Dec. 1990): 381–85; John R. Lott, Jr., "An Attempt at Measuring the Total Monetary Penalty from Drug Convictions: The Importance of an Individual's Reputation," *Journal of Legal Studies* 21 (Jan. 1992): 159–87; John R. Lott, Jr., "Do We Punish High-Income Criminals Too Heavily?" *Economic Inquiry* 30 (Oct. 1992): 583–608.

14. Put differently, six of the specifications imply that a one-standard-deviation change in the number of concealed-handgun permits explains at least 8 percent of a one-standard-deviation change in the corresponding crime rates.

15. Philip Heymann, a former deputy attorney general in the Clinton administration and currently a law professor at Harvard University, wrote, "None of this [the drop in crime rates] is the result of . . . the Brady Act (for most guns were never bought by youth from licensed gun dealers)." See "The Limits of Federal Crime-Fighting," *Washington Post,* Jan. 5, 1997, p. C7.

16. For a discussion of externalities (both benefits and costs) from crime, see Kermit Daniel and John R. Lott, Jr., "Should Criminal Penalties Include Third-Party Avoidance Costs?" *Journal of Legal Studies* 24 (June 1995): 523–34.

17. Alix M. Freedman, "Tinier, Deadlier Pocket Pistols Are in Vogue," *Wall Street Journal,* Sept. 12, 1996, pp. B1, B16.

18. One hundred and eighty-two million people lived in states without these laws in 1991, so the regressions would have also implied nine more accidental deaths from handguns in that year.

19. Given the very small number of accidental deaths from handguns in the United States, the rate of such deaths in the vast majority of counties is zero, and the last two columns of table 5.6 again use Tobit regressions to deal with this problem. Limitations in statistical packages, however, prevented me from being able to control for all the county dummies, and I opted to rerun these regressions with only state dummy variables.

20. For example, see Nicholas D. Kristof, "Guns: One Nation Bars, the Other Requires," *New York Times,* Mar. 10, 1996, sec. 4, p. 3. For some evidence on international gun ownership rates see Munday and Stevenson, *Guns and Violence* (1996): 30.

21. See Ian Ayres and Steven Levitt, "Measuring Positive Externalities from Unobservable Victim Precaution: An Empirical Analysis of Lojack," NBER working paper 5928 (1997); and John Donohue and Peter Siegelman, "Is the United States at the Optimal Rate of Crime?" *Journal of Legal Studies* 27 (Jan. 1998).

22. See notes 12 and 13 above.

CHAPTER SIX

1. Isaac Ehrlich, "Participation in Illegitimate Activities: A Theoretical and Empirical Investigation," *Journal of Political Economy* 81 (1973): 548–51. Except for the political variables, my specification accords fairly closely with at least the spirit of Ehrlich's specification,

though some of my variables, like the demographic breakdowns, are much more detailed, and I have a few other measures that were not available to him.

2. See also Robert E. McCormick and Robert Tollison, "Crime on the Court," *Journal of Political Economy* 92 (Apr. 1984): 223–35, for a novel article testing the endogeneity of the "arrest rate" in the context of basketball penalties.

3. These last two variables are measured at the state level.

4. Phil Cook suggested this addition to me. In a sense, this is similar to Ehrlich's specification, except that the current crime rate is broken down into its lagged value and the change between the current and previous periods. See Ehrlich, "Participation in Illegitimate Activities," p. 557.

5. The natural logs of the rates for violent crime and property crime were used.

6. These estimates are known as two-stage least squares.

7. Ehrlich raises the concern that the types of two-stage, least-squares estimates discussed above might still be affected by spurious correlation if the measurement errors for the crime rate were serially correlated over time. To account for this, I reestimated the first-stage regressions predicting the arrest rate without the lagged crime rate, which made the estimated results for the nondiscretionary law dummy even more negative and more statistically significant than those already shown. See Ehrlich, "Participation in Illegitimate Activities," p. 552 n. 46.

8. Still another approach would be to estimate what are known as Tobit regressions, but unfortunately no statistical package is available that allows me both to control for all the different county dummy variables and to use the Tobit procedure.

CHAPTER SEVEN

1. The Violence Policy Center grew out of the National Coalition to Ban Handguns.

2. Douglas Weil, the research director for Handgun Control, Inc., has publicly disagreed with the claim that most gun-control advocates initially refused to comment on my study. In a letter to the Washington Times, Weil wrote,

> The *Washington Times* editorial ("Armed and Safer," Aug. 14) is misinformed and misguided. The *Times* falsely claims that gun-control proponents "initially refused to read" John Lott's and David Mustard's study of the impact of laws regarding the right to carry concealed guns, and that I attacked the researchers' motivations rather than challenge the study "on the merits." This charge is untrue.
>
> One look at the study would prove the *Times* wrong. On the title page of the study, several pro–gun-control researchers are credited for their comments "on the merits" of the study. Included in this list are David McDowall, a criminologist at the University of Maryland; Philip Cook, an economist at Duke University; and myself, research director for the Center to Prevent Handgun Violence.
>
> Upon reviewing the study, I found Mr. Lott's methodology to be seriously flawed. I told Mr. Lott that his study did not adequately control for the whole range of ways that state and local governments attempt to lower the crime rate. In Oregon, for example, the same legislation that made it easier to carry a concealed handgun included one of the toughest new handgun-purchase laws in the country—a 15-day waiting period and fingerprint-background check on all purchases. . . .
>
> I gladly shared my critique of this study with Mr. Lott and will now reiterate it here; as someone fully credentialed to evaluate Mr. Lott's and Mr. Mustard's work, I would have recommended that the paper be rejected. (See Douglas Weil, "A Few Thoughts on the Study of Handgun Violence and Gun Control," *Washington Times,* Aug. 22, 1996, p. A16.)

While it is true that I thanked Mr. Weil in my paper for a comment that he made, his single comment was nothing like what his letter to the *Times* claimed. Before he explained his concerns to the press, he and I had no discussions about whether I had controlled for "ways that state and local governments attempt to lower the crime rate," possibly because my study not only controls for arrest and conviction rates, prison sentences, the number of police officers and police payroll, but also waiting periods and criminal penalties for using a gun in the commission of a crime.

Mr. Weil's sole comment to me came after two previous telephone calls over a month and a half in which Mr. Weil had said that he was too busy to give me any comments. His sole comment on August 1 was that he was upset that I had cited a study by a professor, Gary Kleck, with whom Weil disagreed. I attempted to meet this unusual but minor criticism by rewriting the relevant sentence on the first page in a further attempt to dispassionately state the alternative hypotheses.

Mr. Weil's claims are particularly difficult to understand in light of a conversation that I had with him on August 5. After hearing him discuss my paper on the news, I called him to say how surprised I was to hear about his telling the press that the paper was "fundamentally flawed" when the only comment that he had given me was on the reference to Kleck. Mr. Weil then immediately demanded to know whether it was true that I had thanked him for giving comments on the paper. He had heard from people in the news media who had seen a draft with his name listed among those thanked. (On August 1, I had added his name to the list of people who had given comments, and when the news of the paper suddenly broke on August 2 with the story in *USA Today*, it was this new version that had been faxed to the news media.) He wanted to know if I was trying to "embarrass" him with others in the gun-control community, and he insisted that had not given me any comments. I said that I had only done it to be nice, and I mentioned the concern that he raised about the reference to Kleck. Weil then demanded that I "immediately remove [his] name" from the paper.

3. This was not my only experience with Ms. Glick. On August 8, 1996, six days after the events of August 2 described above, I appeared with her on MSNBC. After I tried to make an introductory statement setting out my findings, Ms. Glick attacked me for having my study funded by "gun manufacturers." She claimed that I was a "shill" for the gun manufactures and that it was important that I be properly identified as not being an objective academic. She also claimed that there were many serious problems with the paper. Referring to the study, she asserted that it was a fraud.

I responded by saying that these were very serious charges and that if she had some evidence, she should say what it was. I told her that I didn't think she had any such evidence, and that if she didn't, we should talk about the issues involved in the study.

At this point the moderator broke in and said to Ms. Glick that he agreed that these were very serious charges, and he asked her what evidence she had for her statements. Glick responded by saying that she had lots of evidence and that it was quite obvious to her that this study had been done to benefit gun manufacturers.

The moderator then asked her to comment further on her claim that there were serious problems with the study, and she stated that one only had to go to page 2 before finding a problem. Her concern was that I had used data for Florida that was a year and a half old. The moderator then asked her why this was a problem, since I couldn't be expected to use data that was, say, as recent as last week. Ms. Glick responded by saying that a lot of things could have changed since the most recent data were available. I then mentioned that I had obtained more recent data since the study had been written and that the pattern of people not using permitted guns improperly had held true from October 1987 to December 31, 1995.

A more recent exchange that I had with the Violence Policy Center's President, Josh Sugarmann, on MSNBC on February 24, 1997, involved the same accusations.

4. Douglas Weil, from the Center to Prevent Handgun Violence, a division of Handgun Control, wrote the following to the *Washington Times:* "Given that Mr. Lott has published 70 papers in peer-reviewed journals, it is curious that he has chosen a law review for his research on concealed-gun-carrying laws" (*Washington Times,* Aug. 22, 1996, p. A16).

5. Scott Harris, "To Build a Better America, Pack Heat," *Los Angeles Times,* Jan. 9, 1997, p. B1. In many ways, my study was indeed fortunate for the coverage that it received. It appears that no other study documenting the ability of guns to deter crime has received the same level of coverage. MediaWatch, a conservative organization tracking the content of television news programs, reviewed every gun-control story on four evening shows (ABC's *World News Tonight,* CBS's *Evening News,* CNN's *The World Today,* and NBC's *Nightly News*) and three morning broadcasts (ABC's *Good Morning America,* CBS's *This Morning,* and NBC's *Today*) from July 1, 1995 through June 30, 1997. MediaWatch categorized news stories in the following way: "Analysts counted the number of pro- and anti-gun-control statements by reporters in each story. Pieces with a disparity of greater than 1.5 to 1 were categorized as either for or against gun control. Stories closer than the ratio were deemed neutral. Among statements recorded as pro-gun control: violent crime occurs because of guns, not criminals, and gun control prevents crime. Categorized as arguments against gun control: gun control would not reduce crime; that criminals, not guns are the problem; Americans have a constitutional right to keep and bear arms; right-to-carry concealed weapons laws caused a drop in crime." MediaWatch concluded that "in 244 gun policy stories, those favoring gun control outnumbered stories opposing gun control by 157 to 10, or a ratio of almost 16 to 1 (77 were neutral). Talking heads were slightly more balanced: gun-control advocates outnumbered gun-rights spokesmen 165 to 110 (40 were neutral)." The news coverage of my study apparently accounted for 4 of the 10 "anti-gun control" news reports. (*Networks Use First Amendment Rights to Promote Opponents of Second Amendment Rights: Gun Rights Forces Outgunned on TV,* MediaWatch, July 1997.)

6. One of the unfortunate consequences of such attacks is the anger that they generate among the audience. For example, after Congressman Schumer's letter to the *Wall Street Journal,* I received dozens of angry telephone calls denouncing me for publishing my *Wall Street Journal* op-ed piece on concealed-handgun laws without first publicly stating that the research had been paid for by gun manufacturers. Other letters from the Violence Policy Center making these funding claims produced similar results.

Understandably, given the seriousness of the charges, this matter has been brought up by legislators in every state in which I have testified before the state legislature. Other politicians have also taken up these charges. Minnesota State Rep. Wes Skoglund (DFL–Minneapolis) provided one of the milder statements of these charges in the *Minneapolis Star Tribune* (Mar. 29, 1997, p. A13): "Betterman [a Minnesota state representative] uses a much-publicized study by John Lott Jr., of the University of Chicago, to back up her claims about the benefits of her radical gun-carry law.... But what no one has told you about Lott's study is that it has been found to be inaccurate and flawed. And Betterman didn't tell you that the study was funded by the Olin Foundation, which was created by the founder of Winchester Arms."

7. I telephoned Ms. Rand to ask her what evidence she had for her claim that the study was "the product of gun-industry funding" and reminded her that the public relations office at the University of Chicago had already explained the funding issue to her boss, Josh Sugarmann, but Ms. Rand hung up on me within about a minute.

8. Alex Rodriquez, "Gun Debate Flares; Study: Concealed Weapons Deter Crime," *Chicago Sun-Times,* Aug. 9, 1996, p. 2. Kotowski made his remark at a press conference organized by the Violence Policy Center, whose president, Josh Sugarmann, had been clearly told by the press office at the University of Chicago on August 6 that these charges were not true (as the letter by William E. Simon shown later will explain). Catherine Behan in the press office spent an hour trying to explain to him how funding works at Universities.

9. *Chicago Tribune,* Aug. 15, 1996.

10. "Study: Concealed Guns Deterring Violent Crime," *Austin American Statesman,* Aug. 9, 1996, p. A12.

11. The brief correction ran in the *Austin American Statesman,* Aug. 10, 1996.

12. As Mr. Simon mentions, one journalist who looked into these charges was Stephen Chapman of the *Chicago Tribune.* One part of his article that is particularly relevant follows:

> Another problem is that the [Olin] foundation didn't (1) choose Lott as a fellow, (2) give him money, or (3) approve his topic. It made a grant to the law school's law and economics program (one of many grants it makes to top universities around the country). A committee at the law school then awarded the fellowship to Lott, one of many applicants in a highly competitive process.
>
> Even the committee had nothing to do with his choice of topics. The fellowship was to allow Lott—a prolific scholar who has published some 75 academic articles—to do research on whatever subject he chose....
>
> To accept their conspiracy theory, you have to believe the following: A company that derives a small share of its earnings from sporting ammunition somehow prevailed on an independent family foundation to funnel money to a scholar who was willing to risk his academic reputation (and, since he does not yet have tenure, his future employment) by fudging data to serve the interests of the firearms lobby—and one of the premier research universities in the world cooperated in the fraud. (See Stephen Chapman, "A Gun Study and a Conspiracy Theory," *Chicago Tribune,* Aug. 15, 1996, p. 31.)

13. A Gannett Newswire story quoted a spokeswoman for the Coalition to Stop Gun Violence who made similar statements: "But Katcher said the study . . . was funded by the Olin Foundation, which has strong ties to the gun industry. The study has 'been proven by a series of well-known, well-respected researchers to be inaccurate, false, junk science,' she said." (Dennis Camire, "Legislation before Congress Would Allow Concealed Weapons Nationwide," Gannett News Service, June 6, 1997.)

14. John R. Lott, Jr., "Should the Wealthy Be Able to 'Buy Justice'?" *Journal of Political Economy* 95 (Dec. 1987): 1307.

15. "Notebook," *The New Republic,* Apr. 14, 1997, p. 10.

16. After much effort, Randy was eventually able to get Cynthia Henry Thielen, a Hawaiian State Representative, to participate in the radio program.

17. Richard Morin, "Unconventional Wisdom: New Facts and Hot Stats from the Social Sciences," *Washington Post,* Mar. 23, 1997, p. C5.

18. It is surely not uncommon for academics to write letters to their local newspapers or to national or international publications, and indeed such letters were also written (see, for example, *The Economist,* Dec. 7, 1996, p. 8). But to track down the letters of everyday citizens to local newspapers and send replies is unusual.

19. The *Springfield State Journal-Register,* Nov. 26, 1996. Steven Teret, director of the Center for Gun Policy and Research wrote dozens of letters to newspapers across the country. They usually began with statements like the following: "Recently in a letter to the editor dated October 19, Kurt Amebury cited the work of two University of Chicago professors" (*Orlando Sentinel,* Nov. 16, 1996, p. A18); "Recently the *Dispatch* published a letter to the editor citing the work of two researchers" (*Columbus Dispatch,* Nov. 16, 1996, p. A11); "The *State Journal-Register* Oct. 28 published two letters citing research by the University of Chicago's John Lott" (*Springfield State Journal-Register,* Nov. 13, 1996, p. 6); or "A recent letter to the editor . . ." (*Buffalo News,* Nov. 17, 1996, p. H3). In late November, I asked Stephen Teret how many newspapers he had sent letters to. He would not give me an exact count, but he said "dozens" and then listed the names of some major newspapers to which they had

written. It is curious that none of the effort put into responding to my paper by the Center has gone into writing a comment for submission to the *Journal of Legal Studies*, where my original paper was published. Nor has the Center prepared a response for any other scholarly journal.

20. My opinion piece appeared in the *Omaha World-Herald*, Mar. 9, 1997, p. B9.

21. *Virginia Code Annotated*, § 18.2-3088 (1988).

22. This discussion relies on conversations with Clayton Cramer.

23. This point is similar to the "broken-window" argument made by Wilson and Kelling; see James Q. Wilson and George L. Kelling, "Making Neighborhoods Safe," *Atlantic Monthly*, Feb. 1989.

24. Some robberies also involve rape. While I am not taking a stand on whether rape or robbery is the primary motivation for the attack, there might be cases where robbery was the primary motive.

25. Information obtained from Kathy O'Connell at the Illinois Criminal Justice Information Authority.

26. For example, see Douglas Weil, "A Few Thoughts on the Study of Handgun Violence and Gun Control," *Washington Times*, Aug. 22, 1996, p. A16.

27. The durability of these initial false claims about Florida's crime rates can be seen in more recent popular publications. For example, William Tucker, writing in the *Weekly Standard*, claims that "Florida crime rates remained level from 1988 to 1990, then took a big dive. As with all social phenomena, though, it is difficult to isolate cause and effect." See William Tucker, "Maybe You Should Carry a Handgun," *Weekly Standard*, Dec. 16, 1996, p. 30.

28. In an attempt to facilitate Black's and Nagin's research, I provided them not only with all the data that they used but also computer files containing the regressions, in order to facilitate the replication of each of my regressions. It was thus very easy for them to try all possible permutations of my regressions, doing such things as excluding one state at a time or excluding data based on other criteria.

29. Dan Black and Dan Nagin, "Do 'Right-to-Carry' Laws Deter Violent Crime?" Carnegie-Mellon University working paper, Dec. 18, 1996, p. 5.

30. In addition, because the regressions use individual county dummy variables, so that they are really measuring changes in crime rates relative to each county's mean, one need not be concerned with the possibility that the average crime rates for the years that are farthest beyond the adoption of the concealed-handgun laws are being pulled down by relatively low crime rates in some states.

31. Ian Ayres and Steven Levitt, "Measuring Positive Externalities from Unobservable Victim Precaution: An Empirical Analysis of Lojack," NBER working paper 5928 (1997). The main issue with their empirical estimates, however, is whether they might be overestimating the impact from Lojack because they do not control for any other responses to higher auto-theft rates. For example, while higher auto theft rates might trigger implementation of Lojack, they might also increase purchases of other antitheft devices like The Club. In addition, the political support for altering the distribution of police resources among different types of crimes might also change.

32. Ultimately, however, the levels of significance that I have tested for are the final arbiters in deciding whether one has enough data, and the results presented here are quite statistically significant.

33. Daniel W. Webster, "The Claims That Right-to-Carry Laws Reduce Violent Crime Are Unsubstantiated," The Johns Hopkins Center for Gun Policy and Research, copy obtained March 6, 1997, p. 5.

34. Jens Ludwig, "Do Permissive Concealed-Carry Laws Reduce Violent Crime?" Georgetown University working paper (Oct. 8, 1996), p. 12.

35. "Battered Woman Found Not Guilty for Shooting Her Husband Five Times," *San Francisco Examiner*, Apr. 9, 1997.

36. In Chicago from 1990 to 1995, 383 murders (or 7.2 percent of all murders) were committed by a spouse.

37. For a detailed discussion of how Black's and Nagin's arguments have changed over time, see my paper entitled "If at First You Don't Succeed . . ." : The Perils of Data Mining When There Is a Paper (and Video) Trail: The Concealed-Handgun Debate," *Journal of Legal Studies* 27 (January 1998), forthcoming.

38. Black and Nagin, "Do 'Right-to-Carry' Laws Deter Violent Crime?" Carnegie-Mellon working paper, version of December 18, p. 5, n. 4.

39. The December 18, 1996, version of their paper included a footnote admitting this point:

> Lott and Mustard weight their regression by the county's population, and smaller counties are much more likely to have missing data than larger counties. When we weight the data by population, the frequencies of missing data are 11.7% for homicides, 5.6% for rapes, 2.8% for assaults, and 5% for robberies.

In discussing the sample comprising only counties with more than 100,000 people, they write in the same paper that "the (weighted) frequencies of missing arrest ratios are 1.9% for homicides, 0.9% for rapes, 1.5% for assaults, and 0.9% for robberies."

40. For rape, 82 percent of the counties are deleted to reduce the weighted frequencies of missing data from 5.6 to 0.9 percent. Finally, for robbery (the only other category that they examine), 82 percent of the observations are removed to reduce the weighted missing data from 5 to 0.9 percent.

41. The reluctance of gun-control advocates to share their data is quite widespread. In May 1997 I tried to obtain data from the Police Foundation about a study that they had recently released by Philip Cook and Jens Ludwig, but after many telephone calls I was told by Earl Hamilton on May 27, "Well, lots of other researchers like Arthur Kellermann do not release their data." I responded by saying that was true, but that it was not something other researchers approved of, nor did it give people much confidence in his results.

42. See William Alan Bartley, Mark Cohen, and Luke Froeb, "The Effect of Concealed-Weapon Laws: Estimating Misspecification Uncertainty," Vanderbilt University working paper (1997).

CHAPTER EIGHT

1. Allison Thompson, "Robber Gets Outgunned on Westside," *Jacksonville (Florida) Times-Union,* Sept. 24, 1997, p. B1.

2. Craig Jarvis, "Pizza Worker's Husband Shoots Masked Bandit," *Raleigh News and Observer,* Dec. 11, 1996, p. B3.

3. Other work that I have done indicates that while hiring certain types of police officers can be quite effective in reducing crime rates, the net benefit from hiring an additional police officer is about a quarter of the benefit from spending an equivalent amount on concealed handguns. See John R. Lott, Jr., "Does a Helping Hand Put Others At Risk? Affirmative Action, Police Departments, and Crime," University of Chicago working paper (July 1997).

4. The cost of public prisons runs about twice this rate; see Mike Flaherty, "Prisons for Profit; Can Texas System Work for Wisconsin's Overflowing System," *Wisconsin State Journal,* Feb. 16, 1997, p. A1.

5. Fox Butterfield, "Serious Crime Decreased for Fifth Year in a Row," *New York Times,* Jan. 5, 1997, p. 10.

6. Michael Fumento, "Are We Winning the Fight Against Crime?" *Investor's Business Daily,* Feb. 5, 1997, p. A34.

214/NOTES TO PAGES 161–163

7. Yet there never was much controversy over this issue: when Congress debated the law, no one, not even the National Rifle Association, opposed background checks. The dispute was over a five-day waiting period versus an "instant check."

8. Fumento, "Fight Against Crime," p. A34.

9. After the Supreme Court decision, Arkansas completely stopped the background checks, while Ohio has essentially gutted the rules by making background checks voluntary. In addition, as "Ohio Deputy Attorney General Mark Weaver said, the responsibility for conducting background checks rests with counties and cities in most states—rather than with statewide agencies—and . . . 'hundreds of counties' stopped doing checks after the Supreme Court ruling." (Joe Stumpe, "Arkansas Won't Touch Gun Checks 'Unwarranted,' Chief Cop Says," *Arkansas Democrat-Gazette*, July 29, 1997, p. 1A.

10. Bureau of Alcohol, Tobacco, and Firearms, *A Progress Report: Gun-Dealer Licensing and Illegal Gun Trafficking*, Washington, D.C.: Department of the Treasury, Bureau of Alcohol, Tobacco, and Firearms (Jan. 1997).

11. Many other restrictions on gun use have prevailed during the last couple of years, even some that appear fairly trivial. For example, in 1996 alone thirteen states voted on initiatives to restrict hunting. The initiatives were successful in eleven of the states. Congressman Steve Largent from Tulsa, Oklahoma, claims that the new rules are "part of a national effort to erode our ability to hunt. . . . It wasn't a local effort. It was a national effort." Not only were the initiatives strongly supported by animal rights activists, but they also received strong support from gun-control advocates. It is probably not lost on gun-control advocates that support for gun control seems to be strongest among those who grew up in households without guns and that making hunting less attractive is one long-term way to alter support for these initiatives. See Janet Pearson, "A 'Fair Chase': Keep the Sport in Hunting," *Tulsa World*, Nov. 17, 1996, p. G1.

12. For most government agencies that try to obtain higher funding, exaggerating the problems helps justify such higher funding. Michael Fitzgerald, a spokesman for the BATF in Chicago, is quoted as saying that 1 percent of federal license holders are estimated to be illegally running guns. "If that figure is accurate, the reduction of . . . dealers should eliminate a substantial number of traffickers." See Jim Adams, "Number of Licenses Falls Dramatically: Crime Law Puts Squeeze on Gun Dealers; Zoning Can Be Used to Keep Gun Sales Out of Private Homes," *Louisville Courier-Journal*, Mar. 20, 1997, p. A1.

13. During the last few years, the BATF has been much more aggressive in harassing law-abiding gun owners and retailers. A recent study using 1995 data, by Jim Couch and William Shughart, claims not only that the BATF refers dramatically more criminal firearm violations to prosecutors in states that have more National Rifle Association members, but that Clinton's own U.S. attorneys have declined to prosecute a much greater percentage of the cases referred to them in these states. They estimate that 54 percent of the variation across states in the BATF's criminal referrals is explained simply by the number of NRA members in a state, and that about a quarter of these higher requests for prosecutions are declined by U.S. attorneys. See Jim F. Couch and William F. Shughart I, "Crime, Gun Control, and the BATF: The Political Economy of Law Enforcement," University of Mississippi working paper presented at the March, 1997, Public Choice Meetings in San Francisco.

14. Alix M. Freedman, "Tinier, Deadlier Pocket Pistols Are in Vogue," *Wall Street Journal*, Sept. 12, 1996, p. B1.

15. Three different types of devices are under development: X-rays, ultrasound, and radar. The first devices capable of functioning on the street are expected in 2001. See Fox Butterfield, "New Devices May Let Police Spot People on the Street Hiding Guns," *New York Times*, Apr. 7, 1997, p. A1.

16. James Q. Wilson sees these devices as an effective means of disarming criminals while allowing law-abiding citizens to keep their guns. In his view, they will provide us

with the best of both worlds, allowing us to retain the benefits of private protection and to disarm criminals. See James Q. Wilson, "Just Take Away Their Guns," *New York Times,* Mar. 20, 1994, sec. 6, p. 47.

17. In airports or courts, for example, such searches would probably be allowed. Whether these devices will be deemed constitutional if used on the street is less clear.

18. I cannot end, however, without at least mentioning several excellent law-review articles on the issue of what was intended in the Second Amendment: see Nelson Lund, "The Second Amendment, Political Liberty, and the Right to Self-Preservation," *Alabama Law Review* 33 (1988): 103–47; Robert J. Cottrol and Raymond T. Diamond, "The Fifth Auxiliary Right," *Yale Law Journal* 104 (1995): 309–42; Don B. Kates, "Handgun Prohibition and the Original Meaning of the Second Amendment," *University of Michigan Law Review* 82 (1983): 204–68; William Van Alstyne, "The Second Amendment Right to Arms," *Duke Law Review* 43 (Apr. 1994): 1236–55; and Sanford Levinson, "The Embarrassing Second Amendment," *Yale Law Journal* 99 (Dec. 1989): 637–89. Legal scholars seem to be in general agreement on the way the Second Amendment's use of the word *militia* is so completely misinterpreted in current discussions of what the amendment means. The only twentieth-century case in which the Supreme Court directly interpreted the Second Amendment was *United States v. Miller,* 307 US 174 (1939). The court was quite clear that historical sources "showed plainly enough that the Militia comprised all males physically capable of acting in concert for the common defense." The court accepted "the common view . . . that adequate defense of the country and laws could be secured through the Militia—citizens primarily, soldiers on occasion."

The framers of the Constitution were also very clear on this issue. James Madison wrote in the Federalist papers that if a standing army threatened citizens' liberties, it would be opposed by "a militia amounting to near a half-million citizens with arms in their hands" ; see Clinton Rossiter, ed., *The Federalist* no. 46 (1961): 299. An excellent discussion of this and related issues is presented by David L. Franklin and Heather L. O'Farrell in their University of Chicago Moot Court brief on *Printz and Mack v United States,* Apr. 18, 1997.

APPENDIX ONE

1. Although this jargon may appear overwhelming, it is actually fairly simple. Consider the following example. Suppose we wish to present findings that height and SAT scores are correlated among college-bound students. Instead of reporting that an additional inch is related to an increase in test scores of so many points, we can compare standard-deviation changes, which would be equivalent to reporting the results as comparisons of changes in percentile height with percentile changes in the SAT-scores.

2. To phrase this in terms of the earlier discussion of standard deviations, with a symmetric distribution, there is a 32 percent probability that a variable will take on a value that is more than one standard deviation different from its mean, and only a five percent probability that it will be more than two standard deviations away from the mean.

APPENDIX THREE

1. U.S. Department of Justice, *Crime in the United States, 1994* (Washington, DC: U.S. Department of Justice, 1994.) I also wish to thank Tom Bailey of the FBI and Jeff Maurer of the Department of Health and Human Services for answering questions concerning the data used in this paper.

2. The Inter-University Consortium for Political and Social Research number for this data set was 6387, and the principle investigator was James Alan Fox of Northeastern University College of Criminal Justice.

3. Dropping the zero crime values from the sample made the "shall-issue" coefficients larger and more significant, but doing the same thing for the accident-rate regressions did not alter "shall-issue" coefficients. (See also the discussion at the end of the section headed "Using County and State Data for the United States" in chapter 4.

4. For further descriptions of the procedures for calculating intercensus estimates of population, see ICPSR (8384): U.S. Department of Commerce, Bureau of the Census, *Intercensal Estimates of the Population of Counties by Age, Sex, and Race (United States), 1970–1980* (Ann Arbor, MI: ICPSR, Winter 1985). See also Bureau of the Census, *Methodology for Experimental Estimates of the Population of Counties by Age and Sex: July 1, 1975*, Current Population Reports, series P-23, no. 103, and *Census of Population, 1980: County Population by Age, Sex, Race, and Spanish Origin (Preliminary OMB-Consistent Modified Race)*.

5. U.S. Department of Commerce, Bureau of the Census, *Methodology for Experimental Estimates of the Population of Counties by Age and Sex: July 1, 1975*, Current Population Reports, series P-23, no. 103; see also Bureau of the Census, *Census of Population, 1980: County Population by Age, Sex, Race, and Spanish Origin (Preliminary OMB-Consistent Modified Race)*, pp. 19–23.

6. U.S. Department of Commerce, *Statistical Abstract of the United States*, 114th ed., table 746, p. 487.

7. Thomas B. Marvell and Carlisle E. Moody, "The Impact of Enhanced Prison Terms for Felonies Committed with Guns," *Criminology* 33 (May 1995): 259–60.

Bibliography

Akhil Reed Amar. "The Bill of Rights and the Fourteenth Amendment." *Yale Law Journal* 101 (Apr. 1992).

Andreoni, James. "Criminal Deterrence in the Reduce Form: A New Perspective on Ehrlich's Seminal Study." *Economic Inquiry* 33 (July 1995).

Annest, J. L.; J. A. Mercy; D. R. Gibson; and G. W. Ryan. "National Estimates of Nonfatal, Firearm-Related Injuries: Beyond the Tip of the Iceberg." *Journal of the American Medical Association* (June 14, 1995).

Ayres, Ian, and Steven Levitt. "Measuring Positive Externalities from Unobservable Victim Precaution: An Empirical Analysis of Lojack." NBER working paper 5928 (1997).

Bartley, William Alan; Mark A. Cohen; and Luke Froeb. "The Effect of Concealed-Weapon Laws: Estimating Misspecification Uncertainty." Vanderbilt University working paper (1997).

Battalio, Raymond C.; John H. Kagel; and Owen R. Phillips. "Optimal Prices and Animal Consumers in Congested Markets." *Economic Inquiry* 24 (Apr. 1986).

————. "Optimal Prices and Animal Consumers in Congested Markets: A Reply." *Economic Inquiry* 25 (Oct. 1987).

Battalio, Raymond C.; John H. Kagel; Howard Rachlin; and Leonard Green. "Commodity Choice Behavior with Pigeons as Subjects." *Journal of Political Economy* 84 (Feb. 1981).

Becker, Gary S. "Crime and Punishment: An Economic Approach." *Journal of Political Economy* 76 (Mar./Apr. 1968).

Block, Michael K., and Vernon E. Gerety. "Some Experimental Evidence on the Differences between Student and Prisoner Reactions to Monetary Penalties." *Journal of Legal Studies* 24 (Jan. 1995).

Block, Michael K., and John Heineke. "A Labor Theoretical Analysis of Criminal Choice." *American Economic Review* 65 (June 1975).

Blumstein, Alfred, and Daniel Nagin. "The Deterrent Effect of Legal Sanctions on Draft Evasion." *Stanford University Law Review* 28 (1977).

Blumstein, Alfred; Jacqueline Cohen; and Daniel Nagin, eds. *Deterrence and Incapacitation: Estimating the Effects of Criminal Sanctions on Crime Rates.* Washington, DC: National Academy of Sciences, 1978.

Bureau of Alcohol, Tobacco, and Firearms. *A Progress Report: Gun-Dealer Licensing and Illegal Gun Trafficking.* Washington, DC: Department of the Treasury, Bureau of Alcohol, Tobacco, and Firearms, Jan. 1997.

Bureau of Justice Statistics Special Reports." Murder in Large Urban Counties, 1988." Washington, DC: U.S. Department of Justice, 1993.

————. "Murder in Families. Washington, DC: U.S. Department of Justice, 1994.

Cherrington, Ernest H. *The Evolution of Prohibition in the United States of America.* Westerville, OH: Tem-Press, 1920.

Colvin, D. Leigh. *Prohibition in the United States.* New York: George H. Doran Co., 1926.

Cook, P. J. "The Role of Firearms in Violent Crime," in M. E. Wolfgang and N. A. Werner, eds., *Criminal Violence.* Newbury, NJ: Sage Publishers, 1982.

———. "The Technology of Personal Violence." *Crime and Justice: Annual Review of Research* 14 (1991).

Cottrol, Robert J., and Raymond T. Diamond. "The Second Amendment: Toward an Afro-Americanist Reconsideration." *Georgetown Law Review* 80 (Dec. 1991).

Cramer, Clayton E., and David B. Kopel. "'Shall Issue': The New Wave of Concealed-Handgun Permit Laws." *Tennessee Law Review* 62 (Spring 1995). A longer version of this study is available from the Independence Institute, 14142 Denver West Parkway, Suite 185, Golden, Colorado, 80401–3134.

Daly, Martin, and Margo Wilson. *Homicide.* Hawthorne, NY: Aldine de Gruyter Publishers, 1988.

Davis, James A., and Tom W. Smith. *General Social Surveys, 1972–1993: Cumulative Codebook.* Chicago: National Opinion Research Center, 1993.

Donohue, John, and Peter Siegelman. "Is the United States at the Optimal Rate of Crime?" *Journal of Legal Studies* 27 (Jan. 1998).

DiIulio, John J., Jr. "The Question of Black Crime." *The Public Interest* 117 (Fall 1994).

———. "White Lies About Black Crime." *The Public Interest* 118 (Winter 1995).

Dunford, Edward B. *The History of the Temperance Movement.* Washington, DC: Tem-Press, 1943.

Ehrlich, Isaac. "Participation in Illegitimate Activities: A Theoretical and Empirical Investigation." *Journal of Political Economy* 81 (1973).

———. "Crime, Punishment, and the Market for Offenses." *Journal of Economic Perspectives* 10 (Winter 1996).

Ehrlich, Isaac, and Randall Mark. "Fear of Deterrence: A Critical Evaluation of the Report of the Panel on Research on Deterrent and Incapacitation Effects." *Journal of Legal Studies* 6 (June 1977).

Geller, William A., and Michael S. Scott. *Deadly Force: What We Know.* Washington, DC: Police Executive Research Forum, 1992.

Glaeser, Edward L., and Bruce Sacerdote. "Why Is There More Crime in Cities? (Harvard University working paper, Nov. 14, 1995).

Glaeser, Edward, and Spencer Glendon. "Who Owns Guns?" *American Economic Review* 88 (May 1998).

Greenwald, Bruce C. "A General Analysis of the Bias in the Estimated Standard Errors of Least Squares Coefficients." *Journal of Econometrics* 22 (Aug. 1983).

Grossman, Michael; Frank J. Chaloupka; and Charles C. Brown. "The Demand for Cocaine by Young Adults: A Rational Addiction Approach." NBER working paper, July 1996.

Kagel, John H.; Raymond C. Battalio; Howard Rachlin; and Leonard Green. "Experimental Studies of Consumer Demand Behavior Using Laboratory Animals." *Economic Inquiry* 13 (Jan. 1975).

———. "Demand Curves for Animal Consumers." *Quarterly Journal of Economics* 96 (Feb. 1981).

Kahan, Dan M. "What Do Alternative Sanctions Mean?" *University of Chicago Law Review* 63 (1996).

Kahan, Dan, and Martha Nussbaum. "Two Conceptions of Emotion in Criminal Law." *Columbia Law Review* 96 (Mar. 1996).

Kates, Don B., and Dan Polsby. "The Background of Murders." Northwestern University Law School working paper (1997).

Kates, Don, and Dan Polsby. "Of Genocide and Disarmament." *Journal of Criminal Law and Criminology* 86 (Fall 1995).

Kellermann, Arthur L., et al. "Gun Ownership as a Risk Factor for Homicide in the Home." *New England Journal of Medicine* (Oct. 7, 1993).

Kennedy, David M.; Anne M. Piehl; and Anthony A. Braga. "Youth Violence in Boston: Gun Markets, Serious Youth Offenders, and A Use-Reduction Strategy." *Law and Contemporary Problems* 59 (Winter 1996).

Kermit, Daniel, and John R. Lott, Jr. "Should Criminal Penalties Include Third-Party Avoidance Costs?" *Journal of Legal Studies* 24 (June 1995).

Kleck, Gary. *Point Blank: Guns and Violence in America.* Hawthorne, NY: Aldine de Gruyter Publishers, 1991.

———. *Targeting Guns.* Hawthorne, NY: Aldine de Gruyter Publishers, 1997.

———. "Guns and Violence: An Interpretive Review of the Field." *Social Pathology* 1 (Jan. 1995).

Kleck, Gary, and Marc Gertz. "Armed Resistance to Crime: The Prevalence and Nature of Self-Defense with a Gun." *Journal of Criminal Law and Criminology* 86 (Fall 1995).

Kleck, Gary, and E. Britt Patterson. "The Impact of Gun Control and Gun-Ownership Levels on Violence Rates." *Journal of Quantitative Criminology* 9 (1993).

Kopel, David B. *The Samurai, the Mountie, and the Cowboy.* Amherst, NY: Prometheus Books, 1992.

———. *Guns: Who Should Have Them?* Amherst, NY: Prometheus Books, 1995.

Landes, William M. "An Economic Study of U.S. Aircraft Hijacking, 1961–1976." *Journal of Law and Economics* 21 (Apr. 1978).

Law Enforcement Technology magazine. "Gun-Control Survey." *Law Enforcement Technology* (July–Aug. 1991).

Levinson, Sanford. "The Embarrassing Second Amendment." *Yale Law Journal* 99 (Dec. 1989).

Levitt, Steven. "The Effect of Prison Population Size on Crime Rates: Evidence from Prison Overcrowding Litigation." *Quarterly Journal of Economics* 111 (1996).

Lott, John R., Jr. "Juvenile Delinquency and Education: A Comparison of Public and Private Provision." *International Review of Law and Economics* 7 (Dec. 1987).

———. "Should the Wealthy Be Able to 'Buy Justice'?" *Journal of Political Economy* 95 (Dec. 1987).

———. "The Effect of Conviction on the Legitimate Income of Criminals." *Economics Letters* 34 (Dec. 1990).

———. "A Transaction-Costs Explanation for Why the Poor Are More Likely to Commit Crime." *Journal of Legal Studies* 19 (Jan. 1990).

———. "An Attempt at Measuring the Total Monetary Penalty from Drug Convictions: The Importance of an Individual's Reputation." *Journal of Legal Studies* 21 (Jan. 1992).

———. "Do We Punish High-Income Criminals Too Heavily?" *Economic Inquiry* 30 (Oct. 1992).

———. "The Concealed-Handgun Debate." *Journal of Legal Studies* 27 (Jan. 1998): forthcoming.

Lott, John R., Jr., and Larry W. Kenny. "How Dramatically Did Women's Suffrage Change the Size and Scope of Government?" University of Chicago Law School working paper (1997).

Lott, John R., Jr., and William M. Landes. "Multiple Victim Public Shootings, Bombings, and Right-to-Carry Concealed Handgun Laws." University of Chicago Law School Working Paper (1997).

Lott, John R., Jr., and Stephen G. Bronars. "Criminal Deterrence, Geographic Spillovers, and Right-to-Carry concealed Handgun Laws." *American Economic Review* 88 (May 1998).

Lund, Nelson. "The Second Amendment, Political Liberty, and the Right to Self-Preservation." *Alabama Law Review* 33 (1988).

Marvell, Thomas B., and Carlisle E. Moody. "The Impact of Enhanced Prison Terms for Felonies Committed with Guns." *Criminology* 33 (May 1995).

McCormick, Robert E., and Robert Tollison. "Crime on the Court." *Journal of Political Economy* 92 (Apr. 1984).

McDowall, David; Colin Loftin; and Brian Wiersema. "Easing Concealed-Firearm Laws: Effects on Homicide in Three States." *Journal of Criminal Law and Criminology* 86 (Fall 1995).

Miller, Ted R.; Mark A. Cohen; and Brian Wiersema. *Victim Costs and Consequences: A New Look.* Washington, DC: National Institute of Justice, Feb. 1996.

Moulton, Brent R. "An Illustration of a Pitfall in Estimating the Effects of Aggregate Variables on Micro Units." *Review Economics and Statistics* 72 (1990).

Mullin, Wallace P. "Will Gun Buyback Programs Increase the Quantity of Guns?" Michigan State University working paper (Mar. 1997).

Munday, R. A. I., and J. A. Stevenson. *Guns and Violence: The Debate Before Lord Cullen.* Essex, England: Piedmont Publishers, 1996.

Peltzman, Sam. "The Effects of Automobile Safety Regulation." *Journal of Political Economy* 83 (Aug. 1975).

Peterson, Steven; George Hoffer; and Edward Millner. "Are Drivers of Air-Bag-Equipped Cars More Aggressive? A Test of the Offsetting-Behavior Hypothesis." *Journal of Law and Economics* 38 (Oct. 1995).

Plotkin, Martha R., ed. *Under Fire: Gun Buy-Backs, Exchanges, and Amnesty Programs.* Washington, DC: Police Executive Research Forum, 1996.

Polsby, Daniel D. "From the Hip: The Intellectual Argument in Favor of Restrictive Gun Control Is Collapsing. So How Come the Political Strength of Its Advocates Is Increasing?" *National Review,* Mar. 24, 1997.

Quigley, Paxton. *Armed and Female.* New York: St. Martin's, 1989.

Rasmusen, Eric. "Stigma and Self-Fulfilling Expectations of Criminality." *Journal of Law and Economics* 39 (Oct. 1996).

Reynolds, Morgan O. "Crime and Punishment in America." Dallas: National Center for Policy Analysis, June 1995.

Sandler, Todd. "Optimal Prices and Animal Consumers in Congested Markets: A Comment." *Economic Inquiry* 25 (Oct. 1987).

Shields, Pete. *Guns Don't Die, People Do.* New York: Arbor, 1981.

Singular, Stephen. *Talked to Death.* New York: Beech Tree Books, 1987.

Smith, Tom W. "1996 National Gun-Policy Survey of the National Opinion Research Center: Research Findings." Chicago: National Opinion Research Center, Mar. 1997.

Smith, Tom W., and Robert J. Smith. "Changes in Firearm Ownership Among Women, 1980–1994." *Journal of Criminal Law and Criminology* 86 (Fall 1995).

Southwick, Lawrence, Jr. "Self-defense with Guns: The Consequences." *Managerial and Decision Economics* (forthcoming).

Teret, Stephen P. "Critical Comments on a Paper by Lott and Mustard." School of Hygiene and Public Health, Johns Hopkins University, mimeo, Aug. 7, 1996.

U.S. Department of Commerce, Bureau of the Census. *Statistical Abstract of the United States.* Washington, DC: U.S. Government Printing Office, 1995.

Uviller, H. Richard. *Virtual Justice: The Flawed Prosecution of Crime in America.* New Haven, CT: Yale University Press, 1996.

Van Alstyne, William. "The Second Amendment Right to Arms." *Duke Law Review* 43 (Apr. 1994).

Viscusi, W. Kip. "The Lulling Effect: The Impact of Child-Resistant Packaging on Aspirin and Analgesic Ingestions." *American Economic Review* (May, 1984).

Wilson, James Q., and Richard J. Herrnstein. *Crime and Human Nature.* Simon and Schuster, New York, N.Y. 1985.

Wilson, James Q., and George L. Kelling. "Making Neighborhoods Safe." *Atlantic Monthly,* Feb. 1989.

Wolpin, Kenneth. "An Economic Analysis of Crime and Punishment in England and Wales, 1894–1967." *Journal of Political Economy* 86 (1978).

Wright, James D., and Peter Rossi. *Armed and Considered Dangerous: A Survey of Felons and Their Firearms.* New York: Aldine de Gruyter Publishers, 1986.

Zimring, Franklin. "The Medium Is the Message: Firearm Caliber as a Determinant of Death from Assault." *Journal of Legal Studies* 1 (1972).

Index

A "t" indicates material is located in a table or other figure; an "n" indicates material in an endnote.